# HaynesXtreme Customizing
# Honda Civic

**Haynes Publishing Group**
Sparkford Nr Yeovil
Somerset BA22 7JJ
England

**Haynes North America, Inc**
861 Lawrence Drive
Newbury Park
California 91320 USA

# Acknowledgements

Cover photos: Honda Civics shown on the front cover owned by Virgilio Follero and Christine Oliver.

Our sincere thanks to the following Honda Civic owners who allowed us to photograph their outstanding cars for use throughout this book:

APC (American Products Company)
Efrain Gonzalez
Basit Mirza
Paul Smith
Mike Ghadimi
Jeff Huang
Martin Castaneda
Jose Cuellar
Joe Syriani
Tony Contreras
Vince Renteria
Stephanie Lagala-Loza
Edward Otte
Virgilio Follero
Christine Oliver
Laszlo Elo

Photos of the Coustic Honda Civic are used with the permission of Coustic Car Audio, Phoenix, Arizona

© Haynes North America, Inc. 2004
With permission from J.H. Haynes & Co. Ltd.

All rights reserved. No part of this book may be reproduced or transmitted in any form of by any means, electronic or mechanical, including photocopying, recording or by any information storage or retrieval system, without permission in writing from the copyright holder.

ISBN 1 56392 528 1
Library of Congress Control Number 2004100132

Printed by J H Haynes & Co Ltd,
Sparkford, Yeovil, Somerset BA22 7JJ, England.

While every attempt is made to ensure that the information in this manual is correct, no liability can be accepted by the authors or publishers for loss, damage, or injury caused by any errors in, or omissions from, the information given.

04-208

# Be **careful** and know the **law**!

**1** Advice on safety procedures and precautions is contained throughout this manual, and more specifically within the Safety section towards the back of this book. You are strongly recommended to note these comments, and to pay close attention to any instructions that may be given by the parts supplier.

**2** Haynes recommends that vehicle modification should only be undertaken by individuals with experience of vehicle mechanics; if you are unsure as to how to go about the modification, advice should be sought from a competent and experienced individual. Any questions regarding modification should be addressed to the product manufacturer concerned, and not to Haynes, nor the vehicle manufacturer.

**3** The instructions in this manual are followed at the risk of the reader who remains fully and solely responsible for the safety, roadworthiness and legality of his/her vehicle. Thus Haynes is giving only non-specific advice in this respect.

**4** When modifying a car it is important to bear in mind the legal responsibilities placed on the owners, drivers and modifiers of cars. If you or others modify the car you drive, you and they can be held legally liable for damages or injuries that may occur as a result of the modifications.

**5** The safety of any alteration and its compliance with construction and use regulations should be checked before a modified vehicle is sold as it may be an offense to sell a vehicle which is not roadworthy.

**6** Any advice provided is correct to the best of our knowledge at the time of publication, but the reader should pay particular attention to any changes of specification to the vehicles, or parts, which can occur without notice.

**7** Alterations to a vehicle should be disclosed to insurers and licensing authorities, and legal advice taken from the police, vehicle testing centers, or appropriate regulatory bodies.

**8** Some of the procedures shown in this manual will vary from model to model; not all procedures are applicable to all models. Readers should not assume that the vehicle manufacturer has given their approval to the modifications.

**9** Neither Haynes nor the manufacturer give any warranty as to the safety of a vehicle after alterations, such as those contained in this book, have been made. Haynes will not accept liability for any economic loss, damage to property or death and personal injury other than in respect to injury or death resulting directly from Haynes' negligence.

# Contents

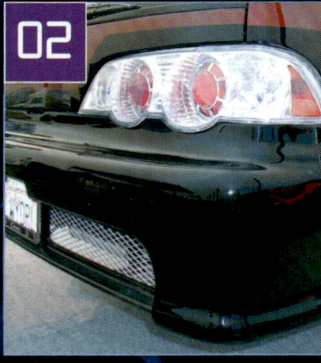

## Introduction 3
Be careful and know the law! 3
From here to there 6
Choosing a tuner 8
The bad with the good 10
A blast through the past 12

## Body and exterior 14
The Ultimate Detail 16
De-badging 20
Aftermarket mirrors 22
Headlights 25
Aftermarket taillight assemblies 27
Install a custom grille 29
Wings 32
Aerodynamic body kits 34
Carbon fiber hoods 39
Neon lighting 41

## Suspension 94
Suspension terms 98
Shock absorbers/struts and coil springs 100
Coilovers 106
Rear suspension 107
Air suspension 109
Nasty side effects 110
Shock tower/strut brace 111
Installing stabilizer bars 113
Understeer and oversteer 115

## Brakes 118
Grooved and drilled discs 120
Uprated discs and pads 121
Painting calipers 124
Painting drums 125

## Engine Performance 126
Engine compartment dress-up 128
Modifying exhaust 140
Turbochargers 146
Superchargers 150

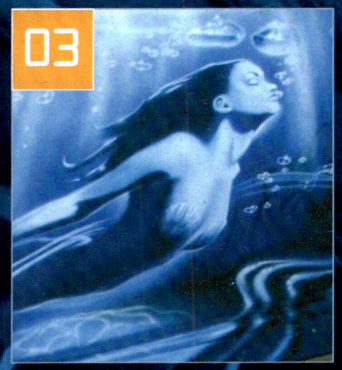

## Custom Painting    42
How to choose a good paint and body shop    44
Vinyl graphics    46

## Interiors    50
Custom styling rings    52
Shift lever knobs    53
Custom pedals    58
Custom floormats    61
Neon lighting    62

Interior trim    66
Gauge face upgrade    70
Installing aftermarket gauges    77
Bucket seats    80
Window tinting    82

## Wheels and tires    84
Choosing wheels    85
Choosing tires    90
Gallery of Wheels    92

Nitrous Oxide    153
Induction systems    156
Ignitions systems    164
Computers and chips    160
Valvetrain Modifications    168
Fuel system    172
Race and Live!    174

## In-Car Entertainment    176
In-dash receivers and players    178
Speakers    180
Amplifiers    184
Choosing the right amp    185
Subwoofer    186
Video    190

## Security    192
Alarms    193
Alarm installation    195
Remote power locks    198

**Glossary**    200
**Safety first!**    203
**Source list**    205
**Haynes list**    207

## 01 From **here** . . .

Ever been to a car show? You'll see the racer with grease under his fingernails, bent over his hood, adjusting his turbo wastegate. You'll see the themed car with matching colors (even under the hood) with a mirror-like paint job reflecting its neon lights. You'll see the rolling sound cannons, with beautifully integrated audio systems, blasting at Richter-scale levels. But you'll also see the daily-driven street cars with custom wheels, body kits and graphics that make them stand out from the other snore-mobiles in the neighborhood. This is truly diversity. And there is no "right" way to customize a car.

# ... to **there**

It seems our cars reflect our personalities, and that's the way it should be. If you're the "all-business" type, you'll probably not care much about your paint job and put the money you save into your engine. For others, looks and appearance are more important, but few of us have the money to "do it all." It's best to figure out what's most important to you and do that first. Look at the number of "unfinished" cars at any show; it illustrates how trying to do it all at once can backfire, especially when you run out of time and money. Most experienced car builders will plan "stages" of modification, each of which can be completed in relatively short periods of time. So, for example, you can get your paint job and graphics, then take some time to save up for your 12-second engine. In the meantime, you can enjoy driving a great-looking car. A die-hard racer might want to do it in reverse, but the principle is the same: it's best not to take on too much at once, unless of course you're the type who wants it all and wants it now - which isn't necessarily a bad thing either.

# Choosing a Tuner

Maybe you've already installed some bolt-on parts or done a tune-up or two before you bought this book. Good. You're not totally clueless! You'll be able to install a lot of bolt-on performance goodies with nothing more than the instructions in this book and the right tools. But when your modifications start affecting driveability (rough idle, loss of low-end power, emissions, noise, etc.), turning a stock Civic into a performance machine will get complicated. That's when you'll need to start looking for help. Sometimes you can find the answers in technical articles in Honda enthusiast magazines or in aftermarket books like this one. Theory is a vital part of the learning process, but it's no substitute for practical knowledge, which can only be gained through lots of experience. So at some point you'll need help from someone who knows how everything under the hood works as a system, how each sub-system is interdependent with and affects every other sub-system. Someone, in short, who's already got The Big Picture. We call this person a tuner.

## What kind of tuner are you looking for?

Some "tuners" just sell high-performance hardware. They know something about the speed equipment that they sell and some of them might even install it for you. But they don't offer custom tuning services such as machining, welding, fabricating and technical advice. In the early stages of a project (when you're upgrading wheels, tires, brakes, suspension and installing other bolt-on high-performance modifications) one of these tuners might be adequate if you have the mechanical ability and the tools to do your own work. But be realistic about your skills. Some bolt-on mods are expensive, and could be damaged or ruined, or could damage or ruin something else (like the engine!) if incorrectly installed.

Other tuners provide technical help to customers, sell them the stuff that they need to improve their Civics' performance, then install it. These tuners can also make any necessary modifications for customers who need help. If your mechanical ability and tools are limited, find a full-service tuner and leave the mail-order emporiums to more mechanically inclined customers. What you need is someone who can serve as your technical guru and help you reach your performance goals by doing some or all of the work for you. Beginners often waste thousands of dollars on inappropriate modifications because they don't take into consideration how one mod affects another. A "full-service" tuner will make sure that you avoid screw-ups by helping you make good decisions on expensive upgrades that require some planning.

## Does the tuner know what he's talking about?

To the tuner, there are just two kinds of experiences: good experiences and ... learning experiences. When a modification works, it's a good experience. When it doesn't, it's a learning experience. A good tuner isn't afraid to make mistakes, but he doesn't repeat those mistakes. He learns from them and moves on.

Good tuners use their own vehicles, not customers' cars, to research and develop new products and services. If you decide to work with a tuner who intends to use your Civic as a test-bed for new ideas or products, make sure that you get compensated for this service in kind with free or discounted parts and labor.

Ask a prospective tuner about his educational background, experience and training. A novice tuner looking for new customers might feel threatened by such questions and might fudge the truth a bit. But an experienced tuner won't. Besides, if you're going to spend thousands of dollars at this establishment, you need to judge for yourself whether the "tuner" standing before you is really qualified to modify your Civic or tell you how to do it. Did he start out taking auto shop classes at a local high school or study automotive technology at a local community college? Did he work for or own an independent Honda garage? Does he have Honda dealership experience? Is he a certified ASE (Automotive Service Excellence) technician or, even better, an ASE-certified Master Automotive Technician (CMAT)? Did he ever work for a professional Honda motorsports team? His answers to these questions will tell you whether this tuner has devoted a chunk of his life to Hondas, or whether he's simply out to make a buck.

Some people will tell you that tuning is art, while others say that it's science. But it's neither. Tuning is engineering. Not that one needs a degree in mechanical engineering to become a successful tuner. Most tuners probably aren't "real" engineers. But the good ones do have engineering minds: they understand the complexities of modern automotive technology well enough to define a problem in engineering terms, and then solve it the way an engineer would. A good tuner can back up his advice with sound data, and will be happy to show it to you.

Some of the best tuners gained their special knowledge and skills working for Honda as an engineer or technician or while turning wrenches for a Honda racing team. A former Honda factory employee might not only have vast experience with the Civic you want to modify, he might also maintain some "backdoor," i.e. unofficial, relationship with the factory. Such connections often enable tuners to gain insights into the mysterious inner workings of the engine management system and other esoteric subjects that are unavailable to their competitors.

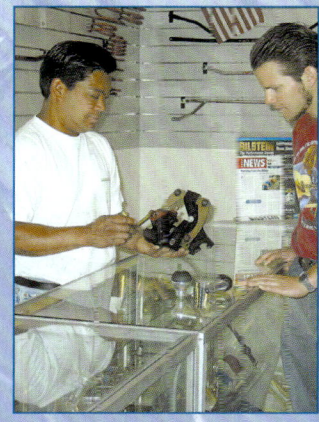

## Does the tuner do the work on time?

Patience is a must when you're putting together a project Civic with a tuner's help. Still, nobody wants a tuner who is unable or unwilling to deliver goods or services in a timely manner, particularly if the project vehicle is also the daily driver. Ideally, it's a good idea to have a back-up car as a daily driver.

## Is the tuner easy to get along with?

Most tuners are helpful and supportive. But some are eccentrics or egomaniacs. This is probably unavoidable in a field that's filled with self-made, self-promoting small businessmen whose success is tied to their accomplishments. If you find that your tuner is patronizing or talking down to you, lecturing you or grumbling about the stupidity of other customers and/or his competitors, get rid of him. You want results, not therapy. A truly hard-working professional doesn't have the time to talk trash about his customers or fellow tuners. He's too busy taking care of business.

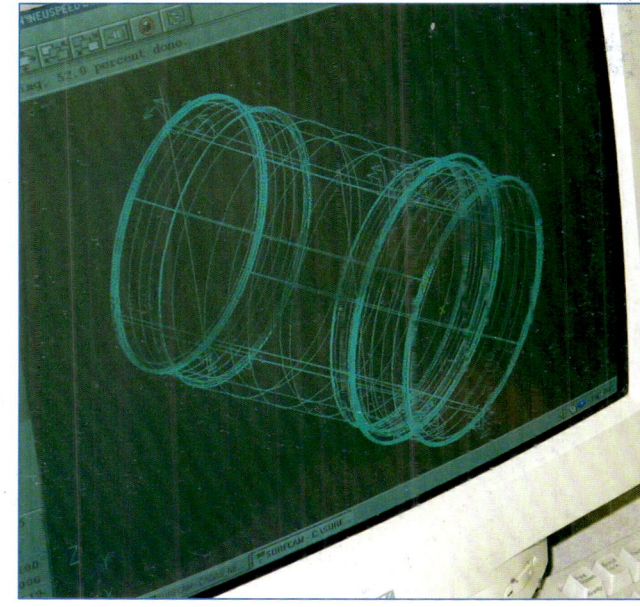

# The Bad with the Good

Customizing your car can get complicated in a hurry. What the manufacturers of high-performance and custom parts don't tell you is that there's usually a price to be paid for each "upgrade" you decide to make. For example, if you install big wheels and low-profile tires, be ready for a slightly rougher ride and be sure to stay away from potholes and curbs, since these wheels damage easily. If you install an intake tube, you're going to start hearing the air flowing into your engine (is that a good thing or a bad thing?). If it's a cold-air intake, you're going to have to watch out for deep puddles, or you might wind up with water in your engine (definitely a bad thing). If you lower your car, you're more likely to damage your suspension or destroy a tire from "fender rub." And speed bumps will become your worst enemy. Well, you get the idea. Your Civic was extremely well designed as it came from the factory. It was designed to provide long life, a comfortable ride and excellent fuel economy. These are all attributes we'd like to keep, if possible. So talk to as many people as you can who've actually done the modifications you're planning. Chances are they'll tell you some of the drawbacks that didn't show up in the magazine ad. And, on the other hand, they may let you know about some pleasant surprises they discovered after adding some custom pieces. Sometimes, you just don't know for sure, which is why you need to go in prepared to accept a little of the bad with the good!

Here are some common issues you may run into:

| Component | For | Against |
|---|---|---|
| **Performance computer chip** | Increased power, realize benefits of other engine modifications. | May affect driveability and ability to pass emissions test. |
| **Cat-back exhaust system** | Slight gain in power, especially with other modifications. Louder (see also: Against). | Possible loss of ground clearance; Louder (see also: For). |
| **Exhaust header** | Slight gain in power, especially when combined with other modifications. | More exhaust noise; less ground clearance (with some designs); more possibility of exhaust leaks. |
| **Power adders** (nitrous oxide, turbocharging and supercharging) | Large power increase without tearing deeply into engine. | Greater chance of engine damage or short engine life if not properly set-up. Can cause you to fail an emissions inspection. |
| **Performance camshaft** | Significant power increase, especially when combined with other flow-improving modifications. | On bigger cams, rough idle, loss of low-rpm power; loss of engine vacuum (so power brakes may work poorly); Can cause you to fail an emissions inspection. |
| **Nitrous oxide** | Big power boost. | Power can come at the expense of engine components not up to the task. |
| **Custom paint** | Ultimate statement. | Expensive. At re-sale, will need to find someone else with exactly the same taste as you. |
| **Body kit** | Turns any common run-of-the-mill car into something unique and personal. | Can look cheap if paint and fit are not perfect. |
| **Window tint** | Help stop sun-fade of interior. More difficult for thief to see what goodies you have. Gives clean exterior look. | May or may not be 100% legal in your area. |
| **Custom bucket seats** | New look to the interior. Perfect final touch to other, more subtle, treatments. Can be more comfortable and provide better support over stock. | May not be compatible with standard seatbelt systems. Installation can be difficult if not designed specifically for your car. |

# A blast through the past
## Where'd my Civic come from?

The Japanese Honda Motor Company was founded by a rebellious racer named Soichiro Honda. America was first introduced to his products in 1959, in the form of a small, step-through motorcycle. It was an instant hit. Within a few years, Honda came to dominate the world's motorcycle market and produced its first car in 1963. Honda automobiles first hit American streets in the 1970's. The first American Honda cars were odd-looking, ultra-compacts sold through Honda's motorcycle dealers – demand was relatively low. That quickly changed with Honda's introduction of the Civic in 1973.

The first Civics weighed only about 1500 pounds, yet could carry four passengers with ease. The transversely mounted 1.2 liter engine was one of the first of this design that Americans had seen – it was a marvel at the time. Even more of a marvel was that the Civic could get over 40 miles to the gallon, in an era when most so-called "economy" cars were getting half that much. With a price under $2,300 and a slogan "it will get you where you're going," the Civic was on its way. Almost immediately, the Civic became the worldwide standard for an economy car – a title it has not relinquished since. Honda continued producing its first-generation Civic through 1979, steadily improving it, adding features and increasing the engine power (from 50 horsepower in 1973 to 63 horsepower in 1979). In 1975, Honda introduced its highly efficient Controlled Vortex Combustion Chamber (CVCC) engine. This revolutionary design improved combustion efficiency and eliminated the need for a catalytic converter (at least for a while).

Capitalizing on early success, Honda introduced its second-generation Civic in 1980. Although similar in appearance to the first generation, this car was a bit larger, more stylish and had more interior room. This upgraded chassis design continued to use the CVCC engine, but now available was a larger 1500cc displacement, which increased torque significantly. Performance enthusiasts saw their first sporty Civic, the Civic S, which got the 1.5 liter engine, as well as upgraded suspension and tires.

In 1984, Honda introduced its first truly new Civic since 1973. The striking modern-looking design was an immediate hit, becoming so popular that dealers could not keep them on their lots. Although small by modern standards, this new Civic was larger and heavier than its predecessor. It also had an all-new 1.5 liter 12-valve engine that produced 76 horsepower. This next-generation Civic continued to sell very well through 1987. From a performance standpoint, the most interesting car in this era is probably the CRX, which had a lightweight, sporty body. The CRX Si, with fuel injection, boasted 90 horsepower and had performance equaling many "muscle-cars" of the time.

The fourth-generation Civic was introduced in 1988. This lower, sleeker, longer car now featured sophisticated double-wishbone suspension and an available D16 1.6 liter 16-valve engine that produced 105 horsepower. Even the base Civic was now a sporty car. Demand for this new model rose so high that Honda began making Civics in Ohio. In the four year run of this model, Honda continued to improve the design and add features, such as four-wheel disc brakes and luxury accessories. The sporty CRX model continued, but its last production year was 1991.

The fifth-generation Civic was introduced in 1992. This car continued the trend toward larger, more stylish design. More contoured and aerodynamic, this new Civic also introduced the first variable valve timing (VTEC) engine, with horsepower up to 125. In 1993, the del Sol was offered, continuing the CRX tradition of a sporty body on a Civic chassis. By 1994, the del Sol was available with a 160-horsepower engine and upgraded suspension – the first real "rocket" of the Civic line.

In 1996, the Civic was re-styled again, receiving larger headlight and taillight housings. The basic Civic platform was similar to earlier years, but styling was greatly changed, both inside and outside the car. Commonly referred to as the "Sixth Generation," this Civic continued to refine the highly successful fifth generation. In 1999, the Civic Si became the new king of Civic performance. The Si had firmer suspension, 15-inch wheels, four-wheel disc brakes, spoilers and even a strut-tower brace. Combined with the 160-horsepower B16 VTEC engine, this car quickly became a favorite among tuners.

2001 began yet another generation of Civic that was again a bit larger and heavier than its previous generation. The Si model continued into the seventh generation, offering upgraded performance and styling over other Civic models. While the basic engine designs remained similar to the previous generation, the engine displacement grew from 1.6 liters to 1.7 liters. The hot performance engine became the K20 2.0 liter VTEC engine used in Si models. While this engine has the same horsepower rating as the B16 of the previous generation, it has more torque than the smaller B16, meaning it can provide better overall driveability.

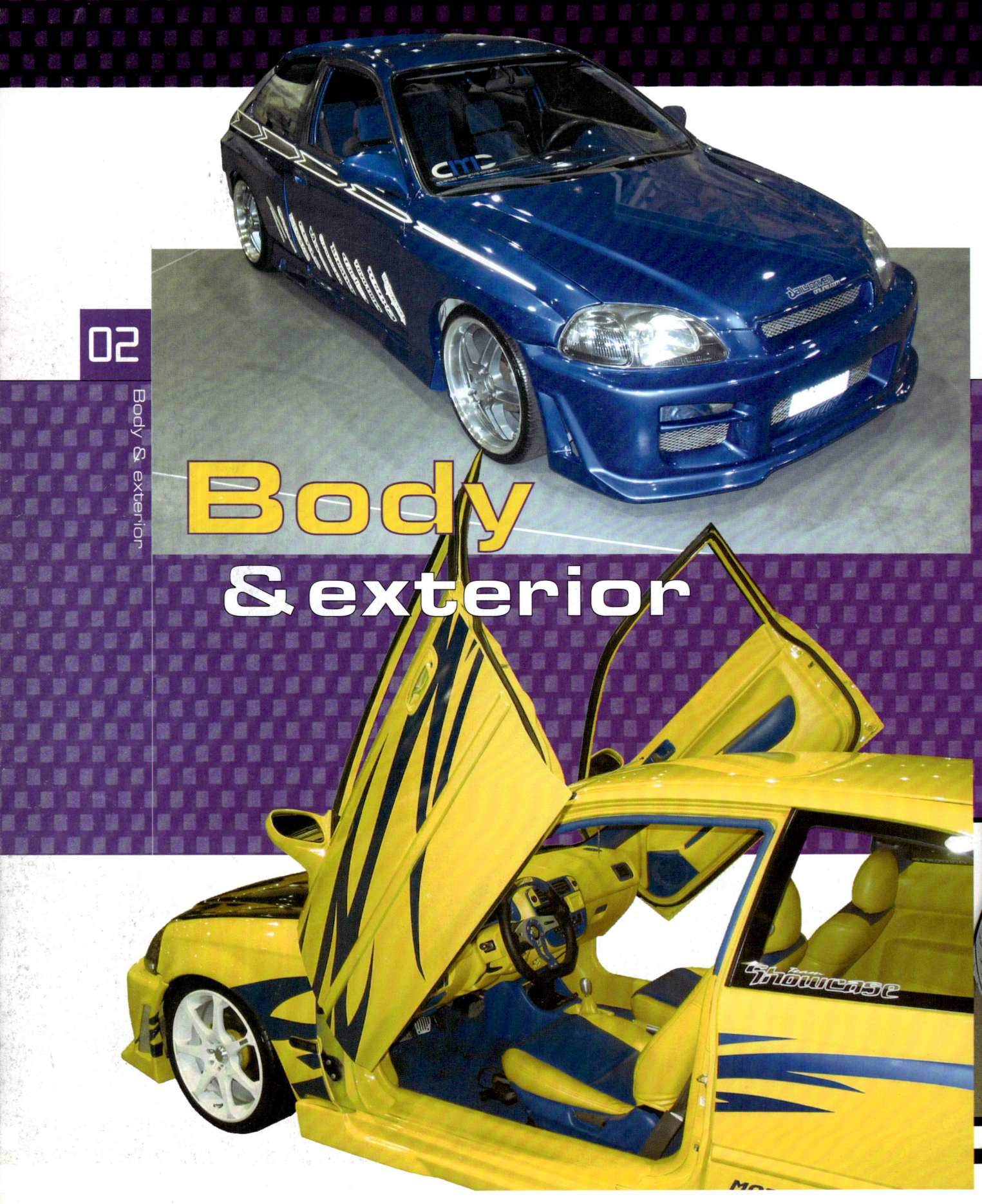

# 02
## Body & exterior

Aerodynamic/styling package, streamlined mirrors, trick taillights, de-badged decklid, custom paint - with the *right* combination of exterior modifications, you could have the coolest car on the block.

Get it all *wrong*, however, and your precious project could end up looking more like some silly vehicle from a bad science fiction movie!

One way to avoid the latter outcome is to decide how you want to alter the appearance of your car and then do a *lot* of R & D: pore over catalogs and magazines, look at other guys' cars at shows, ask manufacturers the right questions *before* you buy anything.

Pay particularly close attention to "fit and finish." How well does a part - air dam, side skirt, rear valance, aero mirror, etc. - fit your car? Look for kits that fit well without requiring a lot of cutting, trimming or other alterations. How well finished is the kit? If it looks like #&*$ in gel coat, is it going to look any better painted? Be forewarned: body kits aren't all equal. Some fit the car they're designed for very well, some don't fit too well at all . . . even after considerable tinkering. Some are fiberglass, some are polyurethane (some of the newer kits are carbon fiber, but the prices of these kits will leave you gasping!).

# The Ultimate Detail

## Step 1  Wash it

**01** Start your detail with a good washing. Don't make the mistake of using the wrong kind of soap. Instead of strong household soaps, use dedicated carwashing soaps, which can be found at your local auto parts store

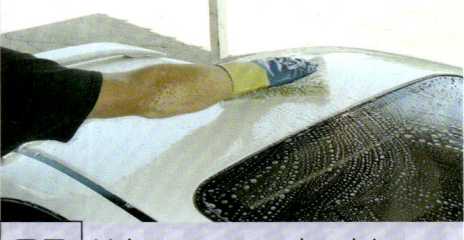

**02** Use a pressure washer or hose nozzle to direct a really strong spray of water on the dirty areas such as the fenderwells, tires/wheels, bumpers, front spoiler and rocker panels. This will help dislodge any heavy deposits of road grime

**03** It's important to wash and rinse a section of your car at a time, and in the shade, to prevent water spots from forming on your paint. Start with the roof and the windows, then the hood, grille and front fenders as the next section, followed by the rear and the sides. Do the tires and wheels last. The reason for doing a section at a time is to get to the rinse phase on each section before the suds and loosened dirt have a chance to dry onto the surface

Achieving good, clean shiny paint is probably the single most important aspect of detailing. The outside of the car is what is seen most, and paint covers 90-percent of the exterior. Once you achieve a good detailing on your paint, future cleaning will be relatively simple, and you'll take continued pride in your vehicle's appearance.

Unfortunately, there is no miracle cure for paint protection, just good protectants applied regularly with equal parts hard work and common sense.

**04** Don't forget to wash the door jambs, interior edges of the trunk lid and the bottom of the hood, as they are difficult to clean later. Door jambs are best rinsed with a clean sponge and water, rather than with a hose which can get water spray on the interior

**05** Proper wheel cleaner sprays can also aid in removing road grime and brake dust from rims

**06** A car can be dried completely with a chamois, but there will be a lot of wrist-bending wringing-out when you get down to the last beads of water. Most pros use terrycloth towels for final drying. Such towels should be 100% cotton, and you should buy and set aside towels just for the drying phase of your detailing. Never use a towel for other aspects of detailing, such as waxing, polishing or wheel-cleaning, and expect to wash that towel out and use it some other time for car-drying

# Step 2
## Really clean the paint

Paint cleaning products come in varying degrees of abrasiveness, from rough compounds that are used only when machine-buffing a new, wet-sanded two-stage paint job, to polishing compounds that are good for getting off stubborn spots or treating really faded paint, to fine polishes and paint "cleaners." The condition of your paint surface determines how abrasive a treatment you need to achieve the shine we're looking for. The more abrasive the product, the more actual paint you will remove in the process of a clean finish, and you want to remove as little paint as possible. When restoring an old, faded paint job, it can be difficult not to polish through the paint and down to the metal! Even when polishing paint with a very fine abrasive, you are still putting scratches into the surface. In all cases, although the array of products you'll find at the store is overwhelming, you are well-served by very carefully reading the directions and cautions in the fine print on the back of the package as to the intended use of the product. The pros tell you to use the least abrasive product that seems to do the job for your application.

**TIP:**
Clearcoated paint requires the use of "clearcoat-safe" products when cleaning or polishing your vehicle's paint. You must read the product labels carefully to find out if they are safe for clearcoat finishes.

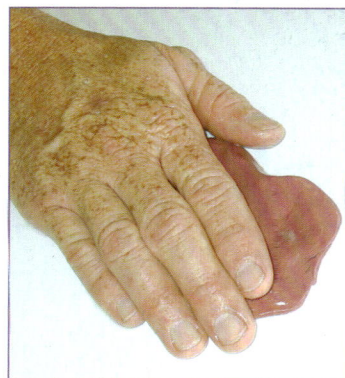

Our experienced detailer uses a polishing clay to clean small areas of the paint surface at one time. While working the clay, he keeps the area he's polishing lubricated with water.

# Step 3
## Glazes and sealers for that brilliant shine

Sealers and glazes require buffing to achieve their effect, and then they must be waxed-over right away or the sun and atmosphere will start to dull them down immediately. So there is considerable elbow grease involved in using them, but if used properly the results may be the shiniest you've ever seen your ride!

When using sealers and glazes, it's vitally important that you read the directions on the product before use. Of course, like any detailing product, they should be used only on cool surfaces, preferably in the shade or indoors, but with plenty of lighting so you can really see where the minute scratches are and how well you're doing on evenly glossing the surface.

Most of the glazes and combination glaze/sealer products must be buffed off before they fully dry. They often contain resins that help them fill in swirl marks left by previous polishing or compounding. Using a back-and-forth motion with your cloth to apply the product, let dry only to a semi-haze . . .

. . . then buff with the same motion, not a circular motion. Buff until there is a high gloss. Some of the many glazes and sealers are very tough to buff out to a gloss if you let them dry fully, so do it in the shade and make sure your phone's answering machine is on when you start the project. You'll love the results of the glaze or glaze/sealer

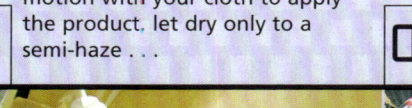

**01**

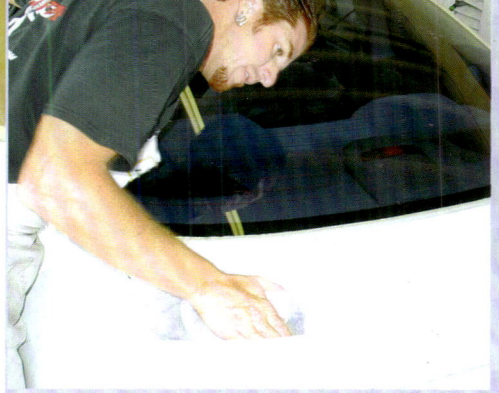

**02**

**Tip**
Use masking tape to protect rubber or plastic trim from glaze or wax residue.

01 Apply the wax of your choice following the manufacturer's directions, usually with a back-and-forth motion with a slightly-dampened cotton terry cloth and allowed to haze all over the car. The wax is buffed off by hand with clean terry cloth towels

 **Tip**
*When waxing around areas such as chrome trim, fender emblems, antenna, etc., you should be cautious not to build up too much wax in the joints of mating surfaces. It may attract dirt later on and also can be hard to remove from detailed areas of trim without tedious work*

## Step 4
## Wax it!

Wax is the final line of defense in your effort to shine and protect your car's paint, and its importance can't be overstated. All of the preparation work you've invested up to this point is lost if you don't wax the vehicle thoroughly and immediately. Everything we've suggested so far is aimed at getting a clean, smooth painted surface free of scratches, tar, bug stains or any other imperfections. Now you can use a good wax to protect all that effort.

02 With compressed air and a small brush like this one, remove wax residue from small cracks or emblems

03 After waxing, a vinyl dressing can be used to renew those faded trim pieces

04 If the fenderwell undercoating flakes-off during a pressure wash, black spray paint can be used to touch-up the fenderwells

**01** Clean the chip thoroughly with a special fiberglass-bristled brush

**02** Use a standard touch-up applicator or a paper match to deposit the touch-up color into the cleaned-out chip, or . . .

**03** . . . if a better match for your paint is available only in a spray can, aim the spray into the cup from the top of the can and then use that liquid paint for touch-ups with a paper match or toothpick for an applicator

## Touch-up

Many minor scrapes and shallow scratches can be eliminated or reduced with nothing more than wax and polishes. Try this first before doing anything more drastic. If that doesn't work, then color it with a touch-up paint.

Most touch-up paint bottles have an applicator inside, or you can use the end of a paper match or a toothpick to apply it. The latter works best in applying only a tiny amount if necessary. The factory brush in the jar puts on way too much paint so that it usually makes a small chip end up looking a lot bigger. If you can't find the color you need for your car in a touch-up bottle, check your auto parts store in the spray-paint racks. There is a much wider selection of "original" touch-up paint colors in spray cans than in little bottles.

We illustrate here a method of repair using a "Chip Kit" which has all the supplies you need for a quality touch-up except the actual color to match your vehicle.

 **Tip**
*Basic touch-up paint available from auto parts stores should be a close match to your car's paint, but due to the myriad colors and shades that come out each year, it can sometimes be difficult to find touch-up paint for more than a few years back. It is suggested that you buy a bottle or two when you buy your car and keep them in the glove box for future use.*

**04** Clear lacquer is applied in several coats after the original color paint has thoroughly dried, which usually takes several days

**05** When the repair is built up to slightly above the surrounding paint, the area is sanded flat with several grades of ultra-fine sandpaper wrapped around a soft rubber sanding block

**06** Very fine polishing compound is then used to blend the repair and sanded area into the rest of the paint

 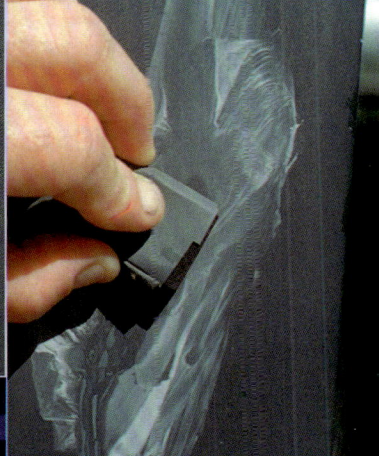 

Body & exterior

# De-badging

You know that old saying about beauty being in the eye of the beholder? Well, you may not see things the same as Honda. Just because Honda put a set of badges on your Civic doesn't mean that you're stuck with these eyesores. They're easy to remove. And your ride will look a whole lot cleaner without them.

**01** To prevent any paint damage to the vehicle, construct a special tool using a scraper with duct tape placed on the end of the blade

**02** Remove glued-on manufacturer badges with a heat gun or hair dryer and your special tool. Try not to scrape off the paint underneath the badge

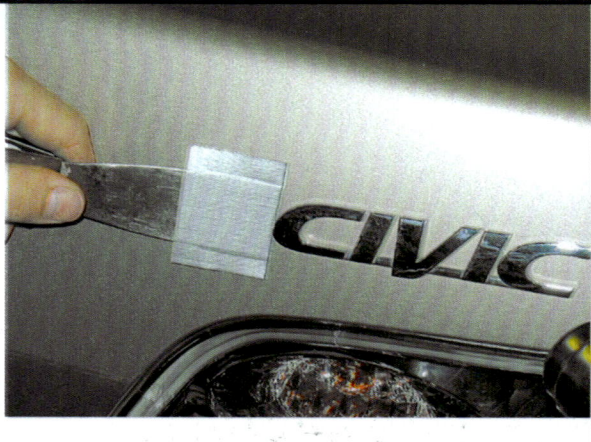

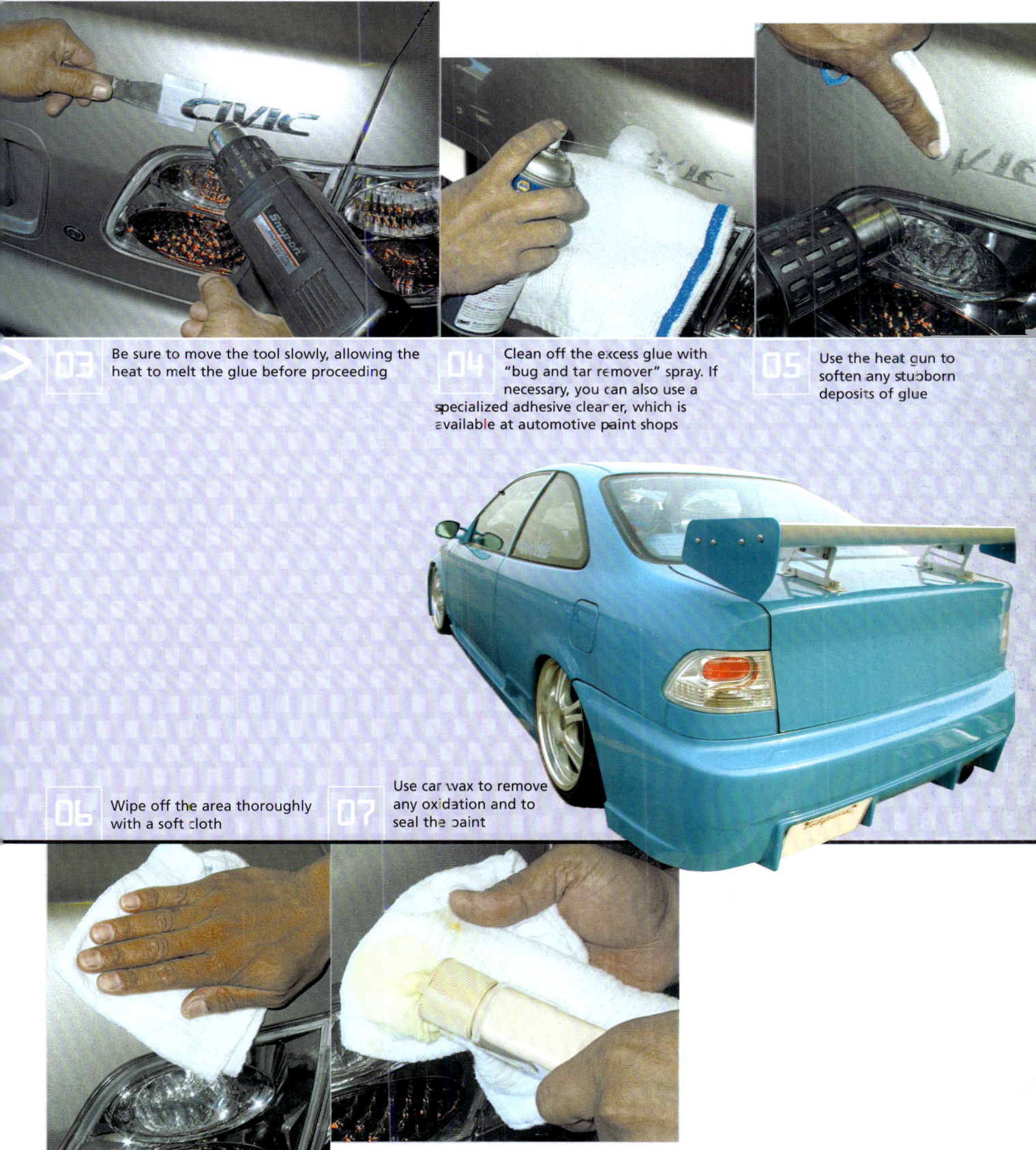

**03** Be sure to move the tool slowly, allowing the heat to melt the glue before proceeding

**04** Clean off the excess glue with "bug and tar remover" spray. If necessary, you can also use a specialized adhesive cleaner, which is available at automotive paint shops

**05** Use the heat gun to soften any stubborn deposits of glue

**06** Wipe off the area thoroughly with a soft cloth

**07** Use car wax to remove any oxidation and to seal the paint

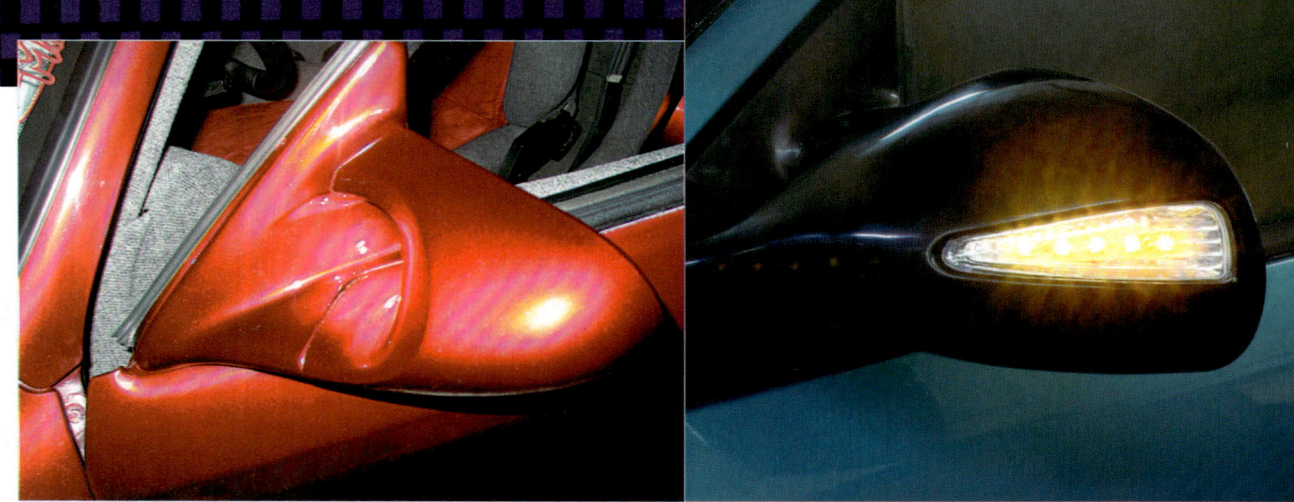

# Aftermarket mirrors

You can install any mirror on any car if you've got the skill. But, while anything may be *possible*, it won't necessarily be *easy*. So if you're a newcomer to the mirror swapping game, we recommend starting out with a set of mirrors designed for your Civic. We liked the look of these M3-style mirrors with integral running lights so much that we obtained a set for our project Civic.

## Installing aftermarket mirrors

**01** First, carefully pry off the triangular trim panel. You should be able to pop it off with your fingers. If it proves difficult to remove, use a panel removal tool or a screwdriver to pry it off (if you're going to use a screwdriver, be sure to tape the end to protect the trim from scratches)

**02** If your Civic has power mirrors, disconnect the battery (see your Haynes manual if necessary), then disconnect the mirror's electrical connector. To detach the mirror assembly, simply remove these three mounting nuts. Be sure to support the mirror with one hand while removing the third nut, so that the mirror doesn't hit the deck!

**03** Using a pair of needle-nose pliers, carefully work the electrical connector (if applicable) through the hole and remove the mirror

**04** Before proceeding, verify that the new mirrors fit correctly by doing a trial fitting. The mirrors shown here, which we obtained from American Products Company (APC) fit perfectly. If your kit doesn't fit correctly, now is the time to decide whether to pull out your utility knife and trim the base (or whether to pull out altogether and get another set of mirrors!)

**05** If you're installing power mirrors, or mirrors with turn signals and/or running lights, remove the door trim panel (refer to your Haynes manual)

**06** Work the electrical connector for the new mirror through the hole, insert the three mirror mounting studs through their mounting holes, install the mounting nuts and tighten them securely

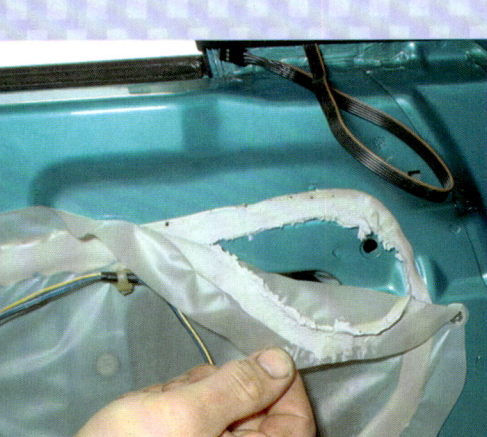

**07** Carefully peel off the plastic vapor barrier (if you're very careful, you'll be able to reattach the old vapor barrier)

**08** To give yourself more room to work, remove the door speaker. The speaker in our Civic is attached to the door with four mounting screws. After removing the screws, pull out the speaker and disconnect the speaker electrical connector

**09** If you're installing mirrors identical or similar to our M-3 style mirrors, the kit includes a small black electronic box, which can be installed with double-sided tape (sometimes included in the kit) or, if equipped with a mounting tab, a self-tapping screw can be used. Before drilling a hole for the screw, make sure that there are no wires or moving parts in the vicinity

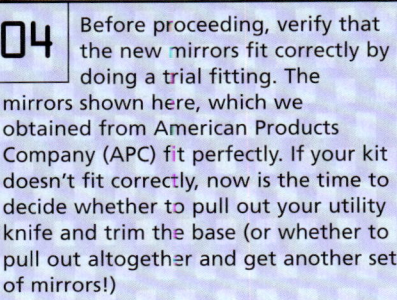

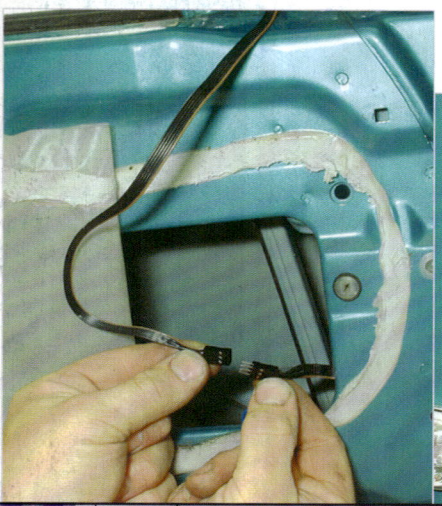  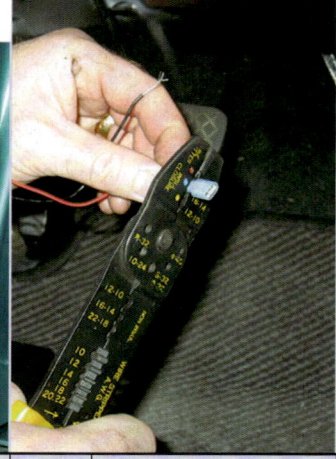 

**10** Once the box is installed, connect the lead from the mirror to the lead from the box. Then reconnect the battery and, if the window is down, close it. At this point, we recommend removing the door to gain better access to the door's wiring harness boot. To reach the fuse panel under the dash, you're going to route your new mirror harness through the same boot used by the door wiring harness. See your Haynes manual if you need help removing the door and, speaking of help, have an assistant standing by. The door is heavy!

**11** Pull the door wiring harness boot out of this hole, then thread your new power and ground wires through the boot. Using a flashlight, snake the new leads over the top of the kick panel and into the under-dash area near the fuse panel

**12** Once you've got your new leads inside the car, strip off 1/4-inch of insulation from the end of the power wire and add the appropriate connector. We added a female spade terminal to our power wire . . .

**13** . . . and plugged it into a spare terminal that's switched on and off by the headlight switch. If your fuse panel doesn't have a vacant switched terminal, locate a parking light or taillight circuit fuse (there's a fuse guide on the fuse box cover and in your owner's manual). Install a fuse tap on one of these fuses (make sure it's on the terminal that has no power when the fuse is removed) and plug in your power wire.

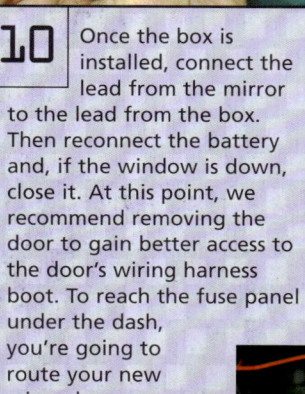  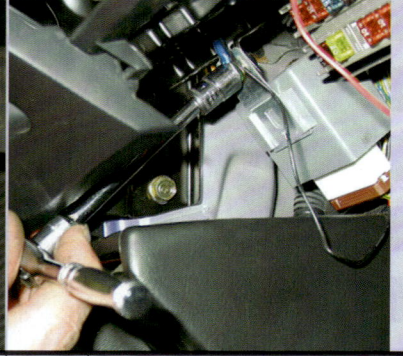

**14** Strip off 1/4-inch of insulation from the ground wire and crimp on a hook terminal . . .

**15** . . . and connect the hook terminal to a convenient ground bolt in the vicinity of the fuse panel. Okay, turn on your headlight switch and verify that the left mirror running light works. Hey, you're halfway there! Now go do the right mirror!

**Before**

# Headlights

**After**

It has been said that "the eyes are the windows to the soul." Assuming that's so, what do you see when you gaze into the soul of your Civic? Right now, you probably see a wide-eyed, innocent econobox; not a very intimidating presence at all.

If that isn't the image you want your car to project, it can be changed with a straightforward headlight housing replacement. There are plenty of high-quality units out there on the market that will transform your car's persona from passive to aggressive - from the front, at least.

**01** For starters, remove the side marker light, followed by the old headlight housing (see the Haynes Automotive repair manual for your Civic if you're not sure how)

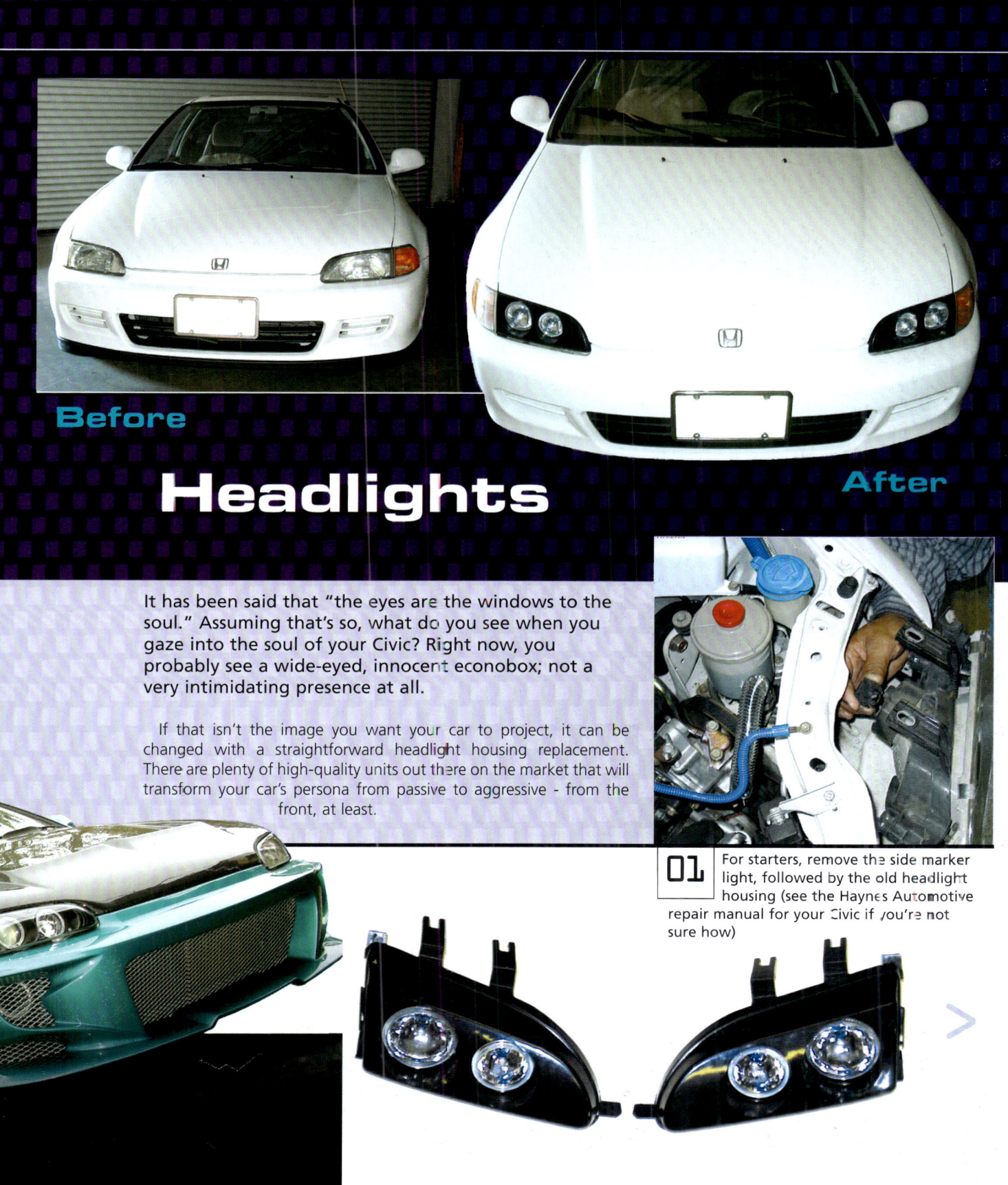

Body & exterior

**02** We connected the marker light to the new headlight housing and installed the self-tapping screw

**03** Time to connect the wiring. Remember, the outer light is the low beam; on our kit the connector with the blue and black wires had to be plugged into this light

**04** Guide the new unit into place, plug in the vehicle's headlight connector into the new headlight connector . . .

**05** . . . then install the unit and its fasteners. Now do the other side, then reinstall everything you had to remove to get the old lights out

**06** You'll probably have to fool around with the adjustment screws for awhile to get your beam pattern how you want it. You can do this in front of garage door or other blank wall to get the pattern close, but it would be a good idea to get an authorized service station to align the lights so you know they're correct (that way you won't blind the drivers of oncoming cars, or get a ticket). There you go - quite the personality change.

# Aftermarket taillight assemblies

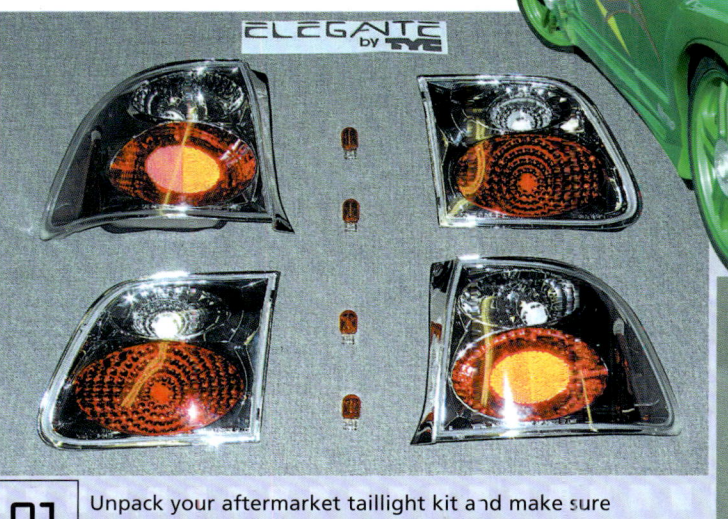

**01** Unpack your aftermarket taillight kit and make sure that everything is there and nothing is damaged.

One of the hottest styling trends is installing clear, smoked or colored aftermarket taillight assemblies. Basically, all you have to do is remove the stock taillight assemblies and replace them with the aftermarket unit of your choice. Don't forget that your running lights and brake lights must be red, your back-up lights clear and your turn signal lights amber. Your stock taillight lenses are already colored red, clear and amber for these lights, but you'll have to install the correct color bulbs with the aftermarket units.

**02** Peel back the trunk carpet for access to the bulbs and fasteners (refer to your Haynes Automotive Repair Manual if necessary)

Before

After

 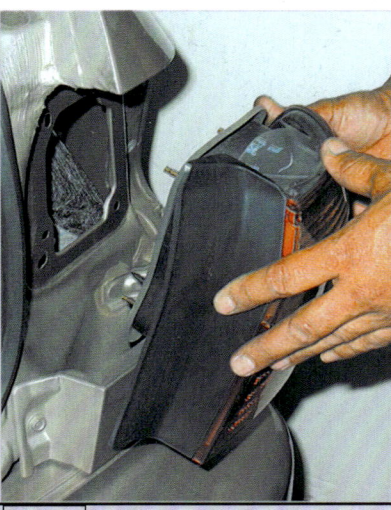 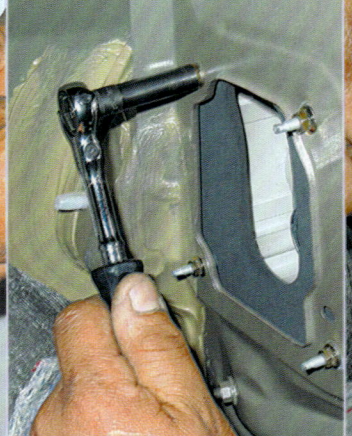 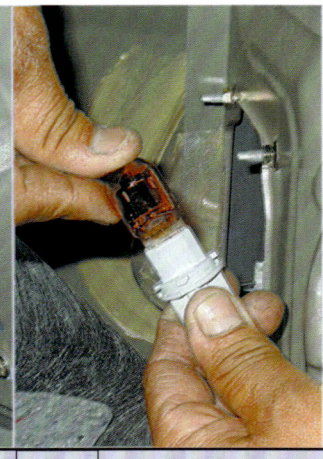

**03** To remove each bulb holder, rotate it counterclockwise and pull it out of the taillight assembly, then unscrew the mounting nuts . . .

**04** . . . and remove the old taillight assembly.

**05** Install the new taillight unit and tighten the four mounting nuts securely

**06** Install the new bulbs in their holders (this is the amber bulb for the turn signal lights) . . .

  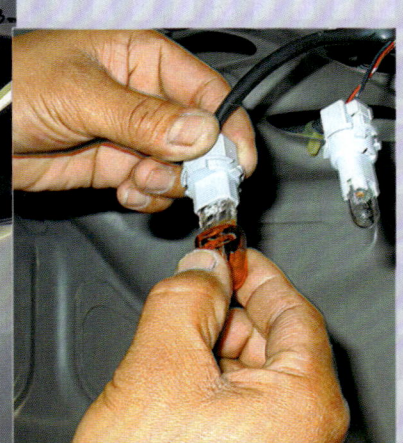

**07** . . . and insert each bulb holder into its socket and turn it clockwise to lock it into place. Okay, that completes the outer light on one side. Now go and do the outer light on the other side

**08** Install the new taillight assemblies in the deck lid. The procedure is pretty much the same as for the outer lights . . .

**09** . . . except the brake lights must be replaced with red bulbs

# Install a custom grille

Nothing tidies up the front end of a project like a custom grille. You lose that dull stock grille, which is usually emblazoned with some goofy corporate logos. And in its place, you get a custom look which really sets your ride apart from the crowd.

And it's also functional because it allows even more cooling air to pass through the condenser, the radiator and the engine compartment. Until a few years ago, if you wanted a mesh grille on your car, you had to make it from scratch. Nowadays, a number of aftermarket manufacturers are offering bolt-on kits that can be easily installed in a matter of hours.

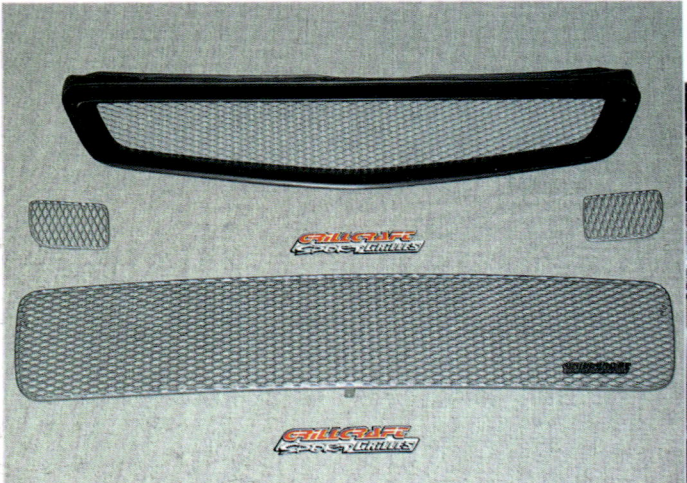

**01** Unpack you new mesh grille kit and make sure that everything, including all fasteners, is there. The kit that we purchased for a late-model Honda Civic includes everything you need to mesh the upper and lower grilles and the small faux brake vents in the bumper cover. Notice that it also includes an (unpainted) upper grille trim bezel, which must be primed and painted to match your car's color before installation

**02** Job One is to remove the stock upper grille and the bumper cover, which houses the lower grille and the faux brake vents; refer to your Haynes manual for the grille and bumper cover removal procedures

**03** Okay, once the stock upper grille and the bumper cover are removed, it's time to get started. First, turn the new grille trim bezel upside down and place the mesh grille in position on the bezel. Position the mesh as high as possible in the trim bezel to avoid any clearance problems with the bumper cover or the bumper cover fasteners

**07** Place the mesh grille trim bezel in place on the bumper cover, install the bezel mounting screws and tighten them securely.

**08** Now grab the new lower mesh grille, place it in position and, using an awl, mark the locations of the mounting holes through the holes in the mounting tabs

**09** Put each faux brake vent grille in position and, using an awl, mark the positions of the two mounting studs. After drilling the holes, install the screws and tighten them securely

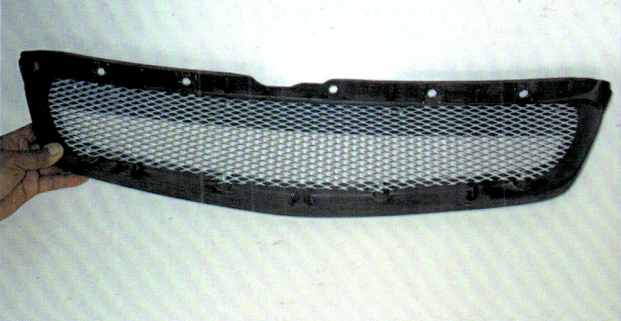
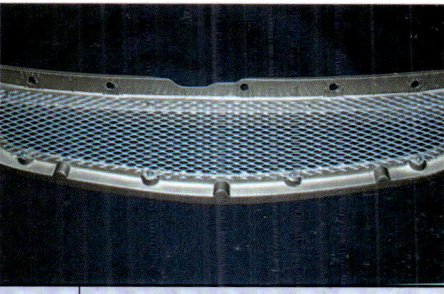

**04** With the mesh grille centered in the trim bezel, drill holes in the bezel and secure the grille to the bezel with screws

**05** There you have it! Now remove the mesh grille so that you can paint the trim bezel or send it out to a professional to have it painted

**06** After the trim bezel has been painted and given enough time to dry thoroughly, reinstall the mesh grille

Before...

...After

31

Body & exterior

# Wings

Let's be frank. If you want to install a rear deck wing because you think it will actually improve the handling of your Civic on the freeway or in fast corners, think again. Because unless you make regular trips at 130 mph, you're not going to realize any real benefits. But if you want to install a wing because it looks cool at any speed (even standing still), well then just do it!

The number and variety of rear wings on the market nowadays is overwhelming. They're available in fiberglass, polyurethane, aluminum and yes, even carbon fiber. They can be installed as part of a full body kit, or on their own. Paint your wing to match the car or paint it flat or glossy black.

## Installing a rear wing

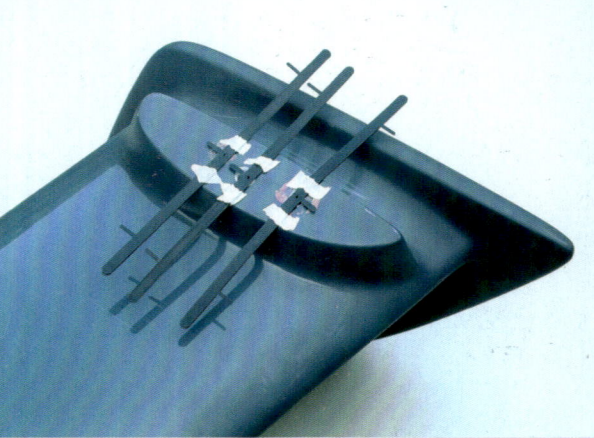

**01** Our "Sky Liner" rear wing, from Wings West, included these mysterious plastic strips taped to each vertical support. If you are installing one of their kits, don't remove these strips, the purpose of which we'll reveal momentarily

**02** Apply a strip of masking tape at each end of the deck lid where you plan to install the wing. Then you can mark the location of the vertical supports and the marks for drilling the mounting bolt holes without marking up the painted surface

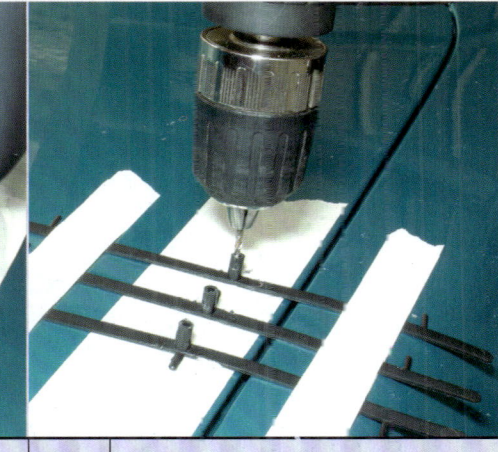

**03** Before placing the wing in position, open the deck lid and note the reinforcement ribs on the underside of the lid. These are the areas where you don't want to drill through! You only want to drill through one layer of sheet metal, so avoid any area that's reinforced. Then close the deck lid, position the wing in the area you've selected and use a ruler to make sure that the leading edges of the vertical supports are equidistant from the rear window

**04** Those mysterious plastic strips are there to help you drill the mounting holes in the right spot. With the wing in position, mark the location of the vertical supports and tape down the plastic strips as shown. Then carefully lift off the wing, leaving the taped strips in place

**05** These little tubes sticking up from the plastic strips indicate the exact location of the mounting holes. Neat, huh? Run a pilot drill down each tube to start the holes, then remove the plastic strips and drill the mounting holes to the size specified in the instructions

Wing kits usually include foam or rubber gaskets that fit between the vertical supports and the deck lid. These gaskets protect the paint from damage and seal out the elements. If you live in an area where it rains a lot, **06** you might want to bolster these potential leak points with some silicone sealant

**07** The wing is now ready to bolt on, except for paint, which you can do yourself, or sub it out to a professional

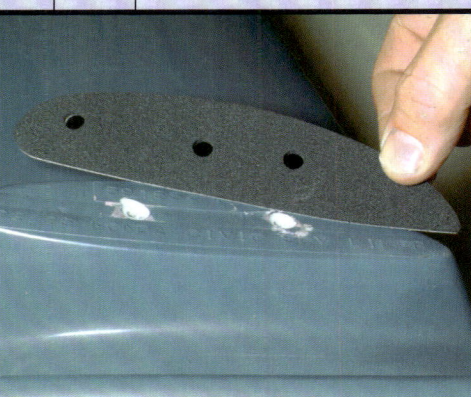
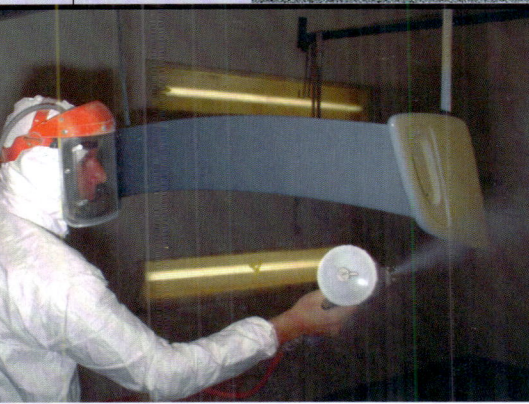

33

Body & exterior

# Aerodynamic body kits

Aside from a set of trick wheels or a custom paint job, an aerodynamic body kit is the biggest visual change you can make to your car.

The newest kits are easy to install because they already fit well, so little if any cutting or trimming is necessary. Some kits are fiberglass, but others use high-quality polyurethane.

Most modern aero body kits come unpainted. And if you decide to purchase a polyurethane kit, it will be a little more difficult to paint than a fiberglass kit because you have to add a flex agent to the base coat. Nevertheless, most automotive painters say that polyurethane requires far less prep work than fiberglass. But, hey, we don't want to let all this talk about painting bore you, or scare you off. If painting's not your thing, fine. Some kit manufacturers will pre-paint their kits (for an additional charge) so that they match most factory colors (but not custom paint).

If you decide to go with an unpainted kit, you will of course have to measure, mark, drill, cut, trim and install some parts, then remove them for prepping and painting, then install them again. Other parts are pre-cut and no drilling is necessary. They're attached to the vehicle surface with double-face tape - really, really strong double-face tape, so they must be painted before installation. Once you stick those pieces on the car, they ain't goin' nowhere!

## Installing a new front bumper cover

**01** Start by removing the bumper cover (refer to your Haynes manual, if necessary). Save the old hardware - you'll need most of it

**02** It's rather unlikely that your new bumper cover will be a perfect fit. This Wings West unit looked good straight out of the box; the holes all lined up fairly well and Wings even meshed it for us. But you might not be so lucky! Typically, some trimming and hole relocation will be necessary, and you might have to install your own mesh. During this "first fitting," you also want to figure out what, if anything, might interfere with installation of the new bumper cover

**03** On our project Civic, there's a now-superfluous splash shield that interferes with installation of the new bumper cover. Go ahead and remove it

**04** A big black "resonator" box (reduces induction noise) which is located at the right front corner of our Civic, also interfered with the new bumper cover, so we removed it, too. If you're worried about affecting engine performance, don't. The missing resonator will make your intake slightly louder, but will have no effect on performance

**05** Even though our new bumper had pre-marked spots for the five upper mounting screws, they weren't perfectly aligned with the holes (a typical problem with body kits). The best strategy for dealing with the slightly off marks is to center the bumper on the vehicle, drill the center hole and install the center mounting screw. Then mark the location of the other holes and drill them where they should be, not where the marks are located

**06** Same story with the mounting screw holes at the ends of the new bumper cover: Hold up the bumper, determine the correct location of each hole and drill it where it has to be, not where the mark is . . .

**07** . . . then install the side mounting screws. At this point, your new bumper cover should look pretty much the way it's going to look, except for the unpainted black plastic finish!

**08** There's one more little job to do - the center mounting bracket underneath - except that our kit didn't include one. The cover won't flap in the breeze without it but it's not entirely rigid either, so we fabricated a makeshift bracket from a strip of metal with a pair of mounting holes drilled into each end. Then attach the mounting bracket between the lower edges of the new bumper cover and the lower radiator crossmember. That's it! Now all you have to do is *paint* your new front end! But first, let's do the rear bumper cover and the side skirts

# Installing a new rear bumper cover

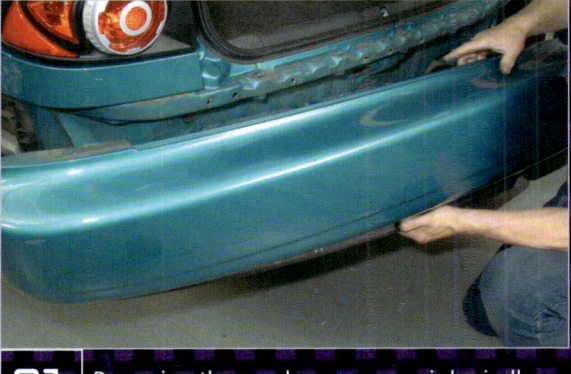

**01** Removing the rear bumper cover is basically the same deal as the front; refer to your Haynes manual if you need to.

**02** Place the new rear bumper cover in position, check the fit and verify that the marks made by the manufacturer do indeed line up with the holes in the vehicle body (not all of them did on our unit)

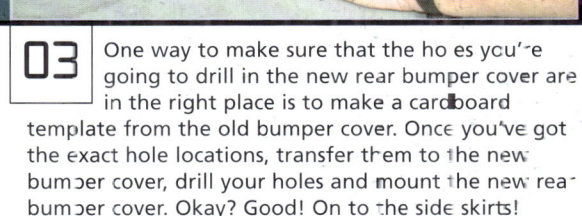

**03** One way to make sure that the holes you're going to drill in the new rear bumper cover are in the right place is to make a cardboard template from the old bumper cover. Once you've got the exact hole locations, transfer them to the new bumper cover, drill your holes and mount the new rear bumper cover. Okay? Good! On to the side skirts!

*Body & exterior*

## Side skirts

Side skirts were first used by Can Am and Formula One cars in the Seventies, which had a very low ride height, and flexible rubber side skirts that provided a flexible seal against the track. Side skirts directed air passing over and around the car from getting underneath the vehicle, where it could upset or negate the downforce produced by the wing and/or the car's shape. Side skirts quickly spread to all kinds of motor racing, then eventually found their way to the street.

Aesthetically, side skirts "tie together" the front and rear bumper covers. They're also a clever way to visually "lower" your Civic, making it look like it's lower to the ground than it really is. But downforce? Get OUTTA here!

**01** Get rid of the mudflaps, if you have 'em. Then check the fit of the new side skirts. Make sure that the doors will open and close without hitting the skirts. If you note any areas that are going to be a problem, mark them with a grease pencil for trimming later. Some Civics also use a plastic trim piece around each wheel housing. If your Civic has these trim pieces, do you want to keep them? Once you install the new side skirts, the wheel housing trim pieces will be trapped by the skirts

**02** Give the rocker panel area and the lower edges of the front and rear wheel housings (where they'll be covered by the new skirts) a good cleaning, then de-grease them completely. If you're going to apply glue to the skirts, de-grease them too. Some skirt kits, like our Wings West pieces, are already equipped with adhesive-backed strips. All you have to do is peel off the adhesive backing to stick them on. If your kit doesn't use adhesive strips, buy some quality adhesive that's suitable for gluing plastic to painted surfaces. Your local automotive paint supply stores can recommend something suitable

**03** If you're going to glue on your skirts, you'll have a little wiggle room after you install the skirt to move it slightly for awhile before the glue sets up. But if your skirt kit uses adhesive-backed strips, you only get one shot at it! In either case, we recommend placing the skirt in position and using a grease pencil to mark the upper line so that you get it right on the first try

**04** Before gluing anything down, you'll need a couple screw holes at the front and rear wheel housings, and two or three along the underside, to really pin each skirt into place. Have a helper hold the skirt in place while you drill the holes

**05** Okay, now you can install the skirts! Line up each skirt with the guide marks you made, then carefully peel off the adhesive backing from each strip and push down on the skirt. If you're using glue instead of the adhesive-backed strips, be sure to remove any excess quickly, particularly between the upper edge and the body. Now install the screws in the wheel housings and in the holes you made underneath the skirt

# Carbon fiber hoods

Carbon fiber is light, strong and expensive. Once used only on taxpayer-funded space shuttles and military aircraft, it eventually trickled down to Formula One and other racing series. Now it's widely available for the street, and it's still light, strong and expensive! There are carbon fiber hoods, mirrors, deck lids, wings, even body kits. None of these pieces are cheap, if they're made from the real stuff. Of course, the most obvious and distinctive carbon fiber upgrade you can make to your Civic is the hood. All it takes is money. The rest is easy.

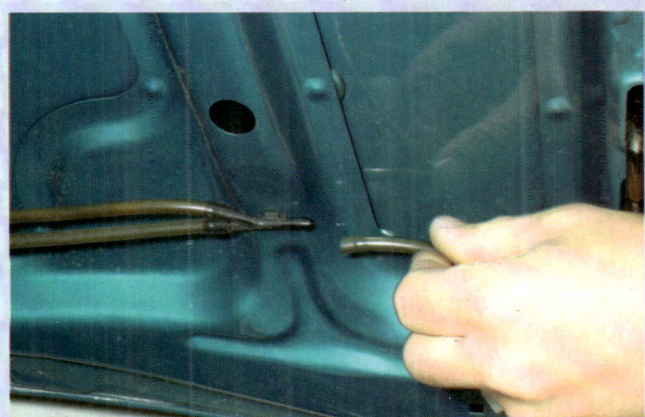

**01** Before removing your steel hood, get help. The hood isn't super heavy, but it's difficult to handle by yourself, and you might just want to reinstall it some day if you sell your car. Okay, first step is to disconnect the windshield washer fluid lines. It's a good idea to indicate which ends are connected together by marking them with numbered pieces of tape

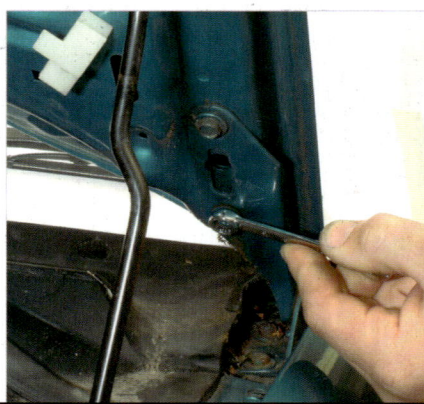

**02** If you think there's a good chance that you'll be installing the stock hood anytime soon, mark the relationship of the hood hinge flange to the hood with a grease pencil or utility marker. Then, with your helper holding one side of the hood while you hold the other, remove the four bolts (two at each hinge) that attach the hood hinge flange to the hood (don't unbolt the hinges from your Civic - you're gonna need 'em)

**03** Carefully remove the old hood and set it down somewhere safe. It's not a bad idea to put some towels or shop rags under the corners to protect the paint. If you've got a garage, the joists are a good place to store the hood until you need it, but you can do that later. Let's get this job finished!

**04** Okay, let's install your new carbon fiber hood! Before you bolt anything down, have your assistant help you place the new hood in position to verify that it's a good fit. Then install the hood hinge flange bolts and tighten them until they're snug, but not too tightly because you need to check the fit of the hood before final tightening of the hood hinge bolts

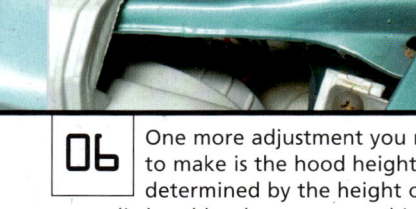

**05** Carefully lower the new carbon fiber hood and note whether the striker (the little hoop on the underside of the hood that secures the hood to the latch when the hood is closed) is correctly aligned with the latch mechanism. If the striker is off-center, the hood isn't correctly aligned. Look at the gaps between the edges of the hood and the surrounding bodywork. If the gap between the left edge of the hood and the left fender is bigger than the gap between the right edge of the hood and the right fender, the hood is cocked slightly to the right, and vise versa. If the hood is slightly off-center, give it a little tweak to the left or right to center the striker in the latch, then look at the gaps again. Hood lined up with both fenders and gaps the same width? Okay, now you can tighten the hood hinge bolts!

**06** One more adjustment you might have to make is the hood height, which is determined by the height of these two little rubber bump stops, which can be screwed in (lowers the hood) or up (raises the hood). Fool around with the bump stops until the hood is flush with the fenders. That's all there is to it! You're done!

# Neon lighting

Inexpensive and easy to install neon lighting is one of the easiest ways to give your ride the "show car" look. With the variety of kits available today, you can install neon to just about any part of your car you want. Just try to keep it away from surfaces that could scrape the ground or get submerged easily in puddles. And check your local laws to be sure you're not doing anything illegal. When wiring, have a separate switch for your neon so it can be turned off when you don't "need" it, which will also help the components last longer.

**03**

Painting and graphics

# Custom Painting

Get some ideas of what you like – go to shows, look at books and magazines – and then find yourself a painter who can make it happen. If you can afford it, a custom paint job is the most effective way to make your car unique.

**Metallic paints** - have microscopic particles of metal in the paint that reflect the light and give off a high luster effect.

**"Metal flake" paint** - is really just metallic paint with bigger chunks of reflective metal in it.

**Candy apple paint** - consists of a reflective base coat of silver or gold metallic, with a translucent color coat on top of it and clear coat on top of that.

**Pearlescent (or simply pearl) finishes** - created by applying multiple layers of paint: first a matte color base, then a colored lacquer coat and finally a clear lacquer coat.

**"Flip-flop" pearl or chameleon paint** - uses high-tech liquid crystal and interference pigments to produce a finish that looks like one color when viewed from some angles but looks like a different color when viewed from other angles.

# How to choose a good paint and body shop

The old adage "you get what you pay for" is especially true of professional bodywork and paint jobs: the best work is very, very expensive. The reason is the labor-intensive nature of the work. It takes a lot of time to do a good job, and time is money.

So, if you decide to take your Civic to a shop for body repairs or painting, be prepared to pay plenty for a first-class job. And shop around before deciding where to have the work done. A little time spent checking out body shops in advance will pay off in the long run.

Don't let a shop's location scare you off. Most shops are located in industrial areas that can't be considered good neighborhoods. However, any good shop, regardless of its location, will have safe, secure storage areas - either indoors, outdoors or both - for customer's cars. If a shop doesn't have well-secured parking, keep looking.

As you drive up to a shop, note its general condition, how the surrounding area is maintained and the types of cars that are waiting for attention. If they all seem to be desirable collectors or luxury cars, you might have stumbled onto a top-notch shop. (You might also need to call your banker for a big loan!) Are completed vehicles stored indoors or outside? Are they covered or not? It might not be obvious at first glance, but details like these can make a difference between a great paint job and a good one, so ask the manager when you get a chance.

Ask the owner or manager to give you a little tour of the shop. Is it relatively neat and clean, or are there body parts and tools scattered all over the place? Is it well lit and roomy, or dark, dingy and cramped? Are the body repairmen and painters wearing neat new work clothes, or grungy old paint-smeared jeans and T-shirts? Is there plenty of room between the cars that are being worked on, or are they jammed together? Has any effort been made to protect the interiors of vehicles and the exterior parts that don't require work? What about new replacement parts and the old parts that have been removed from vehicles during repairs? Are they shoved into the interiors of the cars, or are they labeled and stored neatly in a separate area?

Look for a frame-straightening fixture, MIG, TIG and oxyacetylene welding equipment, and separate masking and painting booths.

Try to get a close look at some recently completed paint jobs. Note whether any dirt or lint is trapped in the paint. Look for runs and sags and see if the coverage is uniform and complete. Was everything carefully masked off? Or is there paint all over trim pieces? If it looks good, chances are that everything was done right.

If everything so far checks out, there's one more thing you should do: Ask the owner or manager if he would be willing to allow you to contact some recent customers so that you can ask them whether they're satisfied with the work done on their vehicles. If there's any hesitation at all, thank the person you're dealing with and leave. If the owner or manager is willing to put you in touch with recent customers, and if they're happy with the work done on their cars, you need look no farther.

Painting and graphics

# Vinyl graphics

Custom vinyl graphics are a relatively inexpensive way to transform your Civic. A good vinyl graphics kit can be a lot wilder than a custom paint job for a lot less money.

But vinyl isn't perfect. For one thing, it's not that easy to install. Vinyl sorta goes on like a decal, but some vinyl graphics (like the kit shown on the following pages) are often much larger, and far more difficult to install, than a mere decal. And unlike paint, which can be quickly removed with reducer if you screw up, vinyl is pretty much toast if you commit a Major Mistake while applying it.

# Installing custom vinyl graphics

**01** First, round up the stuff you'll need for applying your vinyl graphics kit. We used a special stripping cleaner, isopropyl rubbing alcohol, a spray bottle with a slightly soapy water solution (mix a gallon of water with a single DROP of dishwasher soap), a heat gun, scissors, a gasket scraper (taped to protect the paint), masking tape, lint free shop towels and a squeegee (not shown)

**02** Clean off the entire side of the vehicle with the special stripping cleaner

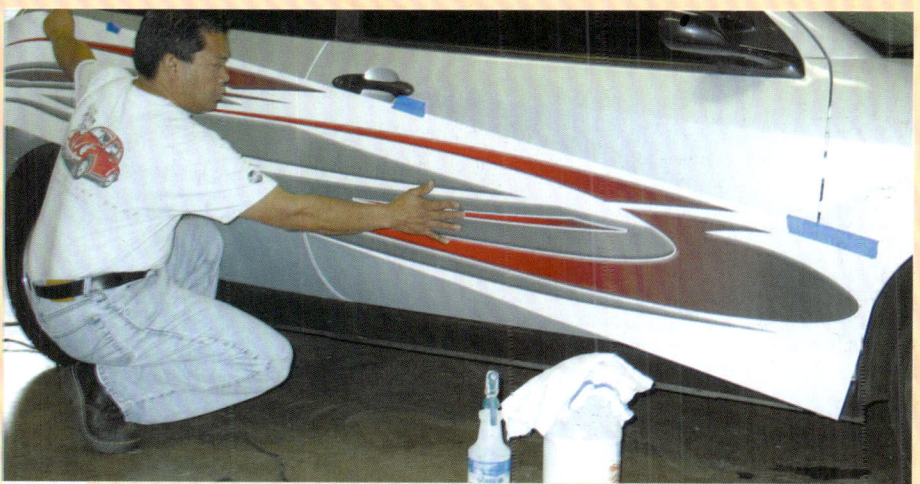

**03** Using a few little pieces of masking tape to "hang" the graphic, figure out where you want to put it. Once you've determined the location and the orientation of the graphic, tape it to the car along the entire upper edge of the graphic pre-mask. This long piece of tape will serve as the "hinge" so that you can flip the graphic up and out of the way as necessary during the installation process

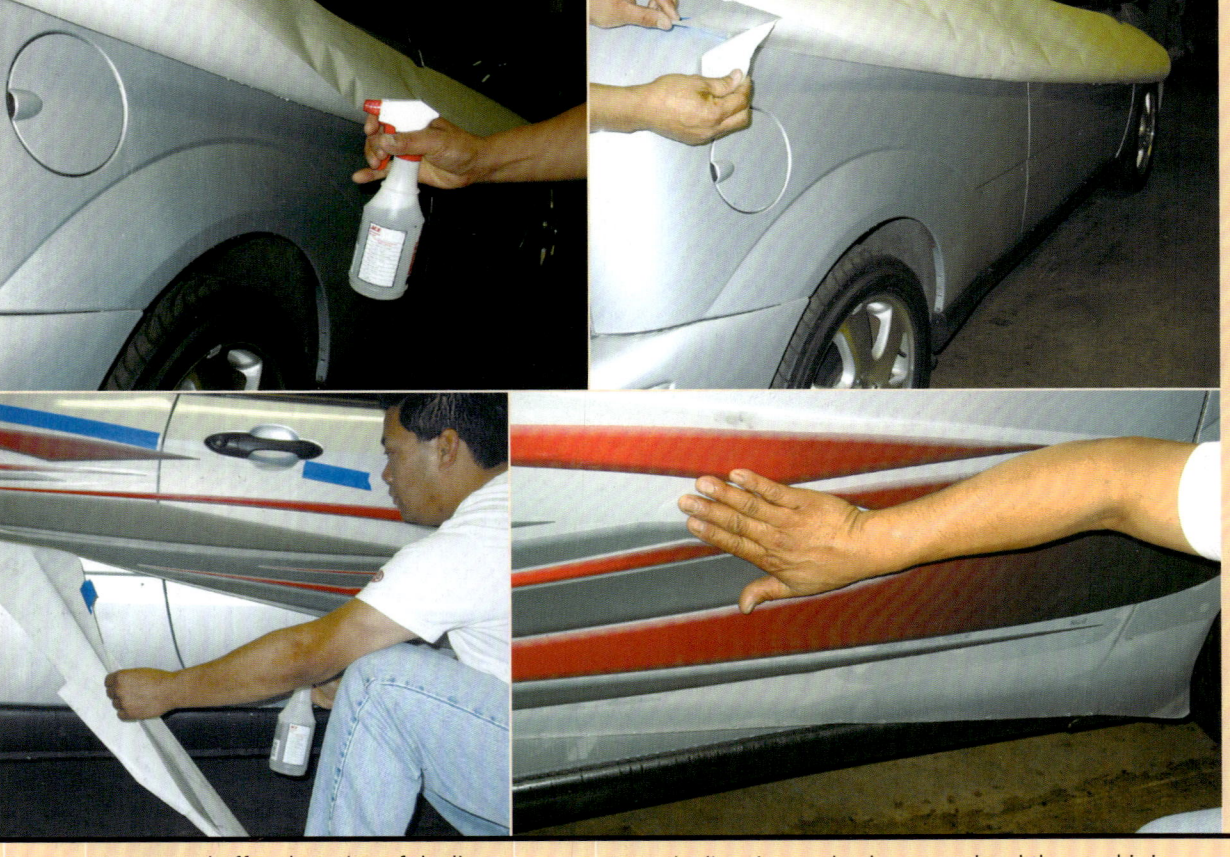

**04** Okay, flip up the graphic and secure it to the window with a piece or two of tape, wipe off the area to be covered with alcohol, then spray the surface liberally with your slightly soapy water solution

**05** Starting at the back (or the front, if you want), peel off the liner (the white backing sheet) from the graphic, working your way down in sections

**06** As you peel off each section of the liner, spray the exposed back side of the vinyl graphic itself with liberal amounts of the semi-soapy water and apply the vinyl graphic to the car, spraying and peeling off the liner as you go

**07** Once the liner is completely removed and the graphic is applied to the vehicle surface, work out the air and water bubbles with your hand first, keeping the graphic flat and preventing it from moving around. Start at the upper middle part of the graphic and work your way down and out toward the ends to prevent the graphic from bunching up

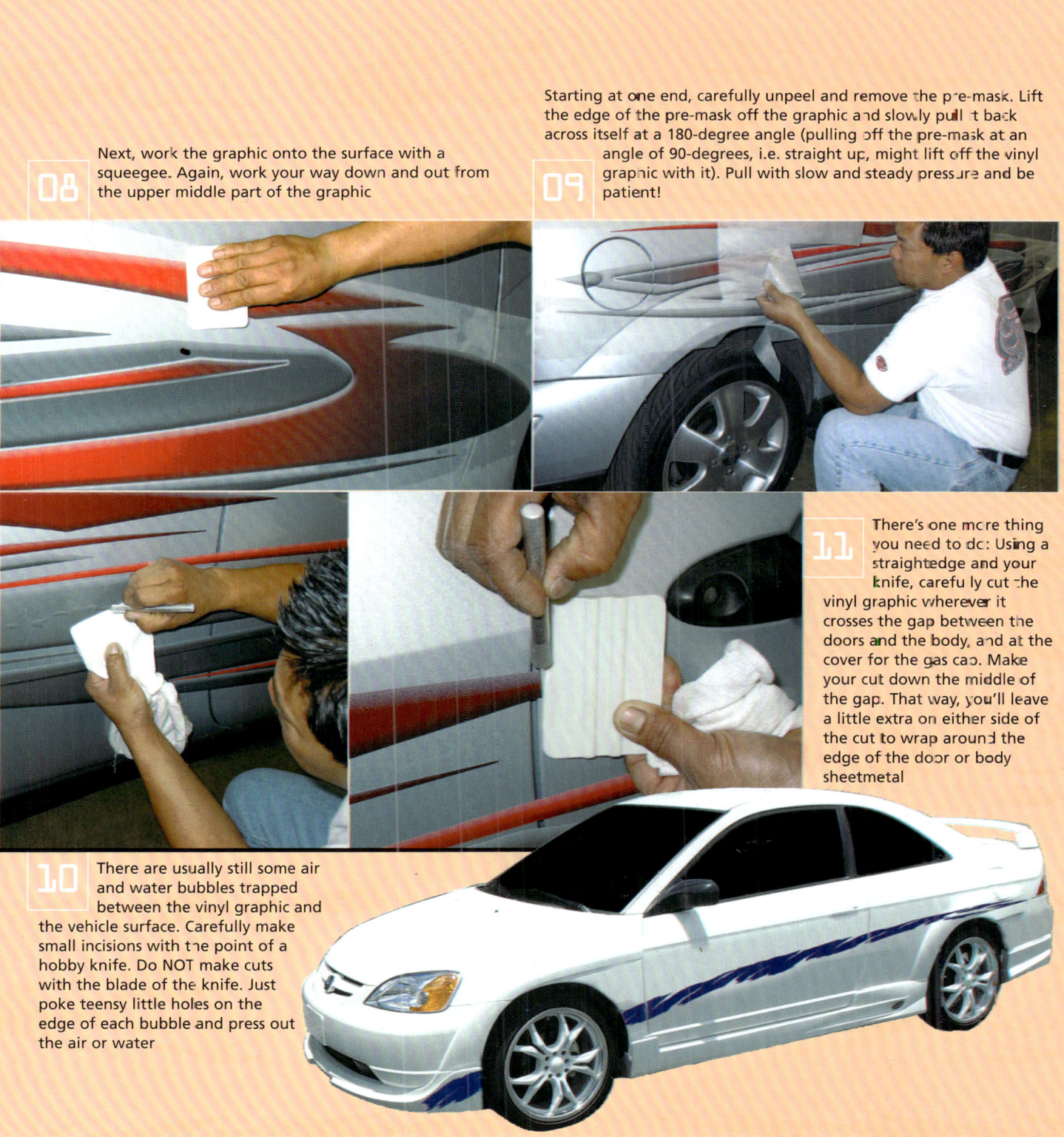

**08** Next, work the graphic onto the surface with a squeegee. Again, work your way down and out from the upper middle part of the graphic

**09** Starting at one end, carefully unpeel and remove the pre-mask. Lift the edge of the pre-mask off the graphic and slowly pull it back across itself at a 180-degree angle (pulling off the pre-mask at an angle of 90-degrees, i.e. straight up, might lift off the vinyl graphic with it). Pull with slow and steady pressure and be patient!

**11** There's one more thing you need to do: Using a straightedge and your knife, carefully cut the vinyl graphic wherever it crosses the gap between the doors and the body, and at the cover for the gas cap. Make your cut down the middle of the gap. That way, you'll leave a little extra on either side of the cut to wrap around the edge of the door or body sheetmetal

**10** There are usually still some air and water bubbles trapped between the vinyl graphic and the vehicle surface. Carefully make small incisions with the point of a hobby knife. Do NOT make cuts with the blade of the knife. Just poke teensy little holes on the edge of each bubble and press out the air or water

# 04 Interiors

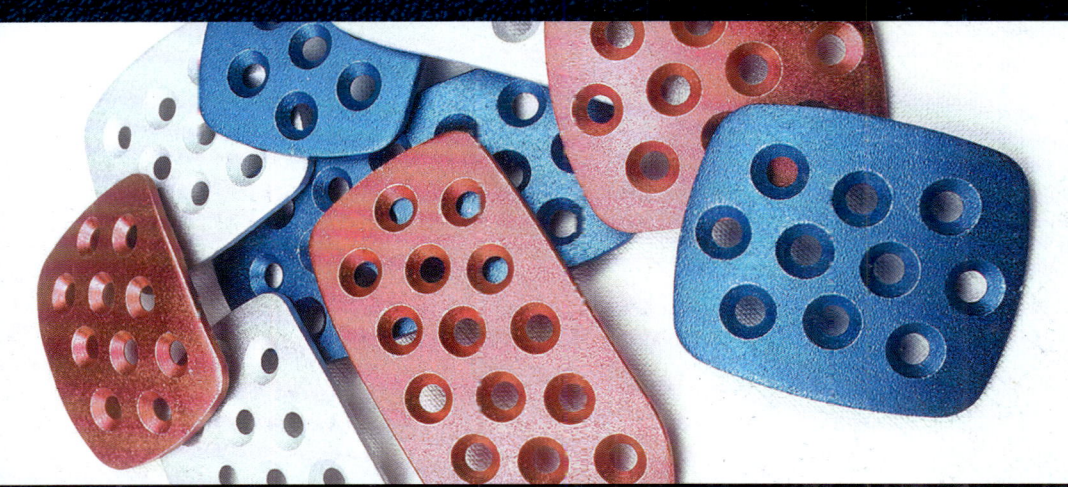

Are you sitting on an original equipment seat that bottomed out sometime back in the Nineties? Are you still wrapping your hands around a dull round blob of pebble-grain plastic posing as a steering wheel? Are you looking at a set of gauges that are hard to read at night and don't tell you much anyway? Are you surrounded by a dull expanse of faded and scuffed plastic trim panels on the dash, console and doors?

Well, lovers of style and color, rejoice! It's easy, and inexpensive, to do away with all this dullness

There has never been such a wide range of colorful, stylish and attractive products for interior upgrades as there is today. From steering wheels to racing seats, from control pedals to trim panels, the only limits to what you can do to your Civic's interior are your budget and your creativity.

## Installing a custom styling ring

**01** Unpack your styling ring kit and then read the instructions

**02** Clean off the steering wheel with a mild degreaser. Remove all dust, oil and silicone protectant

# Custom styling rings for airbag-equipped steering wheels

Even though you can't legally replace an airbag-equipped steering wheel with a custom aftermarket steering wheel, you can upgrade the appearance of your stock wheel with a custom styling ring. Each ring is custom molded to fit over the stock steering wheel. Styling rings are available in decorator colors like blue, red, silver, white, and yellow; in carbon fiber; and in simulated woodgrain such as burlwood or rosewood. They're easy to install and they can turn an ordinary airbag-equipped steering wheel into a stylish, elegant "new" steering wheel.

Carefully position the styling ring over the steering wheel. Before pressing it onto the steering wheel, make sure that the spoke covers on the ring are perfectly aligned with the spokes on the steering wheel. Then press the styling ring onto the steering wheel. Work your way around the circumference of the wheel, pressing down firmly all the way around to make sure that the styling ring is firmly attached. Easy, huh?

 **03** Clean off the inside of the styling ring . . .

 **04** . . . and peel off the protective strip covering the adhesive

 **05**

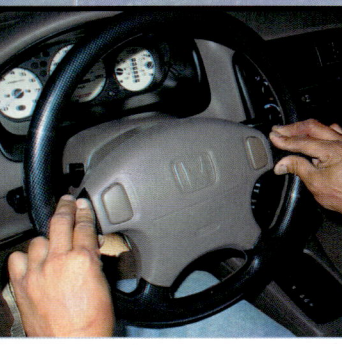

## Installing a custom shift lever knob and dust boot (manual transaxle)

# Shift lever knobs

Think about it: Besides the steering wheel, there's no part of your Civic that you handle more than the shift lever knob. Shift lever knobs and boots are a fairly inexpensive way of modifying the look of your Civic's interior. So why not upgrade to something that looks and feels good. There are hundreds of aftermarket knobs in a riot of colors and materials that will fit your Civic shift lever. And one of them has your name on it!

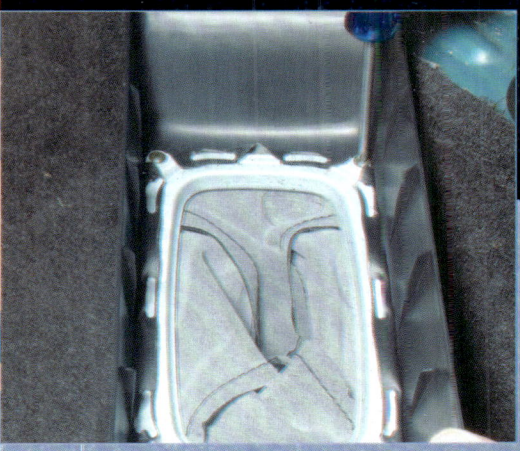

**01** First, remove the center console, or the part of the console that houses the shift lever mechanism (see your *Haynes manual* if you don't know how to remove the console). Once you've removed the part of the console that houses the shift lever, flip it over, remove the dust boot retaining screws (on our project Civic the boot is attached with four screws) . . .

**02** . . . then unclip the dust boot from the surround

**03** We drilled several holes through our new shift lever dust boot and through the surround . . .

**04** . . . and used self-tapping screws to fasten the dust boot to the surround

**05** Pop the dust boot surround back into place in the console . . .

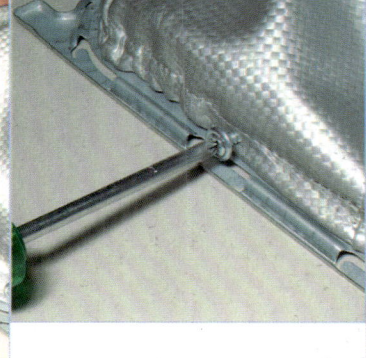
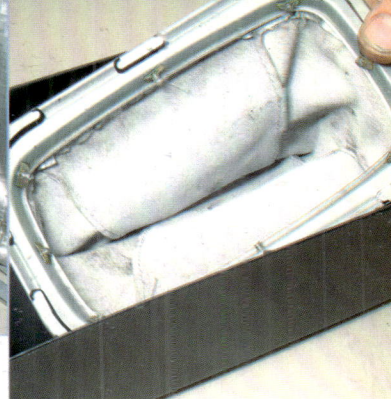

   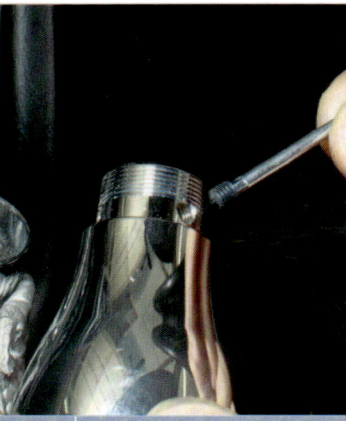

**06** . . . then reinstall the console (again, see your Haynes manual for help if you need it). Now let's do the new knob!

**07** Begin by installing the threaded ring to the shift lever . . .

**08** . . . then install the correct size plastic bushing (forget to install the bushing and the shift lever knob will be a very loose fit!)

**09** Install the three set screws in the threaded holes in the neck of the new shift lever knob

**10** Install the knob on the shift lever, push down firmly and tighten the three set screws uniformly to ensure that the knob is correctly centered on the lever. Make sure that the set screws are tight

**11** Screw the threaded ring onto the threaded lower portion of the knob

**12** Slide the dust boot up under the knob and either secure it with the Velcro collar or tie up the laces (different dust boots use different methods for securing the boot to the top of the shift lever). That's it! Good job!

# Installing a custom shift lever knob on an automatic

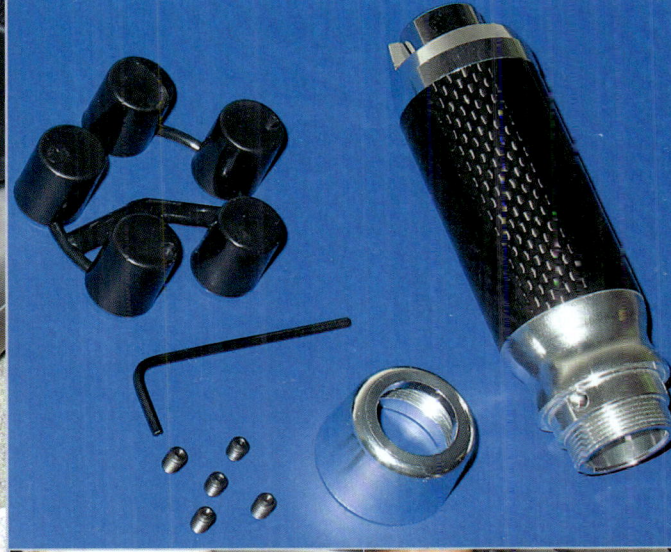

**01** First, unpack your automatic shift lever knob kit and make sure that all the components are there: The kit should include the knob itself, a set of plastic sleeves, some set screws, an Allen key to tighten the set screws and a threaded collar

**02** Remove the set screw from the factory shift knob

**03** Some Civic automatic shift knobs are equipped with *two* set screws

**04** Press the shift control button and remove the knob from the shift lever

**05** Determine which diameter sleeve is correct for your shift lever

55

**06** Using a pair of diagonal cutters, remove the correct sleeve from the kit

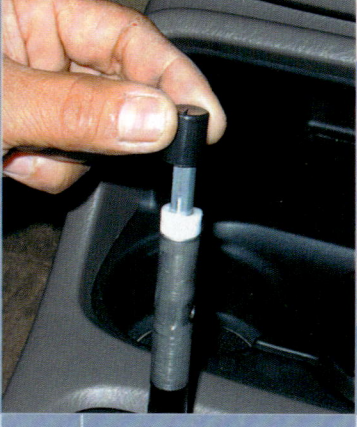

**07** Install the sleeve onto the shift lever

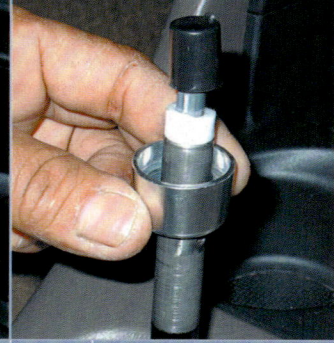

**08** Next, install the collar onto the shaft. Make sure that the threads are facing up, toward the shift knob

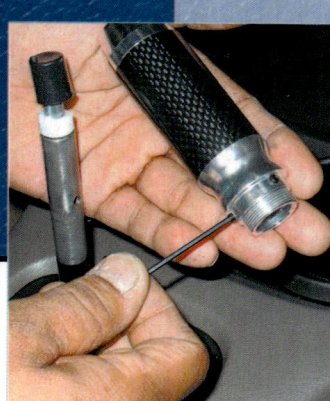

**09** Install the set screws in the shift knob but don't tighten them down yet

**10** Install the knob onto the shift lever with the cutout for the button facing toward the rear so that the button is accessible to the driver

**11** Tighten the set screws securely

**12** Screw the collar onto the shift knob. That's all there is to it!

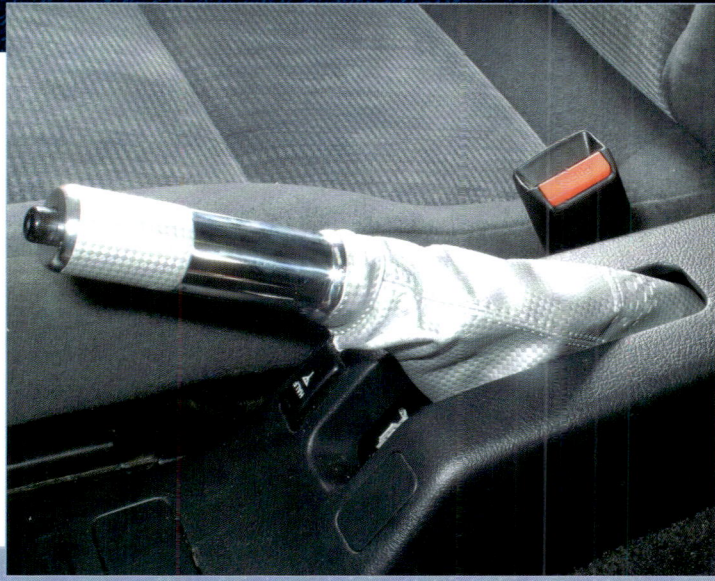

## Installing a custom handle and dust boot on the parking brake lever

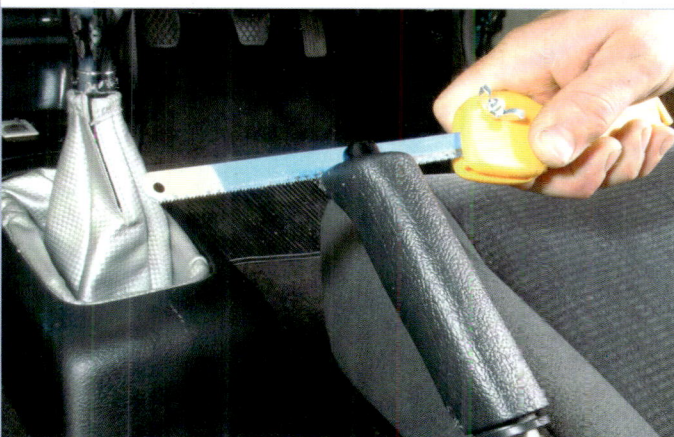

**01** First step is to remove the rear part of the center console (the part that houses the parking brake lever). If you're unsure how to do this, consult your Haynes manual. Then remove the stock parking brake lever handle. On some Civics the handle is permanently attached to the lever, so you'll have to hacksaw it off (on other models, simply remove a set screw or two and pull off the handle)

**02** Once the old handle is removed, slide off the old parking brake lever dust boot

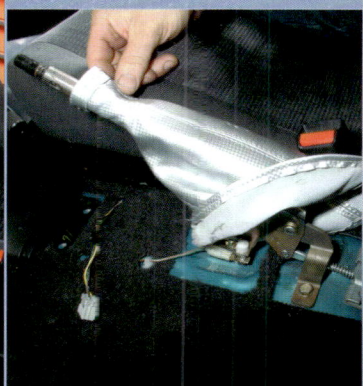

**03** Slide on the new parking brake lever boot . . .

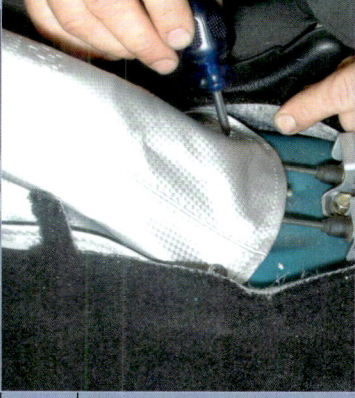

**04** . . . and secure the base with a couple of self-tapping screws (make sure that neither the boot nor the screws interferes with the parking brake cables)

**05** Install the rear section of the center console

**06** Slip the new handle onto the parking brake lever and tighten the set screws securely. Now test the parking brake mechanism and make sure that the new handle is not just pretty but also functional! Finally, fold the dust boot around the base of the handle to hide the set screws and you're done

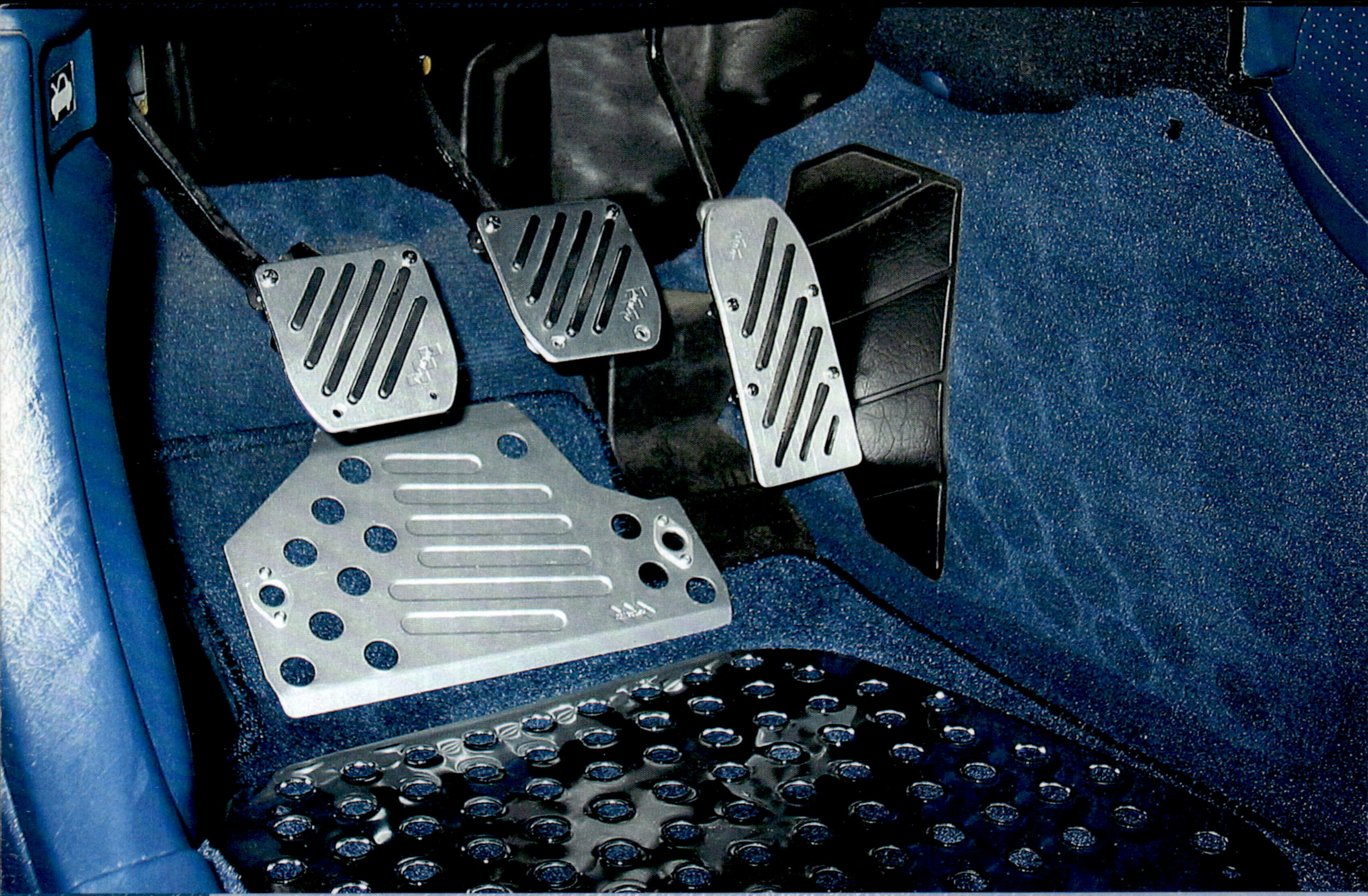

# Custom pedals

## Race replica pedal covers

Have you ever noticed the accelerator, brake and clutch pedal pads on a racecar? They're not heavy rubber-covered steel pads like streetcar pedals. Instead, they're aluminum, with holes drilled in them for lightness. In other words, no frills - stripped for action!

But until recently, when the rubber pads on your Civic pedals wore out, you simply replaced them with new rubber pads because that was your only option. Real racing pedals were hard to find, and expensive. Now you can pick a set of race replica pedals from literally hundreds of styles: brushed or polished aluminum, color-anodized, with or without lightening holes, with or without color-coordinated inserts. Some of the latest high-end pedals are even available in carbon fiber. The inserts (the small projections attached to the upper face of the pedal, to provide traction on the slippery surface of the pedal) are nylon, plastic, rubber or carbon fiber. Combined with other racy interior upgrades, a set of pedal pads gives your street Civic a racecar look.

## Selecting a new set of pedal covers

When selecting a set of race replica pedal covers for your Civic, pay close attention to a couple of things. First, the new pedal covers will have three or four mounting bolt holes in them. When installing the new pedal covers, you'll be using these mounting holes to attach the new covers to the old steel pedal footplates. But you'll also have to drill mounting holes in the old footplates, and those holes must be aligned with the mounting holes in the new covers. So it's a good idea to either take the dimensions of your old steel pedal footplates with you when you go to buy new pedal covers, or to be able to take the new covers out to the parking lot, place them in position on your pedals and "eyeball" the dimensions. If the new pedal covers have mounting holes sitting over nothing but thin air when you position them over the old rubber pedal covers, think seriously about a different set of aftermarket pedal covers! The stock pedal footplates must be large enough so that you'll be able to drill mounting holes in them without having to relocate any of the new pedal covers. Relocating the pedal covers could cause clearance problems between the pedals. And, more importantly, it could be dangerous to offset the pedals because you might accidentally depress the wrong pedal at the wrong time.

Inexpensive, "easy-to-install" pedal covers, which slip over the pedal pads and clamp into place, are widely available. Just be aware that, even when installed properly, they have the potential of slipping and interfering with another pedal, which could cause an accident.

## Installing a set of race replica pedal covers

 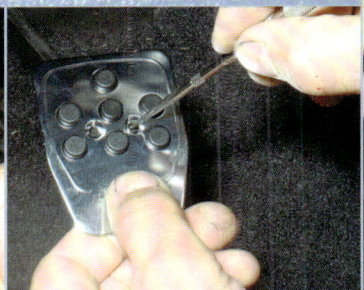  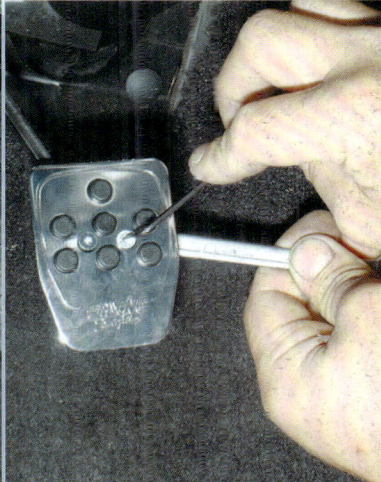

**01** First peel off the old rubber pedal covers from the brake and clutch pedals (we're going to walk you through the brake and clutch pedals first because they're identical and because they're easy; the accelerator pedal installation, which begins with Step 6, is a little more involved)

**02** Hold the new pedal in place with one hand and using an awl or a grease pencil, mark the location of the holes for the pedal cover mounting bolts. Make sure that the holes aren't too close to the pedal arm, or you won't be able to fit the nuts onto the mounting bolts

**03** Before you drill any holes in the pedals, use a center punch to make a deep enough impression in the spots you marked for drilling so that the drill bit doesn't slip and slide all over the pedal. Then support each pedal with a block of wood as shown to prevent the pedal from being pushed down when you apply some pushing power to the drill

**04** These pedal covers are secured to the pedal footplates with a couple of Allen bolts. Insert the Allen bolts through their holes in the footplate, install the nuts and tighten the Allen bolts securely. We can't overstress the importance of making sure that the pedal cover bolts are tight. It's a good idea to check the tightness of the bolts a few weeks after installing them

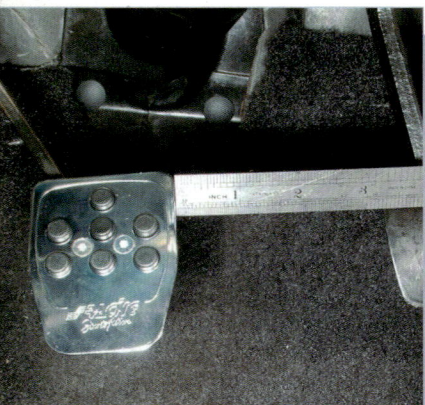   

**05** Some aftermarket manufacturers actually specify the minimum distance between the pedal covers. Because the covers are slightly larger than the footplates they're covering, your feet will take a little while to get used to the slightly different feel from the new larger pedals

**06** On to the accelerator pedal, which isn't quite as straightforward. Right away, we ran into some trouble. We couldn't peel off the old rubber cover from the pedal, so we had to cut it off. We decided that drilling the holes in this pedal would be easier to do on the workbench, so we removed the pedal arm

**07** First, open the hood and disconnect the accelerator cable from the throttle lever

**08** Back under the dash, locate the cotter pin that secures the accelerator pedal pivot pin to the mounting bracket located at the upper end of the pedal arm. Remove the cotter pin, pull out the pivot pin . . .

  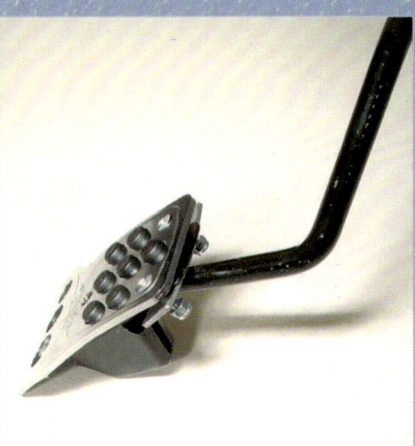

**09** . . . unhook the pedal return spring and remove the accelerator pedal and arm assembly

**10** Place the new pedal cover on top of the footplate, mark the spot for the mounting holes and drill them.

**11** Okay, place the new pedal cover in position, install the mounting bolts and tighten them securely. Now all you have to do is install the pedal and arm assembly and reconnect the accelerator cable

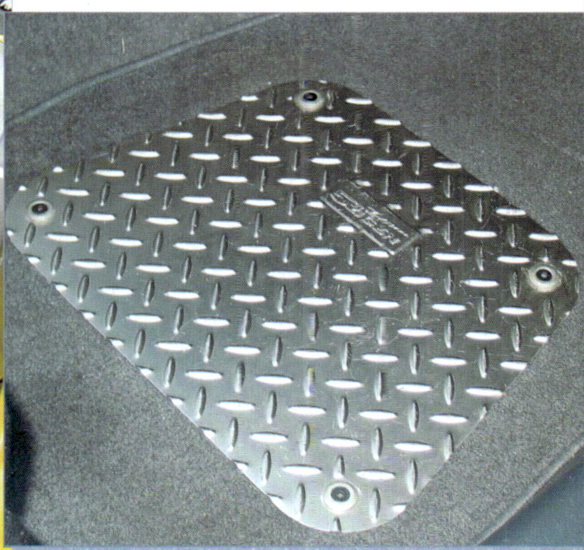

# Custom floormats

Covering up worn and scrappy carpet can easily be accomplished using custom floormats. The types and patterns are endless, depending upon your style.

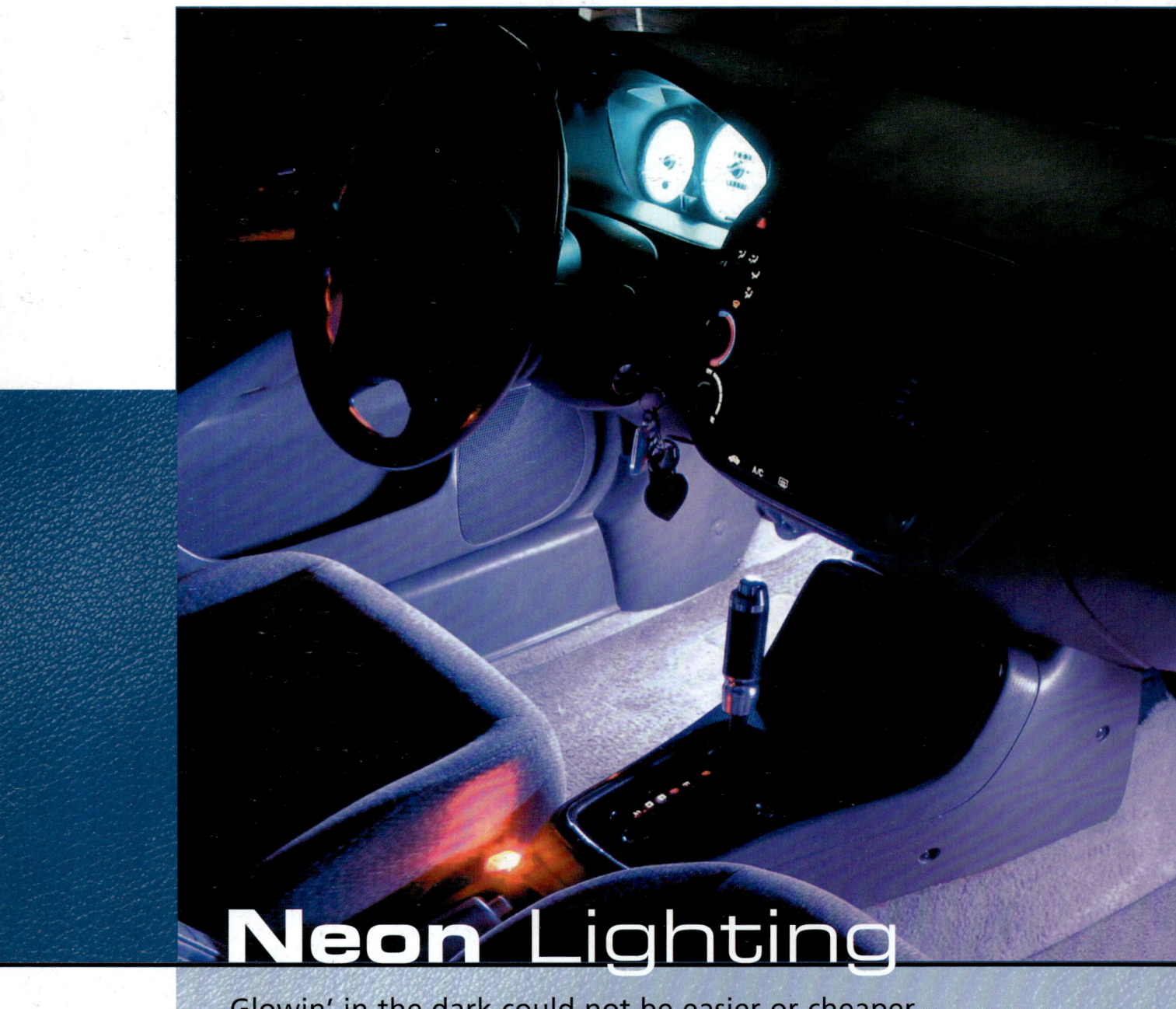

# Neon Lighting

Glowin' in the dark could not be easier or cheaper.
So switch the switch and get with it

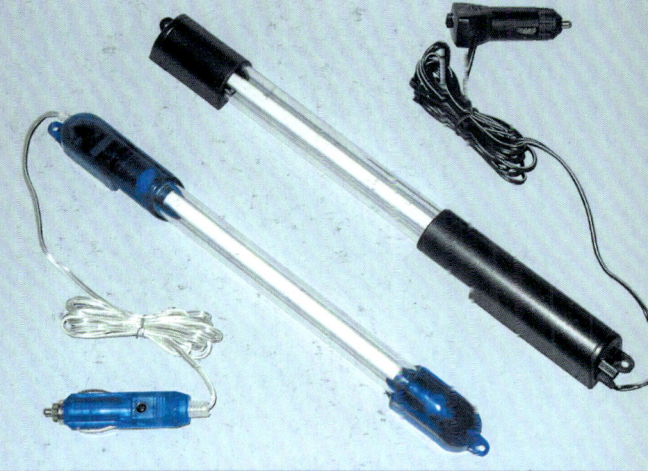

**01** Most kits include an enclosed neon light assembly, an electrical lead, an adapter to plug into the cigarette lighter and the instructions. We decided to install a pair of purple neon lights under the dash of a Honda Civic, one for the driver and one for the front-seat passenger, and a blue neon light in the backseat footwell area

# Installing neon lighting under the dash

**02** Position the neon light assembly under the dash and try to find a place that will provide you with a solid installation. We picked this spot because it was flat and we could drill into it without hitting anything vital

**03** Mark the location of the mounting screw holes

**04** Drill the mounting screw holes with a drill bit a little bit smaller in diameter than the screws you're going to use

**05** Install the mounting screws and tighten them securely, but don't really crank on them. This is a plastic accessory being mounted on a plastic dash, and we all know what happens to plastic when you overtighten it!

**06** Either unplug your cigarette lighter or, if you have an electrical accessory receptacle (like the one we found on this late-model Honda Civic), use that

**07** Plug in the electrical adapter. That's all there is to it for the passenger side. Installing the other neon light for the driver is virtually identical to this procedure, except for one thing . . .

**08** . . . if you install two (or more) neon lights, you can't plug them all into the cigarette light (or an accessory outlet). Of course, you could splice the two electrical leads into one adapter. But at that point you might as well splice the two (or more) leads through a switch you can flip on and off

⚠️ **Warning !**
*The use of neon lighting may not be legal in all areas. Check it out first. Also remember that driving at night with a brightly-lit interior makes it even harder to see out. Neons are best used at shows or in the parking lot.*

## Installing neon lighting in the rear footwell

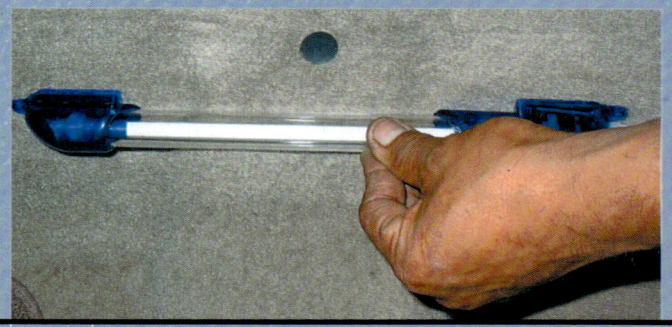

**01** Position the neon light assembly where you want it. We selected the area right below the center of the back seat because we figured one light would provide plenty of illumination for both rear footwells

**02** Using a laundry marker, mark the positions of the mounting screws

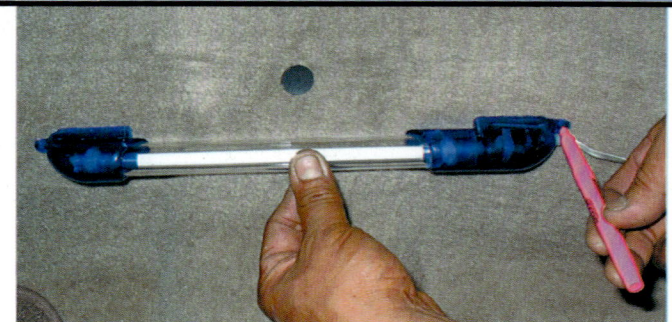

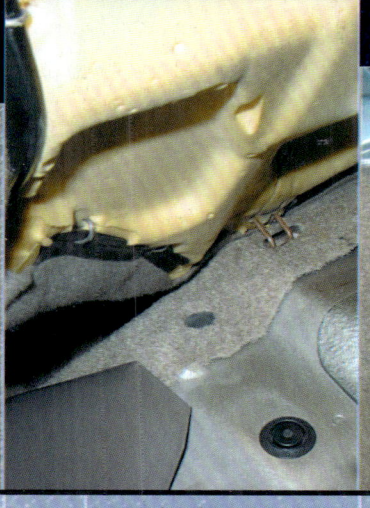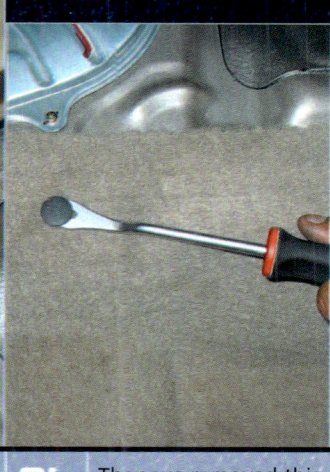

**03** We needed to figure out where to route the electrical lead for the neon light. We decided that behind and under the carpet was our best choice. So we removed the rear seat cushion bolts (see your Haynes manual for the specific rear seat removal procedure for your car) . . .

**04** . . . then we lifted up the rear edge of the back seat cushion . . .

**05** . . . unhooked the forward edge and removed the rear seat cushion

**06** Then we removed this push fastener, peeled back the carpet and routed the neon light's electrical lead down and forward . . .

**07** . . . and then pulled it through the hole in the carpet for the parking brake lever (center console removed). From here, we could route it forward, under the console, to the cigarette lighter or the switch we installed earlier for the front

**08** With the electrical wiring routed under the carpet, place the carpet back in position and install the push fastener

**09** Using the marks you made in Step 2, drill holes through the carpet and the body for the neon light mounting screws

**10** Install the light, secure it with the mounting screws, reinstall the seat and you're done!

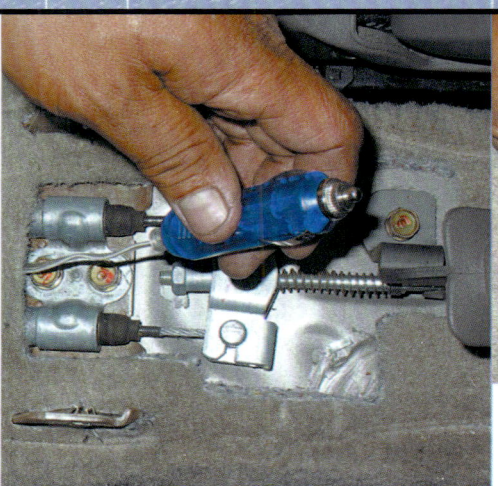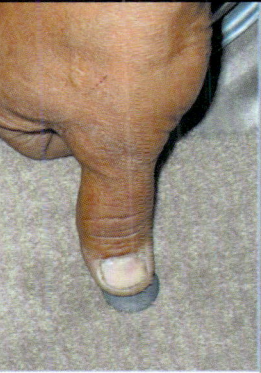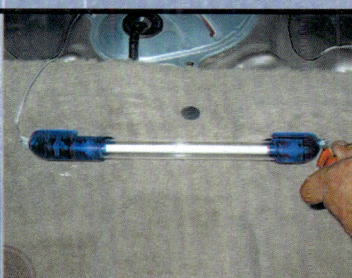

# Interior trim

## Add a little color to your interior

Automotive exteriors come in lots of nice colors, but most stock interiors are still mainly black, gray, or beige. Boring!

But it doesn't have to be that way. There are three ways to add a little (or a lot of) color to your interior: paint it, "film" it or re-cover it with new trim pieces. Interior trim film is a new high-tech product that you can buy in sheets and cut to fit various trim pieces on the dash, the center console and the doors. Film is UV and heat resistant and it's available in a variety of finishes - simulated woodgrain, carbon fiber, etc. - and colors. Trim covers are also available in a similarly wide range of finishes and colors.

## Painting trim

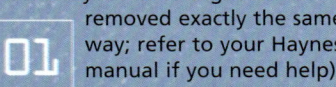

**01** First, remove the trim panel(s) you want to paint. We decided to start with the glove box. Just remove the two screws underneath then remove the glove box (the glove box on your Civic might not be removed exactly the same way; refer to your Haynes manual if you need help)

**02** Break up the glazed surface of the glove box with sandpaper. If you want to keep that "pebble-grain" surface, just sand enough to break the glaze. If you want to get rid of that pebble-grain surface, keep sanding (and sanding!)

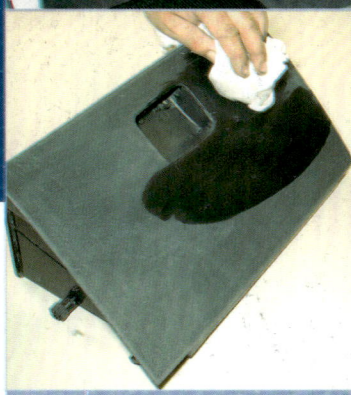
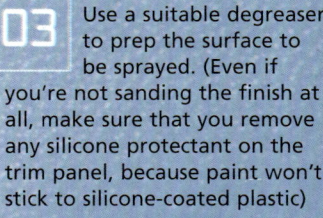

**03** Use a suitable degreaser to prep the surface to be sprayed. (Even if you're not sanding the finish at all, make sure that you remove any silicone protectant on the trim panel, because paint won't stick to silicone-coated plastic)

**04** Mask any areas that you don't want to paint, then apply a "mist coat" of primer. Sand the primer with fine-grit sandpaper, but don't sand off the primer.

**05** Apply the first topcoat very "dusty," which means you must spray from a little further away than normal, letting the paint fall onto the job, rather than blasting it on using the full force of the aerosol spray propellant. Some colors need several coats before they look right. Allow time for each one to dry before applying the next coat

# Applying film

**01** First, remove the trim panel(s) you want to film (refer to your *Haynes manual* for help). Using a suitable degreaser, clean up the surface you want to film. If you're hoping to film a heavily grained finish, be aware that the grain will show through thin film, and the film won't fully stick to a heavily grained surface either

**02** Cut the film to the approximate size and carefully warm up the film and the panel itself with a heat gun. Peel off the backing sheet, and make SURE that the film stays as flat as possible. Also make sure that, when you pick up the film, you don't allow it to stick to itself!

**03** Carefully apply the film. If you're installing a patterned film (like the carbon-fiber-look film shown here), make very sure that you apply the film with the pattern aligned horizontally and vertically. Starting at one edge, work across to minimize air bubbles and creases. If you get a bad crease, unpeel the film a bit and try again. Don't try to shift the position of the film once you've begun to apply it; the adhesive is far too sticky

**04** Before trimming your filmed panel, work out the air bubbles with a soft cloth. Then make sure the film is sticking well by going over it firmly with the edge of a plastic credit card

**05** Trimming the panel can be tricky. It's easier to trim the more complicated edges after heating up the film with a hairdryer or heat gun. But don't overdo it! Also, make sure that the hobby knife you're using is SHARP. A blunt knife will ripple the film, and might even tear it

**06** To get the film to wrap neatly around a curved edge, make several slits almost up to the edge, then heat up the area you're working on, wrap each sliver of film over the edge and stick it on firmly. If you heat the film sufficiently, it wraps around and keeps its shape. Without the heat, the film might spring back, ruining all your hard work

  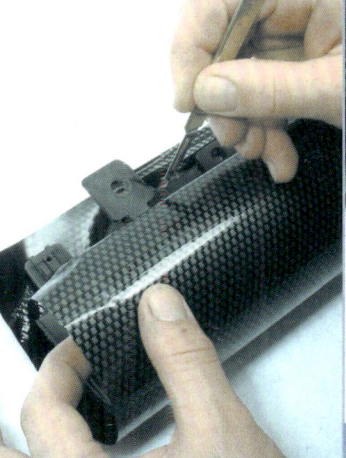 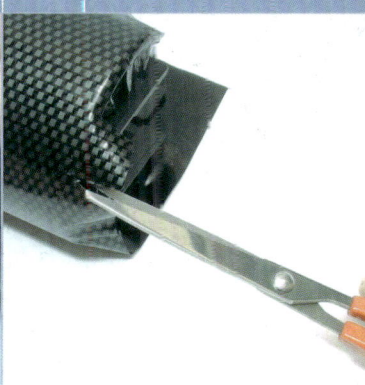

## Installing a custom trim panel kit

Unpack your new trim panel set and make sure that everything is there. And make sure that you have the right kit for your make and model! To keep the adhesive side of each individual trim piece dust-free, don't detach it from the backing paper until you're ready to install it. (And it's not a bad idea to wash your hands thoroughly to remove any oil so that you don't put fingerprints on anything!)

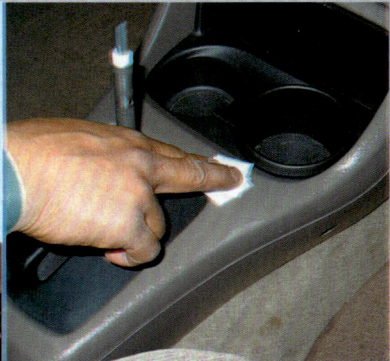

**01** Here's the basic process. Let's start with the center console: First, wipe off all oil, dirt, silicone protectant, etc. with rubbing alcohol

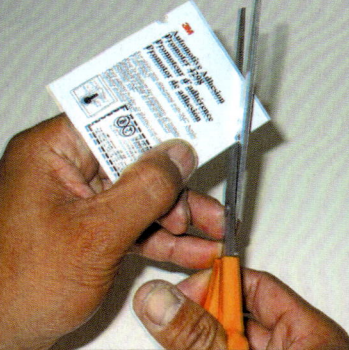

**02** Then break out the promoter . . .

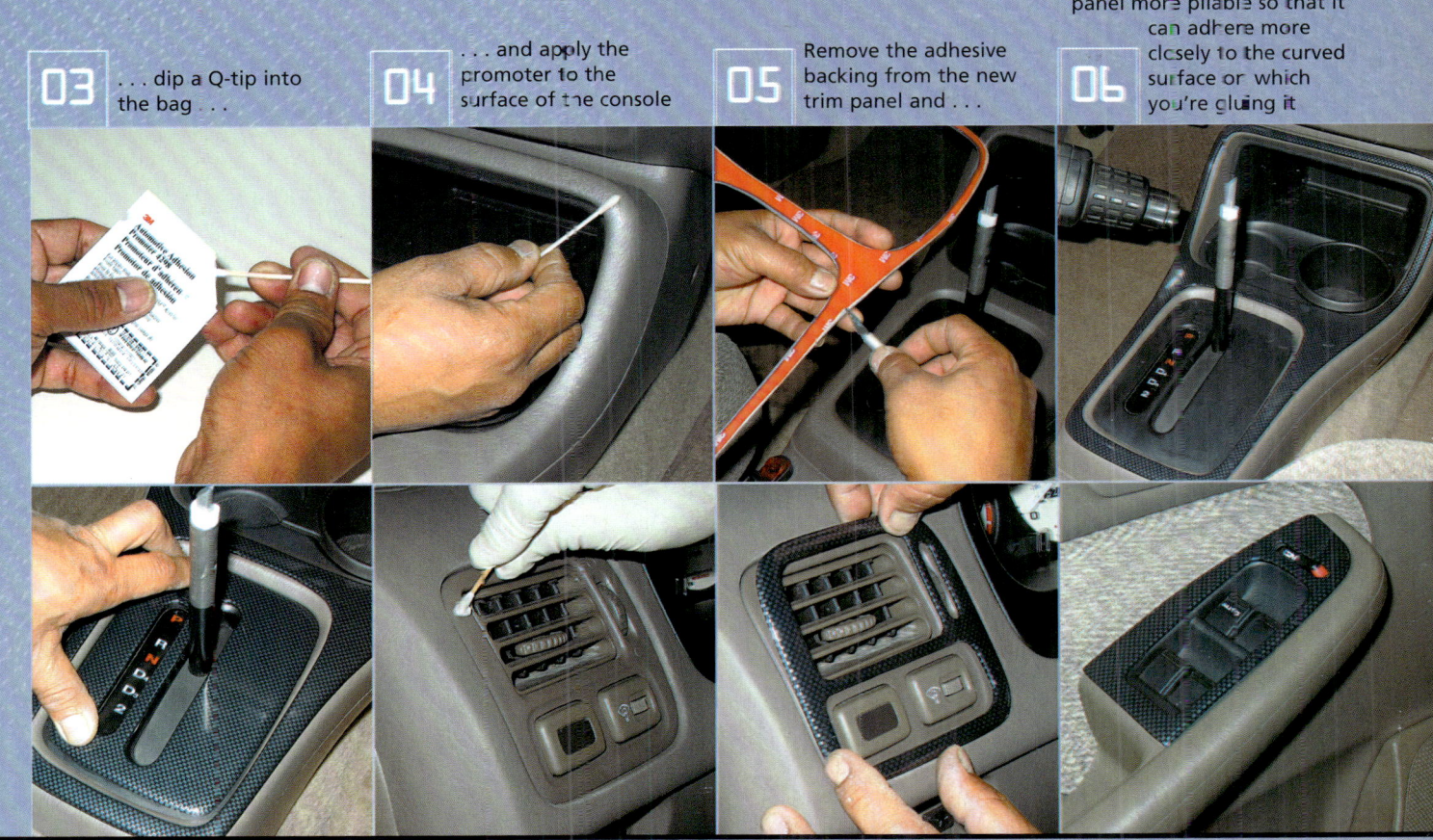

| 03 | . . . dip a Q-tip into the bag . . . |
| 04 | . . . and apply the promoter to the surface of the console |
| 05 | Remove the adhesive backing from the new trim panel and . . . |
| 06 | . . . apply it to the console. On curved surfaces use a heat gun to warm up the new trim panel and then press it down again. The heat makes the panel more pliable so that it can adhere more closely to the curved surface on which you're gluing it |
| 07 | Work your way around the interior putting the remaining pieces in place. Take your time |

# Gauge face upgrade

**White, colored, even glow-in-the-dark . . . changing out your stock black gauge faces will really add a custom touch to your dash**

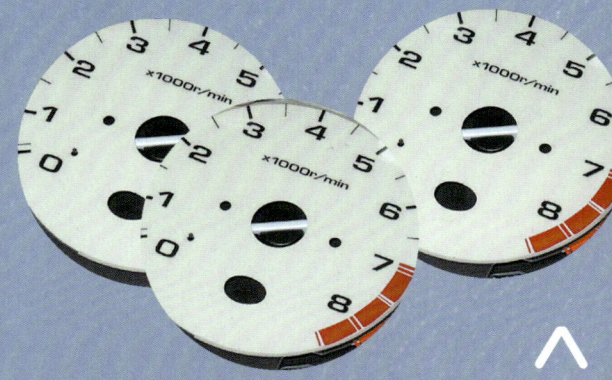

**01** Unpack your electro-luminescent gauge face kit and make sure that everything is there. Then read through the instructions carefully before proceeding. Make sure that you understand the procedure. If you're nervous about any phase of this project, have a more experienced friend, preferably someone who's already installed luminescent gauge faces, help you. Or farm it out to a professional installer

**02** The instrument cluster trim bezel for this Honda Civic is pretty typical of sport compacts. It has two upper retaining screws. The cluster trim bezel on your Civic will have at least two retaining screws and, depending on the year and model, as many as four screws. Refer to your Haynes manual if you're not sure

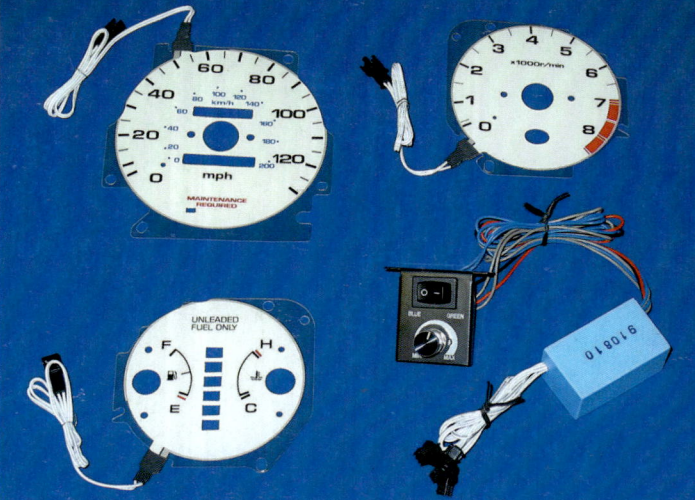

**03** Using a short Phillips screwdriver, remove the instrument cluster trim bezel screws, then remove the bezel. If the bezel doesn't come right off, grab a penlight and inspect the entire perimeter of the bezel for "hidden" screws. On some vehicles, the screws are hidden under small plastic caps. Don't ever try to force a trim bezel loose or you will end up breaking off retaining tabs or the bezel itself. Ouch! These pieces are more expensive than they look

**04** Once the cluster trim bezel is out of the way, find the (usually four) instrument cluster retaining screws (upper screws not visible in this photo) . . .

**05** . . . remove the lower screws . . .

**06** . . . remove the upper screws . . .

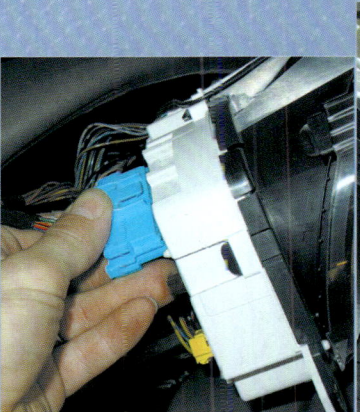 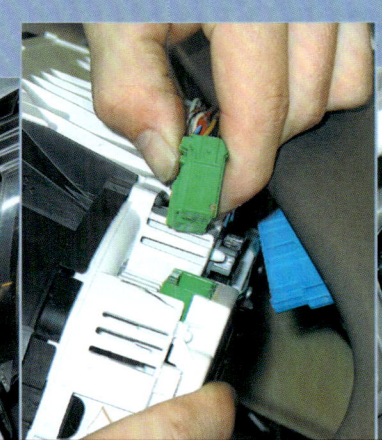 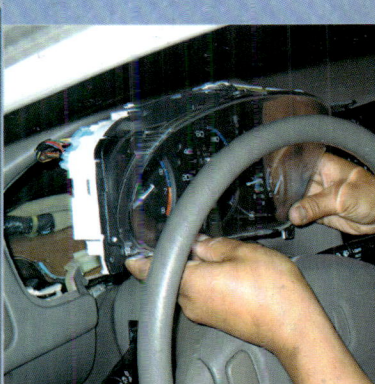

*Just make sure you get the right kit for your car, and don't start stripping anything until you're sure it's the right one. Look carefully at every detail. Applications for replacement faces should be very specific for model and model year. This is one mod that is not ONE SIZE FITS ALL.*

**07** . . . pull out the instrument cluster far enough to unplug the electrical connectors from the back . . .

**08** . . . and the top as well . . .

**09** . . . make sure that everything is disconnected and then carefully remove the cluster

71

**10** Okay, put the cluster on a clean workspace and take it apart. Our cluster was held together by a bunch of little locking tabs. We took apart our feeler gauge set and used the thin metal strips, inserting them into the slots for the locking tabs, to hold the tabs down. Don't try to pry each of the locking tabs loose with a screwdriver; as soon as you let go of one tab and go to the next, the previous tab will snap back into place

**11** Hey, it might look a little goofy, but it works!

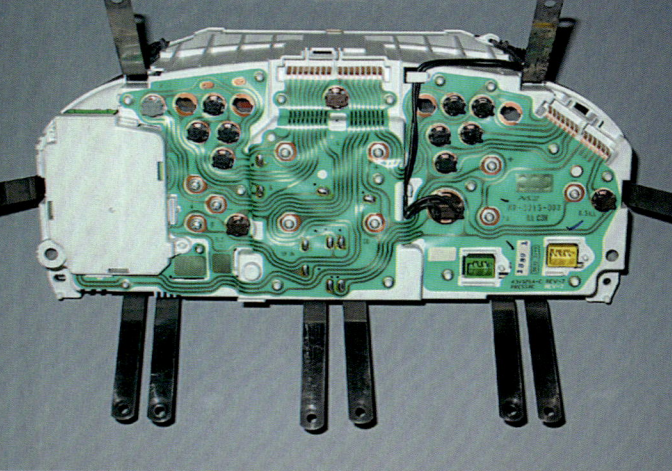

**12** There's one more little thing you need to do before you can separate the two halves of the cluster assembly: remove any gauge illumination bulb holders with leads that cross the split line between the two halves of the cluster. Before proceeding, make sure that there are no wires or anything else routed between the two halves of the cluster

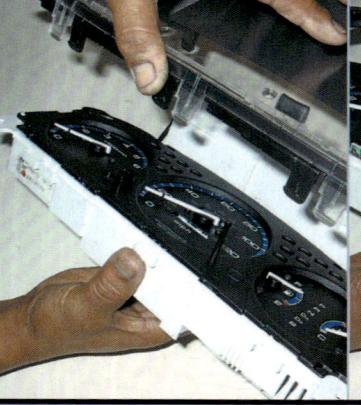

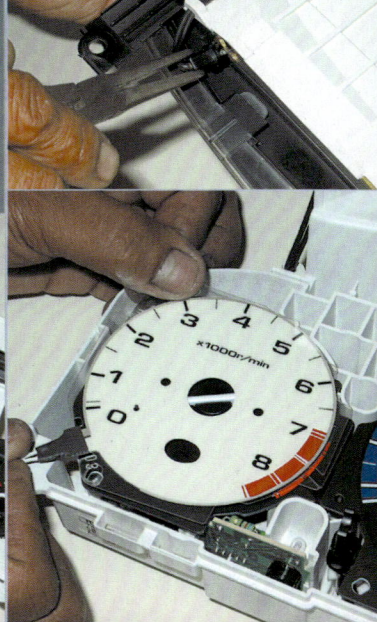

**13** Using a screwdriver, very carefully pry the two halves of the cluster apart. Take your time and gently work the two halves apart by prying all the way around the perimeter of the cluster assembly. If you find an area that's difficult to separate, check the locking tab(s) in that area and make sure that it's still released

**14** Separate the two halves of the cluster assembly and set the lens half aside

**15** Remove the gauge faceplate from the cluster

**16** Before further disassembly of the cluster, position each of the electro-luminescent gauge faces precisely over the old faces and make sure that the hole in the middle of each new gauge face is big enough to fit over the indicator needle hub. If it isn't, you've got the wrong kit for your car!

**17** Remove the screws from the old tachometer gauge face and put them in a bag or some place where you won't lose them (they're small!)

**18** Wash your hands. Make sure that there's no oil or grease on your fingers. Then very carefully work the new gauge face onto the tachometer by working the tach sweep needle up through the hole in the center of the new face and then slicing the face sideways until it's centered over the needle hub. Don't break off the tach needle or you'll be buying a new tach!

**19** Holding the new tachometer face with one hand, turn the cluster over and look for a hole through which you can thread the electrical lead for the new faceplate. We lucked out and found this hole. We also found one for the fuel level and coolant temperature gauge, but had to make our own for the speedometer (see Step 21). If your cluster doesn't have a convenient hole for the tach lead, make one

**20** Retrieve the old gauge face retaining screws and install them but don't tighten them yet. You're going to center the new gauge faces when you install the faceplate that surrounds the gauge faces. If you tighten the screws now, the new gauge faces won't be free to move.

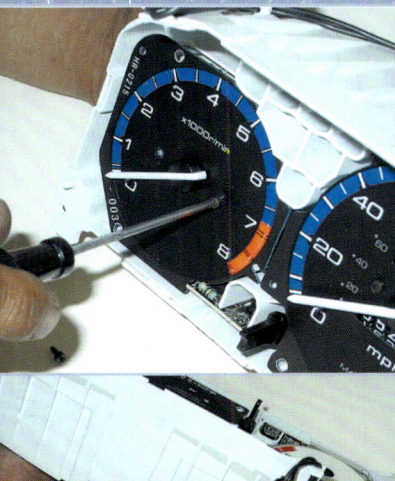
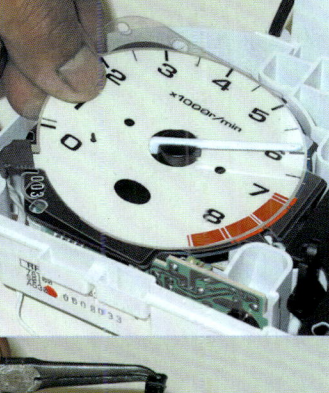
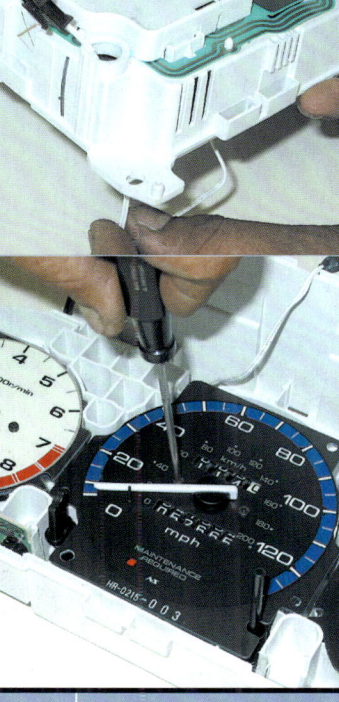
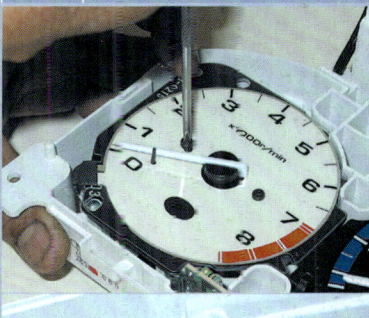

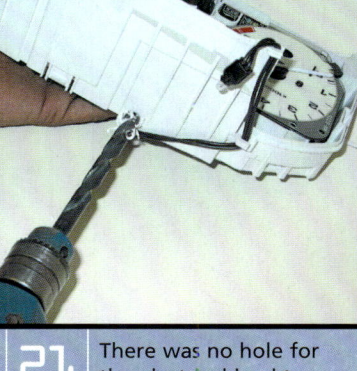
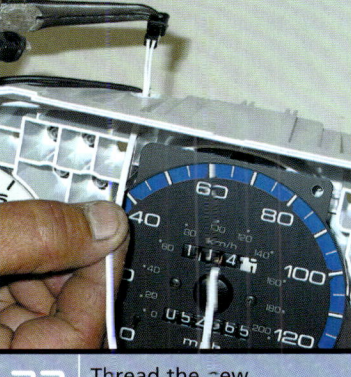

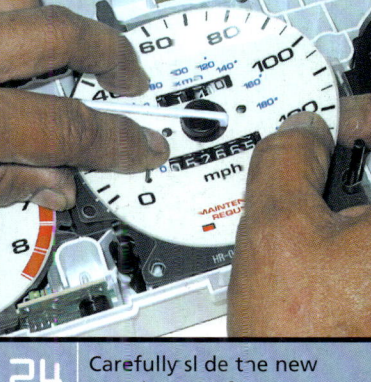

**21** There was no hole for the electrical lead to the new speedometer face, so we drilled one in an area where we wouldn't hit anything expensive. Start with a smaller bit and then gradually work your way up to a 1/4-inch bit

**22** Thread the new speedometer face electrical lead through the hole you made

**23** Remove the retaining screws from the old speedometer face and stash them in the baggie or in someplace safe

**24** Carefully slide the new speedometer face over the speedo needle and into position. Then grab your speedo face retaining screws and loosely install them.

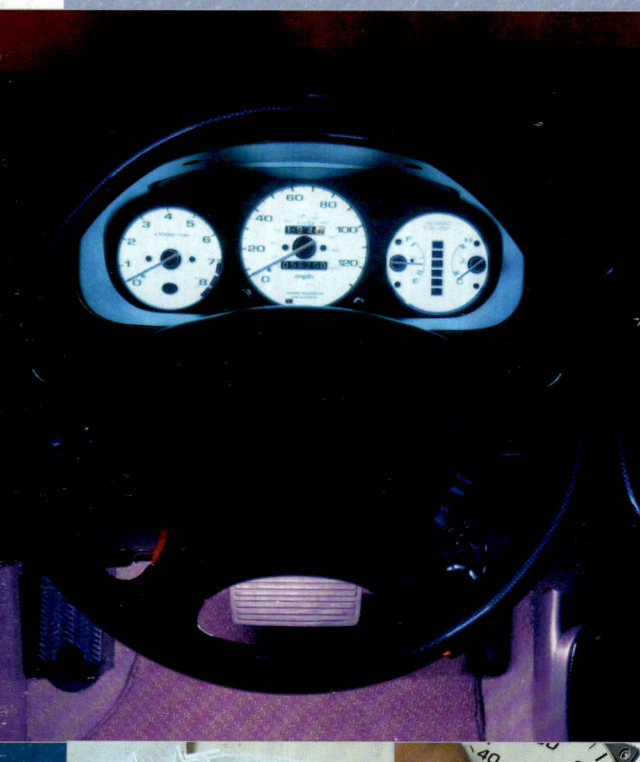

**25** Look for a hole for the lead for the new fuel level/coolant temperature gauge face and thread it through the hole. If there is no hole, make one

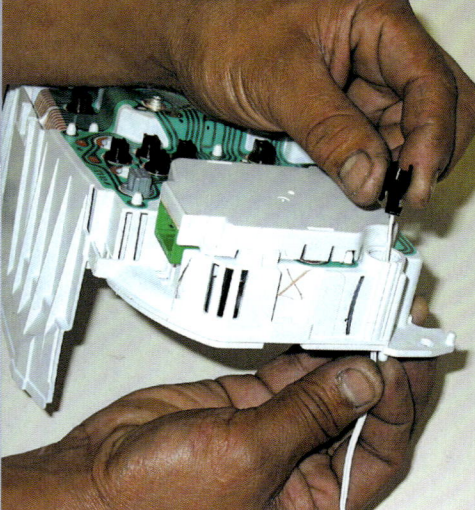

**26** Remove the fuel level/coolant temperature gauge face retaining screws

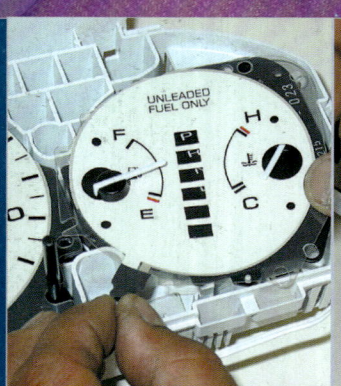

**27** Carefully install the new gauge face for the fuel level and coolant temperature. This one's a little tricky because there are two needles and hubs to deal with, but you'll figure it out! Just be careful and don't break off either of those needles!

**28** Install the old gauge face retaining screws. Again, make sure that they're not tight yet

**29** Place the faceplate in position

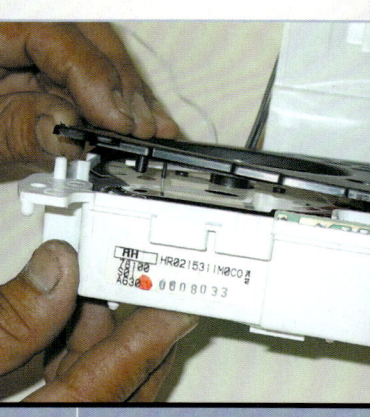

**30** Make sure that the locator pins on the underside of the faceplate fit through the holes stamped through the transparent plastic edges of the new gauge faces. This centers each of the new gauge faces and locks them into position when the cluster is reassembled

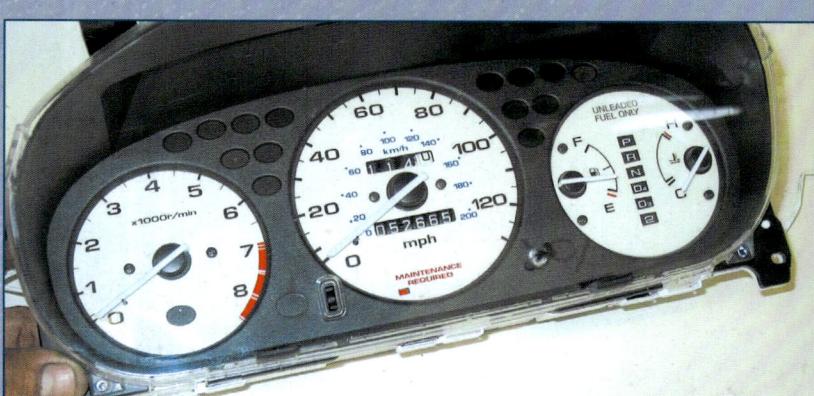

**31** Now you can tighten the gauge face retaining screws! Just snug them. It's not necessary to really crank on them, or you'll strip out the threads

**32** Holding the actual cluster in one hand, with the gauges and faceplate facing up, place the lens half of the cluster assembly in position and snap the two halves together. Make sure that all the locking tangs snap into place

**33** Be sure to reinstall any illumination bulb holders you removed before disassembling the cluster and reroute the electrical lead through any guides or clips, just as it was before

**34** Then combine the leads for the new gauge faces into a small harness and bundle them together with two or three small cable ties

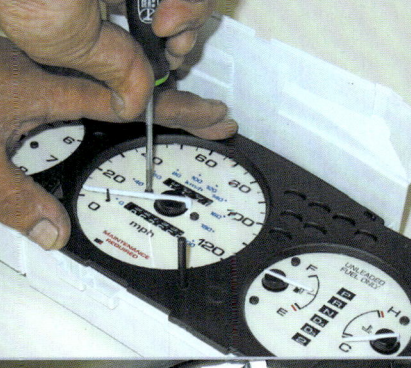

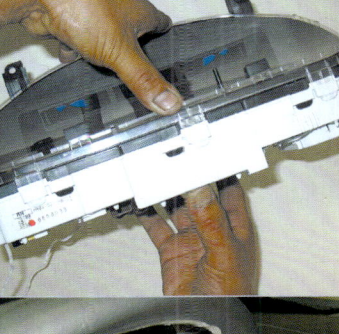

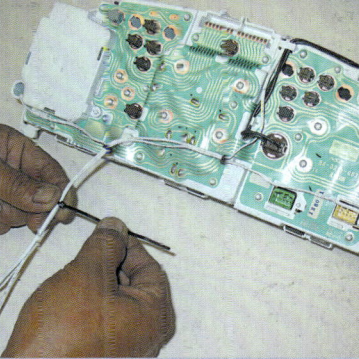

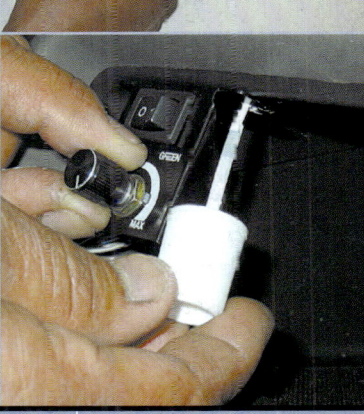

**35** Okay, you're ready to install the cluster in the dash

**36** Install the cluster mounting screws and tighten them securely. But don't install the cluster trim bezel just yet

**37** Look for a good place to install the color selection switch and rheostat. We found a suitable location in the storage receptacle at the forward end of the center console

**38** Mark the location of the switch/rheostat and mark the location of the holes you're going to drill for the switch mounting screws

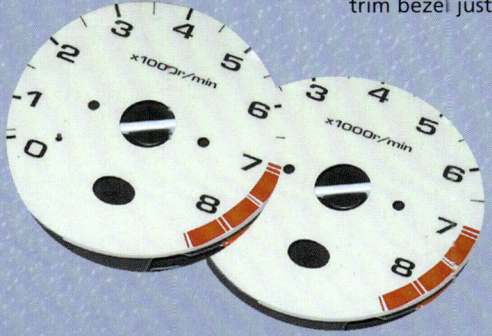

**39** Drill the mounting holes

**40** Look for a place to route the switch wires. We inserted our wires through this gap between the upper and lower parts of the storage receptacle. If nothing is handy, drill a small hole nearby. Just keep in mind that you're going to route the wires toward the instrument cluster so that you can hook up with the three leads from the new gauge faces

**41** Install the switch/rheostat mounting screws and tighten them snugly but not so tight that you strip out the holes

**42** Now fish out those three leads to the new gauge faces . . .

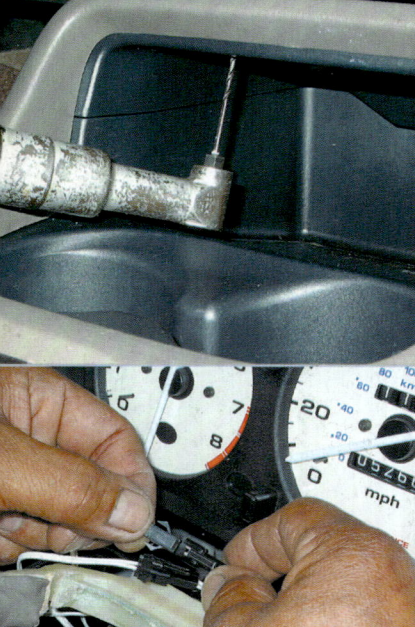
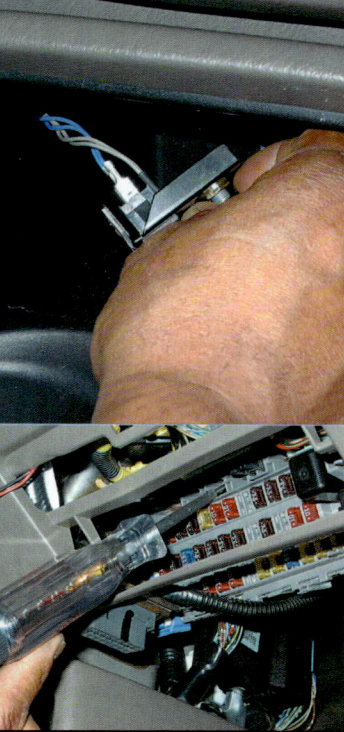
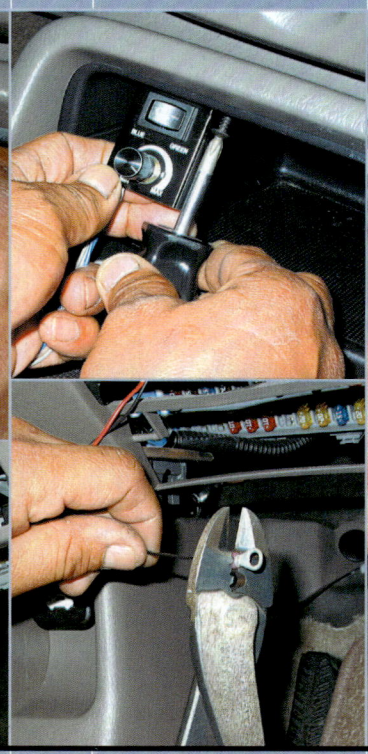

**43** . . . and plug them into the leads from the switch/rheostat. (Most kit switches will have three or four leads for this purpose, so you'll have an extra lead just in case you decide to reface another gauge later)

**44** Now look for a terminal on the fuse panel that's hot when the parking lights are turned on

**45** Strip off a 1/4-inch of insulation from the ground wire, crimp on a ground terminal and bolt the ground wire to a convenient metal-on-metal screw somewhere under the dash. Dash reinforcement bracket screws are good, and so are screws used to attach other ground wires. Just make sure that the ground screw makes a good connection to the body or floorpan

**46** Strip off a 1/4-inch of insulation from the power wire, crimp on a suitable spade connector and connect the power wire to the hot-when-the-parking-lights-are-turned-on terminal at the fuse panel. That's it! You're done! Enjoy!

# Installing aftermarket gauges

## Installing pillar pod gauges

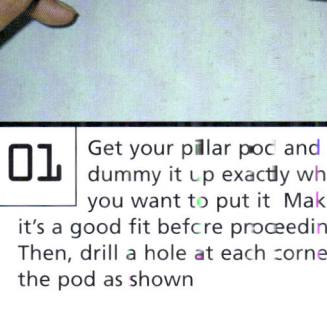

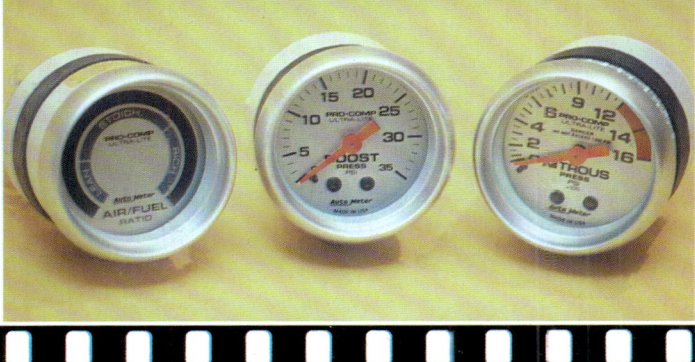

**01** Get your pillar pod and dummy it up exactly where you want to put it. Make sure it's a good fit before proceeding. Then, drill a hole at each corner of the pod as shown

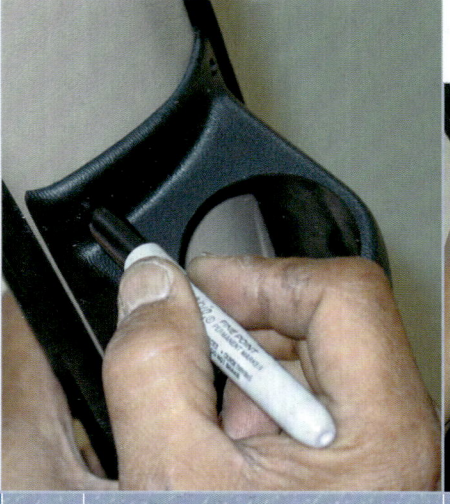

Interiors

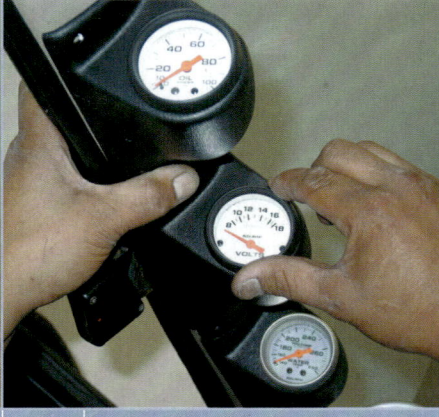

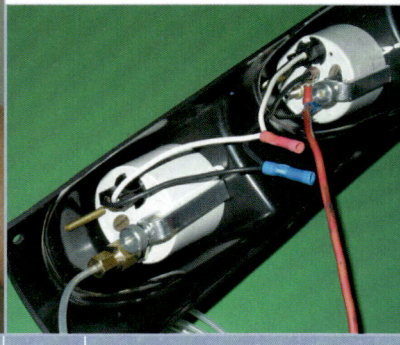

**02** Place the pod in position on the pillar and mark the locations of the four holes you're going to drill. Make sure the holes aren't going to be too close to the edges of the pillar

**03** Insert the gauges into the pillar pod, place the pod in position on the pillar, then rotate the gauges so the "OIL" and "VOLTS" on the gauge faces are horizontal and parallel to each other.

**04** Remove the pillar pod and clamp the gauges into place with the clamps provided by the manufacturer, then connect the wires. Note how we spliced the two illumination bulb wires and the two ground wires together.

**05** Route the wires and the oil line for the oil pressure gauge through the gap between the end of the dash and the A-pillar, then install the pillar pod/gauge assembly on the pillar and attach it with the four mounting screws. Don't overtighten the screws or you'll strip out the holes. When you're done with this phase, hide the wires with some convoluted tubing.

# Installing aftermarket gauges

## Installing a tachometer

**01** It's recommended to mount the tach where it's easy to see without taking your eyes off the road. Make sure that the dash material is substantial enough to support the tach. Once you've settled on the perfect spot for your tach, mark the position of the mounting bracket.

**02** Remove the tach from the mounting bracket and mark the position of the bracket holes for drilling. Verify that your drill bit (and mounting screws) won't hit anything important like electrical wiring or vacuum lines

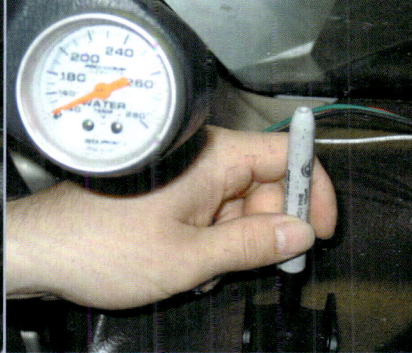

**03** Install the tach in its mounting clamp, then bolt the clamp to the mounting bracket. Before tightening the mounting bolt and nut, hop in, adjust the seat to your regular driving position and adjust the angle of the tach so that it's facing directly at you

**04** Hook up all the wiring exactly as instructed by the tach manufacturer, take your time for a clean, trouble-free installation

**05** Unlike the other wires, the signal wire must be routed through the firewall to the engine compartment. Look for a convenient cable grommet (throttle, clutch, hood release, etc.) in the firewall and make a hole in it with an awl. We used the clutch cable grommet because it's big and because it's easy to get to

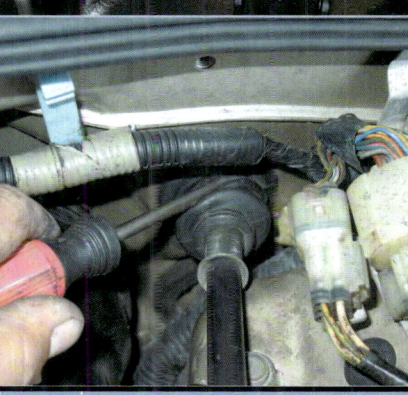

# Bucket seats

**If you're doing a complete makeover of the interior, sooner or later you'll have to decide what to do with the old seats.**

If you've already discovered how difficult it is to brace yourself during hard cornering in a seat with no support, you're probably ready to replace the front seats with something a little sportier. And if your tired old La-Z-Boys just happen to be bottomed out, broken, stained or threadbare, then the decision's made! Make a pair of aftermarket bucket seats the centerpiece of your new interior. Nothing says serious go-fast car like a pair of racing buckets (with racing harnesses, of course). Bucket seats are available in a wide variety of colors and styles and features: Recliners and non-recliners; fabric, leather, vinyl, velour, suede (and pseudo-suede!); integral headrests and separate headrests; heated and non-heated; lumbar support and no lumbar support; and . . . well, you get the idea. Somewhere out there are two front seats with your name on them! But before you go seat shopping, here are some things to think about.

First, keep in mind that the seat mounting brackets and the "runners" (the rails on which the seat assembly slides back and forth) are proprietary. In other words, they're part of the original seat assembly, and a new seat won't necessarily fit without some modification. So make sure that there is a mounting kit for the seats you want so that you'll be able to install them in your car. If there isn't, then either think about some other seats, or be prepared to do some fabrication.

Original equipment seats may not be very supportive, but they are adjustable fore-and-aft and they can recline, i.e. the seatbacks can be tilted to a number of positions. Most aftermarket sport buckets are also adjustable fore-and-aft, and most of them are recliners. Installing recliners in a coupe will allow you to keep using the rear seats, if that's important. But if you're planning to install real racing seats, be forewarned: real racing seats are not recliners. If you decide to install non-recliners, the seatback angle will be fixed, so make sure that the seating position is comfortable for you. Also, consider that non-recliners will make access to the rear seats in a coupe difficult, if not impossible. If you're also planning to install racing harnesses with the new seats, you will render the rear seats essentially inaccessible. So plan on turning your car into a two-seater if you decide to go this way.

Are you going to install a racing harness with each new seat? If so, make sure that the new seats have holes in the headrest for the shoulder straps. Racing harnesses can be installed in cars with seats that don't have these holes, but they won't look as integrated, or as racy. The good news is that you don't have to use (non-reclining) racing buckets to get those shoulder-strap holes. Many recliners are also equipped with these holes as well.

# Removing the old front seats

> **⚠ Warning !**
> If your Civic is equipped with side-impact airbags or seat belt pre-tensioners, refer to your Haynes manual and disable the supplemental restraint (airbag) system. It is essential that you disable this system before proceeding

**01** Move each front seat all the way forward to access the rear seat bracket mounting bolts and remove the small plastic trim covers hiding the bolts (if equipped) . . .

**02** . . . remove the bolts . . .

**03** . . . then move the seat all the way to the rear to access the front retaining bolts. Before removing the old seat, have a look underneath and be sure to disconnect any electrical connectors (power seat motor, heated seat, adjustable lumbar support, airbag, etc.)

**04** And out she comes! That was easy. Now go remove the passenger seat!

  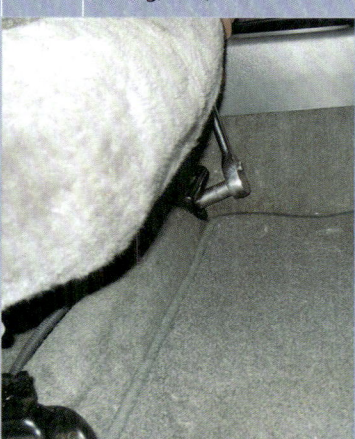 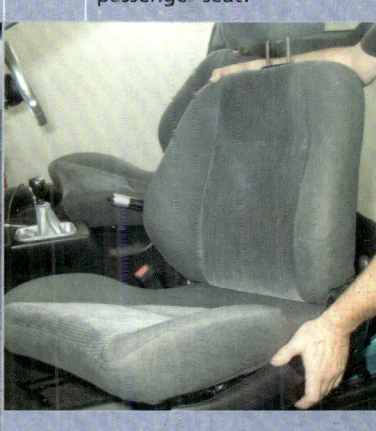

# Installing racing bucket seats

If you're going to buy a pair of racing buckets, make sure that the manufacturer has the right brackets to fit the stock mounting bolts holes in the floorpan. These holes are a government-specified diameter and thread pitch, and they're located at spots in the pan that are specially reinforced to withstand the tremendous forces involved in the event of a collision. You don't even want to think about making new holes in the floorpan for seat bolts. So make sure that your kit includes brackets designed to fit your Civic. If you get the right mounting kit, installing a bucket seat can be as easy as one-two-three . . .

**01** Place the new racing bucket mounting bracket in position and bolt it down to the floorpan

**02** Place the new racing bucket in position on the mounting bracket . . .

**03** . . . and secure it to the mounting bracket. That's all there is to it! Now go do the other one!

 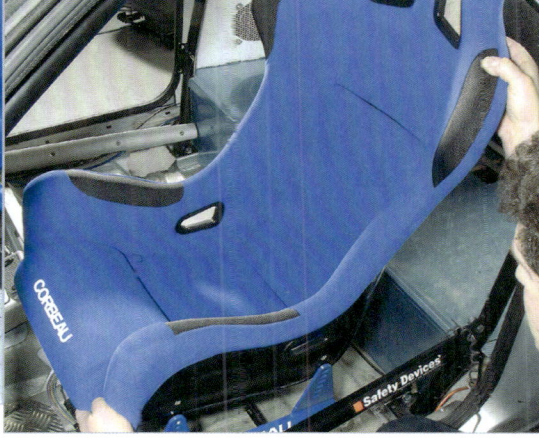 

# Window tinting

First, pick your day, and your working area, pretty carefully - on a windy day, there'll be more dust in the air, and it'll be a nightmare trying to stop the film flapping and folding onto itself while you're working. Applying window tint is best done on a warm day (or in a warm garage), because the adhesive will begin to dry sooner. Don't try tinting when it's starting to get dark!

**01** Step one is to get the window that will be tinted extra clean inside and out. Do not use glass cleaners or any other product using ammonia or vinegar, since both of these ingredients will react with the film tint or its adhesive and create a mess. It is also worth cleaning the working area around the windows because it is too easy for stray dirt to attach itself to the film tint. On door windows, lower them down partially to clean all of the top edge then close them tight to fit the film tint

**02** Before you even unroll the film tint, beware - handle it carefully! If you crease it, you won't get the creases out. Unroll the film tint and cut it roughly to the size of the window

The downside to tinting is that it will severely try your patience. If you're not a patient sort of person, this is one job which may well wind you up - you have been warned. Saying that, if you're calm and careful, and you follow the instructions to the letter, you could surprise yourself.

In brief, the process for tinting is to lay the film on the outside of the glass first, and cut it exactly to size. The protective layer is peeled off to expose the adhesive side, the film is transferred to the inside of the car (tricky) and then squeegeed into place (also tricky). All this must be done with scrupulous cleanliness, as any muck will ruin the effect (difficult if you're working outside). The other problem which won't surprise you is that getting rid of air bubbles and creases can take time. A long time. This is another test of patience, because if, as the instructions say, you've used plenty of spray, it will take a while to dry out and stick.

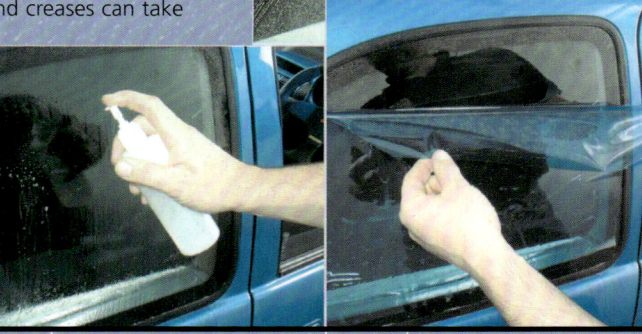

**Legal eagle:** The laws on window tinting vary from region to region and are sometimes confusing at best. Do some research on the film you intend to use and then contact your local authorities. Otherwise, install the tint with the understanding you could get stopped and have to strip it off.

**03** Spray the outside of the window with a weak, soapy water solution. Some film tint kits will provide a cleaning solution for your vehicle, but if not, use a little bit of dish soap in a spray bottle and apply the solution sparingly to the windows

**04** Lay the sheet of tint onto the glass, with the protective film (liner) nearest you. Check this by applying a small piece of sticky tape to the backside and front side of the corners of the tint and film and carefully separate them. It will then become obvious which side is the sticky side of the tint and which side is the protective film

**05** Spray the outside of the film with soapy water

**06** Use a squeegee to get rid of the air bubbles and place the tint on the outside of the window glass. Remember, the protective film (liner) will be facing out

**07** Use a sharp knife and be sure not to damage your paint or window rubber. Trim the perimeter of the tint to the outside of the window. On some rear glass and tailgate glass there are wide black bands on the edges of the glass. Cut your tint to the inside of these bands or the tint will not fit when it is transferred inside. Use a straight edge when cutting the tint

**08** Now go inside the vehicle and prepare the glass for receiving the tint. Tape some plastic sheet to the door trim panel to prevent water damage when the tint is applied. It is a good idea to remove the door trim panel first, before going ahead with the job. Spray the inside of the glass with a soapy solution. Remember, no ammonia products such as glass cleaner or vinegar

**09** Working on the outside of the glass, it is time to separate the tint from the protective film. Use two pieces of tape to pull apart the film at the corner

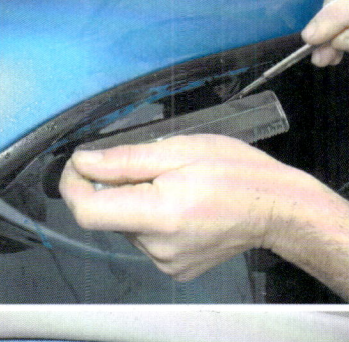
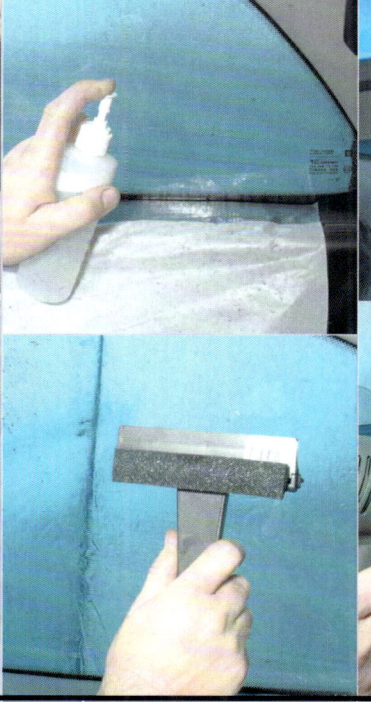
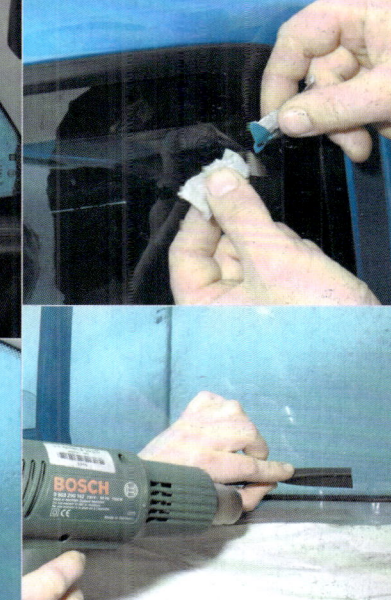

**10** As the film comes apart, spray more solution on the tinted piece underneath to help it come apart cleanly. Try not to lift the tint off the glass too much as this will cause excess creasing. Have the assistant stabilize the tint to prevent any movement while the protective film is being removed from the tint layer

**11** Have the assistant help transfer the tint from the outside of the window to the inside of the window. Peel the tint off the outside of the glass and keep it flat as possible. Remember, in this position, the outside tint layer contains the adhesive. Utilizing two people and without letting the tint fold, place the tint onto the inside window glass as close as possible to the correct position. The outside layer of tint now should be the adhesive side on the inside window. Carefully slide the tint into the corners, keeping the tint flat

**12** Spray the tint with soapy water and carefully squeegee it into place, working from the top to the bottom. It is easier to use the squeegee blade separated from the handle to access the corner spots

**13** You may end up with an area at the bottom of the glass that will not stick. Do not panic. First, soak up any excess water at the base of the tint with paper towels. Use a hot air gun to gently warm the tint at the base to assist with the adhesion. Be very careful when using a squeegee on a dry surface. Do not lift the tint off the glass. Be patient, the tint will stick. Persistence will pay off

# Wheels & tires

## 05

If there is one crucial first customizing step in the process of making your economy compact into a sport compact, it's the tires and wheels, and of those two it's 90% the wheels. The right wheels can set your car apart in a way that makes it noticeable from two blocks away, even if the rest of the car remains unimpressively stock.

Wheel and brake size brings up questions of fit and appearance - this wheel has plenty of clearance around the brakes, but makes the brake look a bit small

Most street wheels are cast aluminum, with this example being a one-piece design

# Choosing wheels

Two-piece wheels are very popular because they are less expensive than the one-piece, though they may weigh a little more - weight is a factor mostly for racing

Custom wheels are mostly purchased to attract attention, but they do have practical considerations. A wider wheel allows you to install wider tires for better traction. A set of custom aluminum wheels may be lighter than your stock steel wheels and thus reduce the amount of unsprung weight in the chassis, which leads to improved handling. However, the weight savings of the aluminum may be negated if you go much bigger than stock in the new wheels. A 20-inch-diameter aluminum "show" wheel might actually weigh more than your stock 16-inch-diameter wheels!

Have in mind the style of wheel you like long before you enter the tire/wheel store. Once you're in the store, the vast display of wheel choices can make the final selection more headache than fun. Observe the other Civics you see and look at the wheels/tires closely. If you can find the owner of the car, ask him if he had any problems with the tires/rims he chose. Once you spend the money to get new rolling stock, you'll want to be happy with them for a long time to come.

Also look at cars like yours in magazines and see which wheels appeal to you, as well as scoping out the wheel advertisements. When you see wheels you like on a Civic like yours, read further and see what other modifications may have been made to accommodate those tires/wheels. Was the car lowered, and did it have custom wheelwells or an aftermarket body kit? Those custom body alterations may have given the clearance needed for those tires/wheels. Getting a picture of how complicated the simple act of choosing wheels and tires can get?

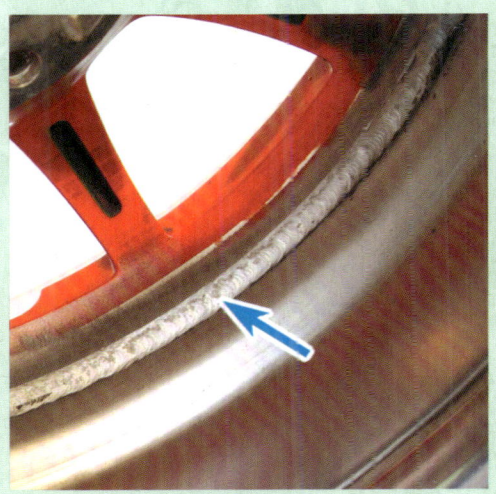

Two-piece wheels have the center section joined to the aluminum rim, either by fasteners or by welding

Rim width on custom wheels is measured at the inside of the wheel lips, not the outside as you might have thought

## Plan ahead

If you're the type who is mostly interested in extracting total performance from the engine, while leaving your Civic pretty much stock as far as suspension and the body are concerned, you can just add tires and wheels that fit your car just the way it is. However, if you think that later on you'll lower your car with some aftermarket springs, you must consider the clearance between the tires and the fenderwell lip. It's cool to have a tire/wheel combo that fills the wheelwell, but not so cool to drive around with the outside edges of your tires worn away from rubbing the body.

A tire/wheel package that fits your car now may create interference when the car is lowered an inch or two. You can tell the guys whose tire-to-body fit is less than optimal. They're the ones who enter the driveway of your favorite hangout really slow and with the car at an extreme angle to the driveway to keep from having rubber meet paint.

If you are thinking of adding flared fenders or a custom body kit to your car at some point, this will have a major impact on your wheel/tire choice. If you want really wide tires and big rims, you almost have to run something aftermarket in terms of bodywear just to clear the tires. On the other hand, you may have a good amount invested in the custom wheels/tires on your car currently and they may look too small if you add a body kit. Figure the cost of new rims and rubber into your budget if you are going to utilize a wide-body kit on your car.

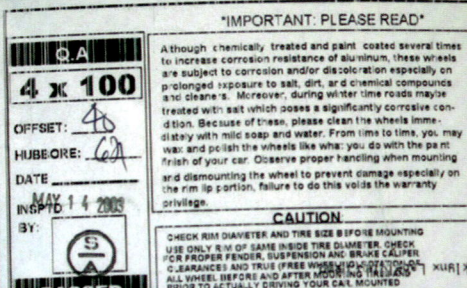

This wheel sticker's information includes: wheel offset, 40mm; bolt pattern, 4 bolts on a 100 mm circle; hub bore; and date of manufacture

Wheels make a major statement about your car - if you're going for show, you can't be shy about wheel design or wheel/tire combos - look for a big rolling radius!

## Rolling radius

Rolling radius is the distance from the center of the wheel to the edge of the tire's tread. Most of us simply look at the tire/wheel diameter, rather than the radius. Without having to find the exact center of the wheel, you can measure the diameter with a tape measure simply by going from the ground to the top of the tire. Since tires vary in height as well as width, just knowing that a car has 18-inch wheels doesn't tell you how tall the rolling radius is, but a handy pocket tape measure will.

The existing final drive ratio in your transaxle is affected by the rolling radius of the tire/wheel size you choose. With a taller rolling radius at the tire/wheel, the effect is to make the final drive even more of a "cruising" ratio, which is not what you and I want for acceleration.

If you don't want to increase the rolling radius but still make the upgrade to taller wheels, you'll have to choose a tire that is shorter in section height. If your stock tire was a 75-series or 60-series, for instance, changing to a wider 55 or 50-series tire on your one-inch bigger new wheels may give you the same rolling radius as your stock tires and wheels, without taking away any gearing effect on performance. If you go up one inch in rim diameter, decrease the tire profile one size. A step up in wheel and tire size from a typical stock combo of the factory wheels with 185/65R-14 tires to 15-inch aftermarket wheels and a fatter-but-shorter 205/50 hunk of rubber will give you better handling and traction, but not be so tall in rolling radius as to ruin your acceleration.

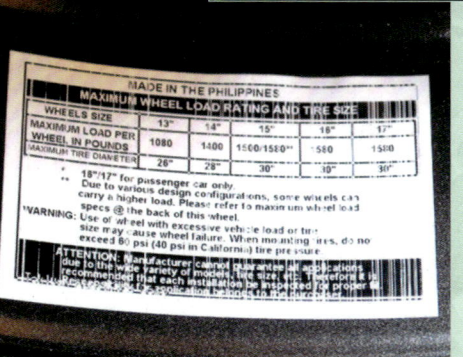

Some wheels are marked only with decals rather than cast-in numbers - this sticker indicates the wheel load rating and the maximum recommended tire diameter (rolling radius)

Confused? Well, a 205/55x15 tire (that's a 15-inch wheel, obviously) has a rolling radius of 607mm. Upgrading to a 17-inch wheel means fitting a 215/40x17 rubber with a nearly-identical rolling radius of 606mm. Stay within ten percent of your original height and you should be okay. Rely on wheel/tire combos that you know have worked successfully on other Civics, plus listen to the advice of a good tire and wheel shop. They've probably seen all the right and wrong combos!

## Wheel weight

If there were no other considerations when buying wheels, we'd always go with the lightest available. Lighter wheels are easier to accelerate or slow down and they are easier on your suspension. Unsprung weight is that weight in your car that has to bounce up and down over the road with your tires. If you have a big set of tires they can improve road grip on corners, but the heavy unsprung weight is like asking the suspension to work harder. Unfortunately, really light wheels are expensive! Most of us are more concerned with the outward appearance of the wheels than their performance benefit at the track, so we pick the wheel for our Civic that has the best compromise between the factors of weight, looks, and price. The cast wheels commonly available are much less expensive than the forged variety.

If you're really serious, use a common bathroom scale to weigh the wheels - the lighter the better for handling

Wheel offset has perhaps the most influence on tire/wheel fit - the off-car wheel here has all the offset possible to tuck the wheel in, while the on-car rear wheel has less offset and more rim showing - to fit a customized body, front and rear wheels may need to be different

To measure a wheel's offset, lay a straightedge across the back of the rim, then measure from there down to the wheel's mounting surface - this measurement compared to the wheel's theoretical center gives you offset

## Wheel offset

There's much more to the measurement of a wheel than its diameter. The amount of wheel offset is critical to fitment problems with the body and even the brakes. That flat, machined section on the back of a wheel that fits directly against your brake disk, drum or hub is the area we're concerned with. If that section is in the exact center of the wheel (in a side or end plane), the wheel is considered to have no offset. If the mounting plane is closer to the back of the wheel than the front of the wheel, that wheel will stick further out from the car than a "centered" wheel.

All wheels for FWD cars have a considerable offset to the inside of the car, meaning that flat mounting surface is closer to the outside of the wheel. Just how much offset is what matters. A wheel with a certain offset or wheel-center design may not clear the brake calipers or some other suspension parts on your car. A wheel with too much offset to the outside may cause the tire to interfere with the fenderwell lip. The correct wheel for you lies somewhere in between. Typical Civic wheels have 35 to 40mm of offset.

There are no universal standards for marking wheels with their offset dimensions. Some have the offset cast into the back of the wheel, some have a sticker on the rim, and some are unmarked. However, the offset of a wheel is easily measured with a ruler and straightedge. Lay the wheel down on a flat surface and measure the height of the rim. If the measurement is 200 mm, then the center of the wheel is at 100 mm. Place

This car has a large wheel and equally oversize brake setup - braking and appearance are equally satisfied

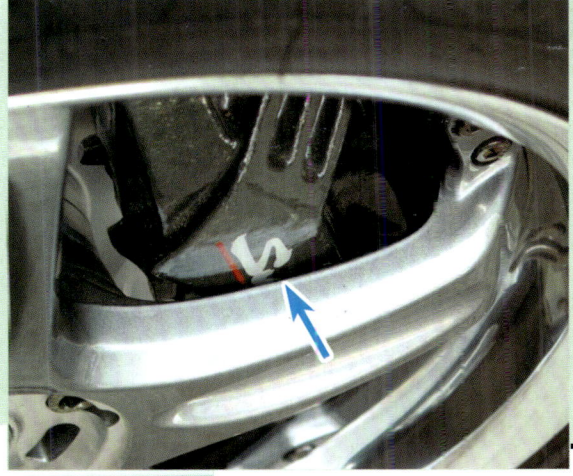

Depending on the shape of the wheel's center, interference with a big caliper may come at the side, not just the outer edge - this one just clears

If you're planning for competition, you'll need the widest tire you can fit, which requires a wheel with lots of offset to tuck the wide tires inside the wheelwheel

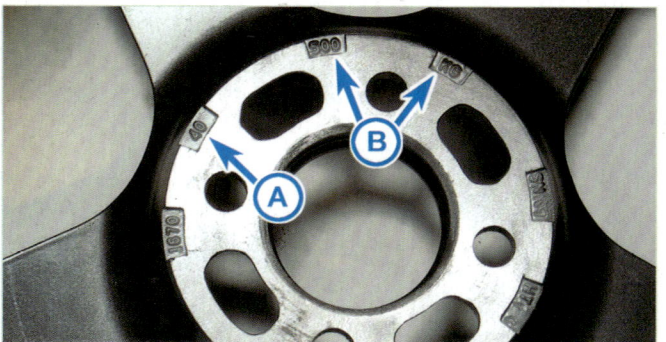

On most wheels, some important information is marked on the backside of the wheel - this one-piece wheel indicates the offset is 40 MM (A), and that the maximum load rating (per wheel) is 500 KG (B), or 1100 pounds (more than enough for any 2300-pound Civic!)

a straightedge across the wheel on the backside and measure from that edge down to the flat mounting surface of the wheel where the bolt pattern is. Let's say that measurement is 140 mm. This measurement is also called the backspacing, and it means the wheel has the mounting surface 40-mm further to the front of the wheel than the theoretical center. The offset is 40 mm.

For purposes of checking a wheel's offset, measuring the width of rim as described works fine, since we're just looking for the centerline measurement. However, when wheel sizes are described, the width measurement that is used is only the space between the tire mounting beads, not the lip-to-lip measurement. A wheel that is nominally 17x8 would be eight inches between the two tire beads. Measuring between the outside edges would be too confusing, since wheel designs vary greatly in the amount of lip width.

## Used wheels

If you tend to swap parts around between your car and your circle of buddies, or you contemplate buying a set of wheels at a swap meet, there are a number of things to check. Bring a tape measure that has both inch and metric measurements. We've just outlined above the simple measurements that determine rim width and offset.

Another thing to worry about when selecting wheels is the bolt pattern. Most cars have four or five nuts or bolts holding each wheel to its hub. Different manufacturers use different bolt patterns for their wheels, so, just because two wheels have the same number of lug nuts doesn't mean they will interchange. Make absolutely sure the bolt pattern is correct before you throw down your hard-earned cash!

Take one of your existing Civic wheels off and make a paper or cardboard template of the bolt pattern. Place the paper over the machined mounting surface at the back of the wheel and rub a lead pencil over the paper until the location and dimensions of the bolt holes are clearly outlined. Keep this paper with you when you are wheel shopping and you won't get stuck with a set of Mitsubishi wheels that won't fit your car. Hold the paper behind the wheel you're examining and all the holes should line up with the bolt holes in the wheels.

Some wheels are made with two different bolt patterns to fit different model cars - this makes them less expensive for the manufacturer, and a good deal for the consumer - here are the two most common Honda patterns, 4 x 100 mm and 4 x 114 mm

## Stay centered

How a wheel is located on a particular vehicle's hub can vary. A "hub-centric" wheel is one that is located on the car's hub by a closely-machined opening in the center of the wheel that is matched to that car's hub diameter. Some wheels are "lug-centric" which means that the center of the wheel doesn't locate perfectly over the hub, but the lug nuts and lug nut holes are tapered to locate the wheel that way.

Your original Civic wheels are machined at the center to locate properly on your hubs. Most good aftermarket wheels are also machined to fit a specific application. There are some companies, however, that make most of their wheels in a basic, one-size-fits-all dimension, and rely on inserts that go behind the wheel to achieve the correct fit to center the wheel on various makes of car. Enthusiasts prefer to have a wheel that is located precisely on their specific car.

Many wheels have plastic or metal rings inserted on the backside to make an exact hub-fit on a particular application, always make sure the ring is in place before mounting a wheel

Extra-long studs protruding through "racing" lug nuts not only gets you through tech inspection, they also look racing-cool on the street

To protect the finish on your wheels during removal/installation, use special plastic liners over your lug socket or wrap the socket with electrical tape

# Wheel lug nuts/studs

The relationship between the wheel studs in your car's hubs and the lug nuts used to secure the wheels on those studs is a critical safety consideration. Where most enthusiasts get themselves in trouble in this area is by using wheel spacers to achieve a look or fit by increasing the offset of a wheel. Spacers go between the wheel and the hub to move the wheel outboard a little.

If you use the same lug nuts that you had originally before the spacers were added, the amount of wheel stud that is threaded into the lug nuts is reduced by the thickness of the spacer.

Most wheel experts dislike wheel spacers, preferring their customers buy the right wheel for the job in the first place. There is no hard-and-fast rule about how many threads need to be engaged between the stud and the lug nut, but you should never reduce this dimension beyond the amount engineered by your car's manufacturer. If your car had 5/8-inch of threads into the lug nuts, stick with that dimension. To achieve this with spacers or some wheels that have thicker mounting areas (like built-in spacers), you should remove the hubs from the car and replace the studs with longer ones.

To protect your investment in cool tires and wheels, you'll want to use a set of locking lug nuts - use one per wheel, and don't lose the special "key" adapter required to remove them

A word to the wise. If you ever contemplate running your car at a track, whether a test run at the dragstrip or weekly assaults on the slalom course, the track officials will examine your lug nuts, specifically to see that enough threads are engaged. On many typical aftermarket wheels, the lug nuts have closed ends. The officials will ask you to remove one of your closed-end lug nuts to check for thread engagement. On wheels with open-end lug nuts, they can see how much thread engagement there is. It varies with the sanctioning body, but most organizations like to see a certain amount of stud threads sticking out beyond the end of an open-end lug nut.

Lug nuts are important! The two types are tapered (left) and straight (right) - the tapered ones (like stock lugs) center the wheel over the hub, while the straight ones don't exactly, so the wheel must have an exact center at the hub

Lug nuts also come either open at the ends or closed - if you ever plan on competing, the inspectors will want you to have the open type, so they can check how much stud is engaged with the lug

Some wheels have a thicker mounting flange than your stock wheels - using a thicker wheel or wheel spacers means you should have longer studs pressed into your hubs for full thread engagement

Lug nuts may look alike, but pay attention to their markings or you could strip your wheel studs - this one is marked "12x1.5", which means it's for a 12 mm stud with 1.5 thread pitch

If you are planning on lowering your Civic, make sure the wheels/tires you purchase aren't going to be too tall or too wide for the body in the lowered stance

# Choosing tires

Along with the custom wheels, tires are an important part of both the looks and performance of your Civic. If you want the ultimate look, you'll get the tires and wheels that are as close as possible to looking like a rubber band has been wrapped around a 21-inch wheel. Not only is this nice to look at, it's race-inspired. In hard cornering, stock tires do not stay centered on the wheel. They "roll under," so that the tread area actually moves away from the center of the wheel. When this happens, the tread distorts, the tire "breaks away" and starts sliding. On low-profile tires, roll-under is almost non-existent, so the tire can keep a consistent tread "patch" on the road. Tires designed for long tread life are usually made from a very hard rubber compound and therefore will last a very long time. But hard-compound tires don't stick to the road as well. So most high-performance low-profile tires are made from softer, stickier rubber compounds that will allow better traction for cornering and acceleration - but the tires will tend to wear out faster.

As you can see, tire design is compromise. No one tire design can do everything well. Think about how much you really want to spend on your tires and wheels, including how often you can afford to replace the tires. If you choose the softer tread compounds for your tires, they'll have to be replaced perhaps twice as often as the original tires for your Civic. That adds up in the long run!

Think about ride quality, too. You may not be an old man with a bad back, but if you do a lot of driving, constant bumping and bouncing can be annoying. Remember that the ultra-low profile tires are not very practical if you do a lot of driving on rough roads. One good pothole hit is all it takes to damage the rim on a bucks-up wheel. A cheaper, higher-profile tire and wheel might absorb a hit from a pothole or curb just fine. The low-profile tires most often seen on sport compact cars that have been customized are going to ride rougher than the OEM rubber, since they have less "cushion" than higher aspect ratio tires. There's just no way around making a real compromise in tire selection.

If you do most of your driving on the street in normal traffic and on the highway, take a closer look at the sidewall markings while you're out tire shopping. First of all, the tire must have a DOT (Department of Transportation) number on it. If there's no DOT number, the tire isn't legal for the street and can only be used for racing on a track. Among the many numbers/letters/codes on the side of street-legal tires are the ratings of that tire for traction, wear and temperature. The ratings are in letter form, with A being the highest rating. It's difficult for a tire to make "straight A's" in every category, but to stretch your tire dollars, make sure you examine the treadwear rating. Likewise, for vehicles that see track action, temperature and traction ratings will be the categories you want your tire to score highest in.

So don't just go into a showroom and point to the wheels and tires that look the best - with that level of research, you're almost sure to be disappointed. Talk to the salespeople and technicians at the tire store and find out about the ride quality and treadlife of each tire, as well as its cost. Tire technicians who install a lot of tires can help you figure out how big a tire/wheel combination you can fit in your car. And if you're planning on lowering the car, tell them about that, too, since it will have an effect on maximum tire size. When in doubt about maximum tire size, contact the tire manufacturer for their recommendations.

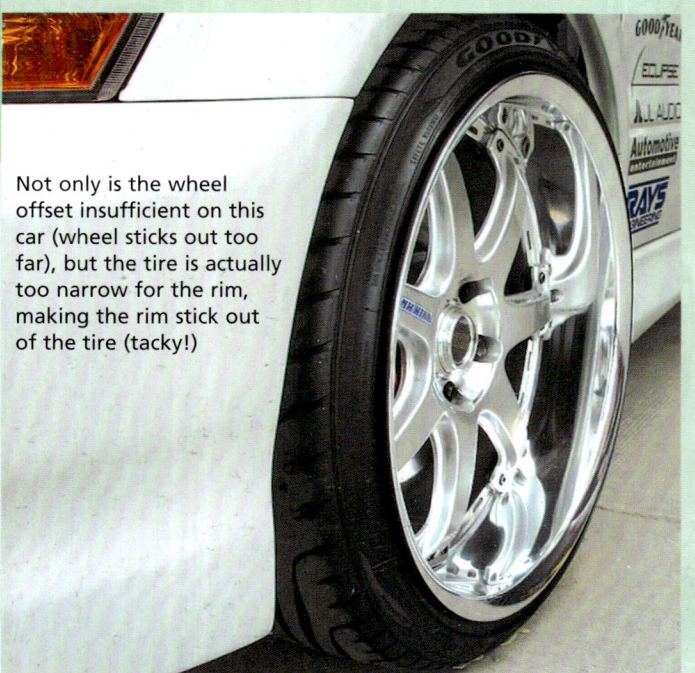

Not only is the wheel offset insufficient on this car (wheel sticks out too far), but the tire is actually too narrow for the rim, making the rim stick out of the tire (tacky!)

Among the important markings on a tire are these ratings for Treadwear, Traction and Temperature performance

Race tires look cool, but don't get caught on the street without a legal-for-street DOT (Department of Transportation) indication or you could get a ticket

Some high-performance tires are "directional" in their design - the arrow marking means it must roll in this direction only, so you can't rotate these tires side-for-side

The most important markings on a tire are these for the tire size, profile and speed rating

Many people try to measure their own wheelwells with a tape-rule to determine how much clearance they have for larger tires and wheels. Even if you take these measurements with the front wheels in their extreme turn positions, there are many other variables that are very hard to calculate. For example, the new wheels will likely have more offset than your existing wheels. Overall tire-and-wheel height and width will be different than the wheel measurements themselves. And don't forget about suspension movement - you don't want to have the tires rub every time you go over a bump! No, it's best to let the experts determine your maximum tire and wheel size, and they are usually happy to help. And if the combination doesn't work, you'll have someone to blame besides yourself!

Enthusiasts who do their own research generally make better buying decisions, and on wheel/tires you need to look at all the examples of modified Civics you can. Check out their tires and wheels and see not only how they look, but also how evenly they are wearing in the application. Look at the backside of the front tires, if possible, and see if the tire or wheels has been rubbing on any suspension or body parts. If the outside edge of the tire's tread is chewed or worn excessively, it could indicate this wheel/tire combo is too wide for the vehicle. Always compare "apples to apples." If the Civic you really like has a body kit or flares on the fenders, don't assume that the wide tires he's sporting are going to fit your stock Civic.

## Tire size markings

All tires carry standard tire size markings on their sidewalls, such as **"195/60 R 15 87H"**.

| | |
|---|---|
| 195 | indicates the width of the tire in mm. |
| 60 | indicates the ratio of the tire section height to width, expressed as a percentage. If no number is present at this point, the ratio is considered to be 82%. This section ratio is also called the aspect ratio or the "profile." A low number here means a low-profile tire that won't be as tall as a higher-ratio tire. |
| R | indicates the tire is of radial ply construction. |
| 15 | indicates the wheel diameter for the tire is 15 inches. |
| 87 | is an index number which indicates the maximum load that the tire can carry at maximum speed. |
| H | represents the maximum speed for the tire which should be equal to or greater than the car's maximum speed. |

Note that some tires have the speed rating symbol located between the tire width and the wheel diameter, attached to the "R" radial tire reference, for example, "195/60 HR 15".

## Speed rating symbols for radial tires

| Symbol | mph |
|---|---|
| P | 93 |
| Q | 99 |
| R | 106 |
| S | 112 |
| T | 118 |
| U | 124 |
| V (after size markings) | Up to 150 |
| H (within size markings) | Up to 130 |
| V (within size markings) | Over 130 |
| Z (within size markings) | Over 150 |

# Gallery of Wheels

Wheels and tires

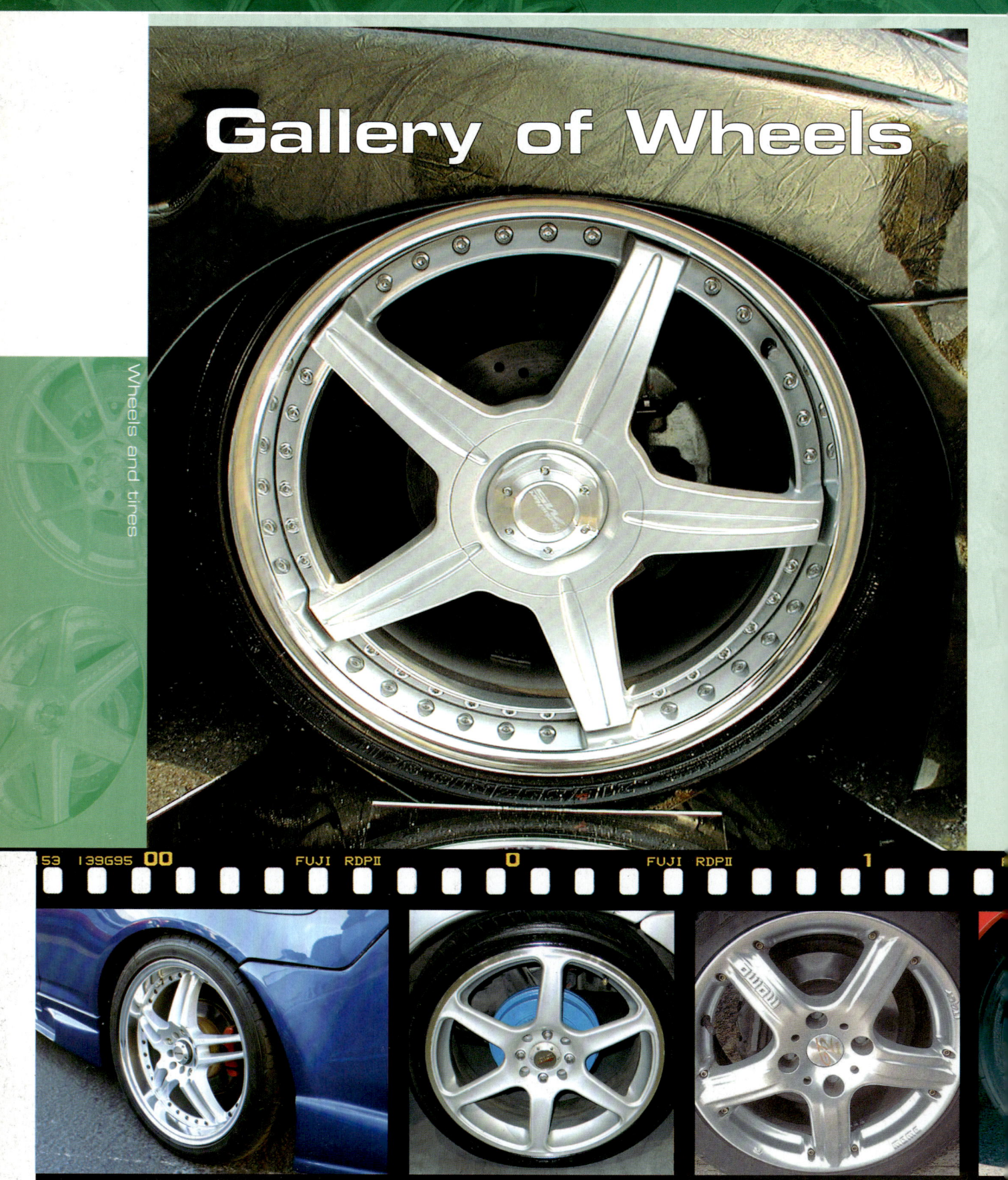

# 06 Suspension

**Altering you car's stock suspension can not only give you that lowered, aggressive look, but, if done right, will improve the handling as well.**

Dropping the car on its suspension brings the car's center of gravity closer to its roll and pitch centers, which helps to hold it to the road in corners and under braking - combined with stiffer springs, shocks and stabilizer bars, this reduces body roll and increases the tire contact patch on the road. But - if improving the handling is really important to you, choose your new suspension carefully. If you go the cheap route, or want extreme lowering, then making the car handle better might not be what you achieve.

*As for what to buy, there are basically four main options when it comes to lowering:*

**1** *Set of lowering springs.*

**2** *Matched set of lowering springs and shock absorbers.*

**3** *Set of "coilovers."*

**4** *Air suspension.*

## How low to go?

Assuming you want to slam your suspension so that your fenders just clear the tops of your monster new tires, there's another small problem - it takes some inspired guesswork to assess the required drop accurately and avoid the nasty rubbing sound and the smell of burning rubber. Lowering springs and suspension kits will only produce a fixed amount of drop - this can range from 3/4-inch to a more extreme drop of anything up to four inches. Take as many measurements as possible, and ask tuning shops or informed friends. Suppliers and manufacturers are also a good source of help. Coilovers have a range of adjustment possible, which can get you exactly the amount of drop you're looking for.

*Suspension*

## High-rate lowering springs

**For:** This option is generally the least expensive way to go. You'll get the low-slung look and handling will be slightly improved.

**Against:** If your shocks are bad or your new springs are badly matched to their damping characteristics, handling could be poor.

**Buy:** Progressively wound springs which give a smooth ride but also cope with bumps, potholes and extreme cornering; springs for use with standard shocks to prevent pogo-stick handling and shock damage; springs that offer a drop of between 3/4 and 1-1/2 inch - any lower will result in poor handling, fender-rub and excess tire wear.

## Matched strut or shock/spring kits

**For:** Massive improvement in handling thanks to well-developed, matched springs and struts or shocks. Some have adjustable damping so you can fine-tune the ride quality. Price can range from fairly reasonable to through the roof!

**Against:** Due to increased damping and spring rates, the ride may be harsh.

**Buy:** Kits with progressive springs - these offer an improved ride without compromising handling; kits with adjustable shock damping; kits with multi-position spring platforms - enabling you to tweak the ride height.

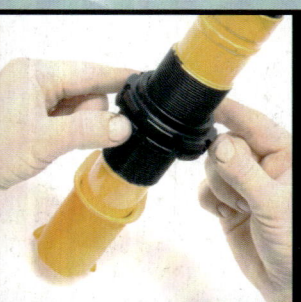

## Coilover kits

**For:** Ride height can be adjusted to the level you want. Most kits offer 3/4-inch to 4 inches of adjustment. Conversion kits are available for use with your stock struts or shock absorber/coil spring units; these are generally only a little more expensive than a set of lowering springs. If you can afford to shell out the big bucks, you can go with a set of matched strut or shock and spring units with the threaded spring adjusters already installed.

On some models, damping can be set as desired. The package can be set up to offer awesome handling on the road and then be dumped for shows and cruises.

**Against:** Coilovers can be hard to set up properly. If they're set to give a big drop, the springs can pop out of the top cups on full extension. Ride is hard - with a capital H.

**Buy:** Kits with helper springs - less spring dislocation; kits with adjustable damping.

## Air suspension

**For:** Instant adjustability of ride height; great for dropping your ride when parked.

**Against:** Irregular ride and handling; possible damage to suspension components and body parts if not set up properly.

**Buy:** Complete kit with compressor, valves, struts (or damper units) and hoses.

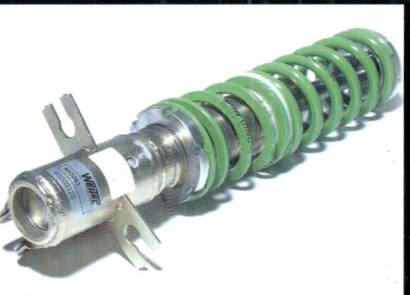

# Suspension terms

## Fender-rub
Fender-rub occurs when the suspension is too low or too soft. Going over a bump, the wheel is forced up as the suspension compresses, rubbing the wheel opening in the fender.

## Circlip
The circlip is a flat, spring-steel clip that fits into a groove on the body of the strut or shock, on which the spring cup sits. On struts or shocks designed for lowering, there are sometimes a number of grooves offering differing ride heights.

## Shock absorbers (shocks)/struts
A shock absorber absorbs the kinetic energy of the of the suspension during compression, or of the spring during rebound, damping further reaction from the spring. Shocks, as they're often called, stop the car from bouncing along the road, resulting in better handling. On cars with MacPherson strut-type suspension, the shock absorber and coil spring are incorporated into a strut that is also a structural member of the car's suspension that keeps the wheel in a vertical position. Many other cars have coil springs joined with the shock absorbers too, but upper and lower control arms handle the task of keeping the wheel upright.

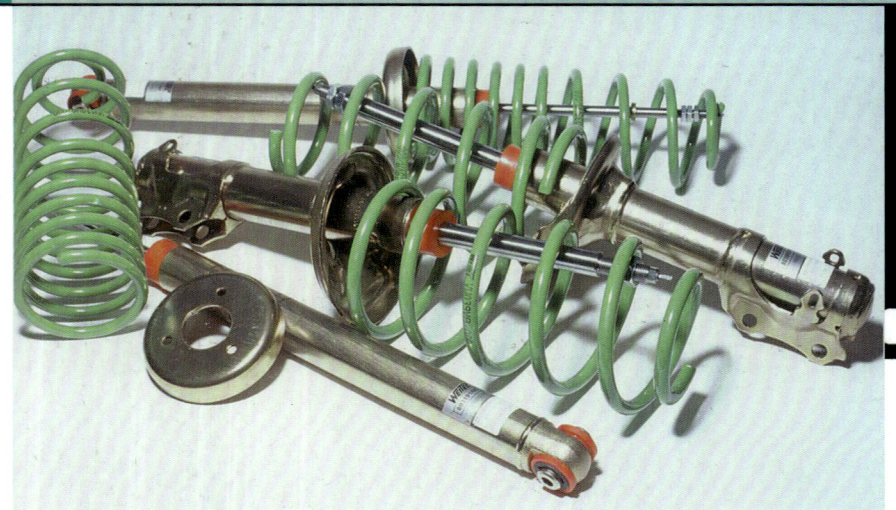

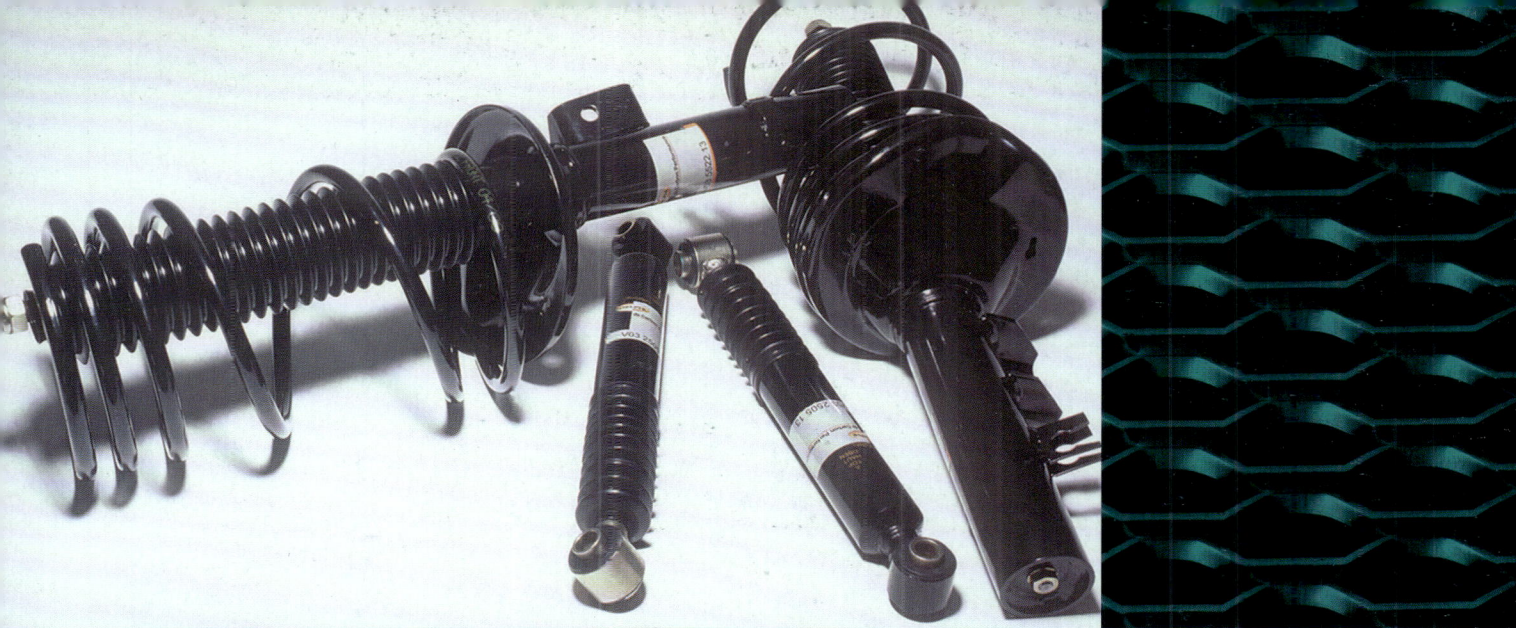

## Damping
Damping is the action of the shock absorber dissipating energy when the suspension is compressed (such as when going over a bump) or during rebound (when the suspension extends after being compressed). On all modern motor vehicles damping is accomplished by forcing fluid through an orifice (or series of orifices).

## Helper spring
Only found on coilover shocks or struts, the helper spring prevents dislocation of the main spring when it is unable to cope with extreme extension. The helper spring offers further extension travel, preventing possible dislocation.

## Progressive wound
The coils on a progressive spring have been wound closer together at one end. This offers decent ride quality until the loose-wound coils are compressed, then, under further compression, the suspension is stiffer. This limits suspension travel and improves cornering without giving a harsh ride during normal driving.

## Ride height
The ride height refers to the height of the chassis from the ground. The height of the springs determines the ride height and center of gravity.

## Shot-peened
Shot-peening is a process in which tiny pieces of metal (shot) are fired at the surface of the steel spring, increasing the spring's surface area and making the spring stronger.

## Spring cups
The spring cup is located on the body of the strut. The bottom of the spring sits in the cup with the help of an internal lug, which prevents dislocation.

## Spring rate
The spring rate translates as the potential resistance against compression of the spring, measured in pounds. A low spring rate means the spring will give a better ride (is "softer"), while a high spring rate means the spring will "give" less and thus has a harsher ride.

# Shock absorbers/ struts and coil springs

Replacing the struts (or shocks) and coil springs is an excellent way to lower a car. Although the car can sometimes be lowered by replacing the springs only, we recommend replacing the shock absorbers or strut assemblies with new ones specifically matched to the springs being installed. Doing this will help prevent fender-rub and result in better cornering. When done correctly, this conversion will get you lower but still retain predictable handling characteristics - this is a must if you like to push your car hard through corners.

Many aftermarket companies sell kits of matched shock absorbers/struts and springs, often referred to as a "suspension kit." Some of the kits are called "adjustable," but check this out carefully so you're sure you know what you're getting. With some kits this adjustment only applies to the damper rates of the shocks, which can be customized by simply turning a knob or screw on each shock or strut. This feature has no effect on the ride height, but provides the ability to adjust for better ride quality or better handling. Other kits - the kind with threaded adjusters for the springs *and* damping adjusters for the shocks - offer the best of both worlds; ride height adjustment and damping adjustment. It's critical that you follow the instructions that will come with the parts. This is not a job for a beginner - if you don't know what you're doing, get help or have the job done for you.

## Front strut or shock absorber/coil spring replacement

If you don't already have a *Haynes Repair Manual* for your specific car, now would be a good time to buy one. We'll take you through the basics here, but the *Haynes* manual will give you the details.

**01** Loosen the wheel lug nuts, raise the car and support it securely on jackstands. Remove the wheel. Unbolt the brake hose bracket from the shock or strut (if applicable). If there is any other wiring that will be in the way of strut or shock removal, such as for the ABS speed sensor, carefully disconnect it and move it out of the way.

### Shock absorber/coil spring assemblies (1988 through 2000 models)

**02** Remove the damper fork pinch bolt . . .

**03** . . . then remove the through-bolt that connects the damper fork to the lower control arm . . .

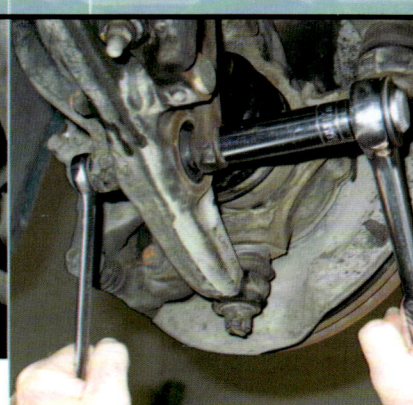

**04** . . . and remove the damper fork from the shock absorber. If it's stuck, carefully tap it off with a hammer.

**05** Support the shock absorber (an assistant would be helpful here) and unscrew the upper mounting nuts. DON'T unscrew the big nut in the center - that's the piston rod nut; it secures the upper mount and harnesses the coil spring! Leave it alone!

**06** Guide the shock absorber/coil spring assembly out from the wheelwell.

## Strut assemblies (2001 and later models)

**07** Remove the cotter pin, then loosen the nut and separate the tie-rod end from the steering arm on the strut using a puller (keeping the nut on the ballstud will prevent the tie-rod end from separating violently). Now unscrew the nut and detach the tie-rod end from the arm.

**08** Mark around the bolt heads and where the strut meets the knuckle; this is to help you retain the current camber setting when you reinstall the strut, just in case camber adjusting bolts have been installed previously (this will be unnecessary if you're installing a different strut). After removing the bolts and separating the knuckle from the strut, support the knuckle securely to prevent it from falling down

**09** Support the strut (get some help, if possible) and remove the upper mounting nuts. DON'T unscrew the big nut in the center - that's the piston rod nut; it secures the upper mount and harnesses the coil spring, so don't mess with it!

**10** Lower the strut out from the wheel well. Make sure the knuckle and hub assembly is securely supported while the strut is removed from the car - if it falls down, the inner CV joint could separate from its housing

# All models

**11** **Warning:** *Disassembling a coil-over type shock absorber or strut is potentially dangerous! Your full attention must be directed to the job, or serious injury may result. If you don't feel completely comfortable working with these assemblies, take them to a professional.* Before disassembling the shocks or struts, make sure you have a good spring compressor and obtain a new piston nut for each strut/shock absorber (the nut should be replaced every time it is removed). Install the spring compressor according to the manufacturer's instructions (or, as shown here, install the shock/strut into the tool) and compress the coil spring until all spring pressure is relieved from the seats.

**12** Remove the trim cap, if equipped, then loosen and remove the piston rod nut, washer and insulator (as applicable). If necessary, retain the piston rod with a Torx or Allen wrench to prevent rotation while loosening the nut. Discard the nut (a new one should be installed during reassembly)

**13** Lift off the upper mounting plate and spring seat . . .

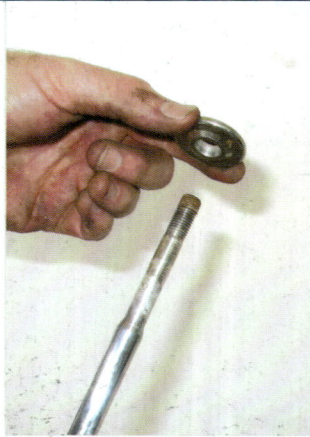

**17** Take off the bump stop plate . . .

**18** . . . and the bump stop. Note how all the parts are installed so you can assemble them the same way

**19** If you're installing a set of matched springs and coilover shocks/strut bodies, jump to Step 20. Otherwise, assemble the strut or shock by reversing the disassembly sequence. Be sure the piston nut is tightened to specification and the spring ends are properly seated in the spring seat, as shown. Then slowly release the spring compressor. The remainder of assembly is the reverse of disassembly. Be sure to tighten all fasteners to specification (see your *Haynes Automotive Repair Manual*). To install the shock absorber/coil spring assembly, go to Step 25.

**14** ... followed by the insulator or bearing, as applicable

**15** If equipped, remove the washer and dust cover

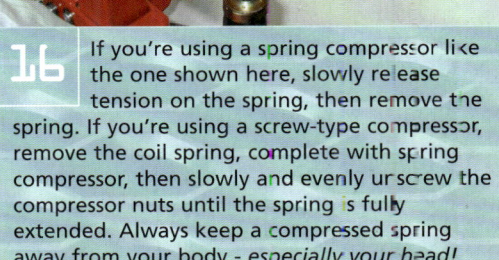

**16** If you're using a spring compressor like the one shown here, slowly release tension on the spring, then remove the spring. If you're using a screw-type compressor, remove the coil spring, complete with spring compressor, then slowly and evenly unscrew the compressor nuts until the spring is fully extended. Always keep a compressed spring away from your body - *especially your head!*

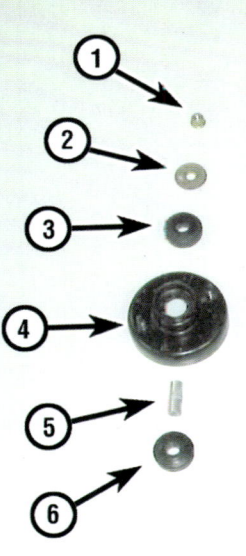
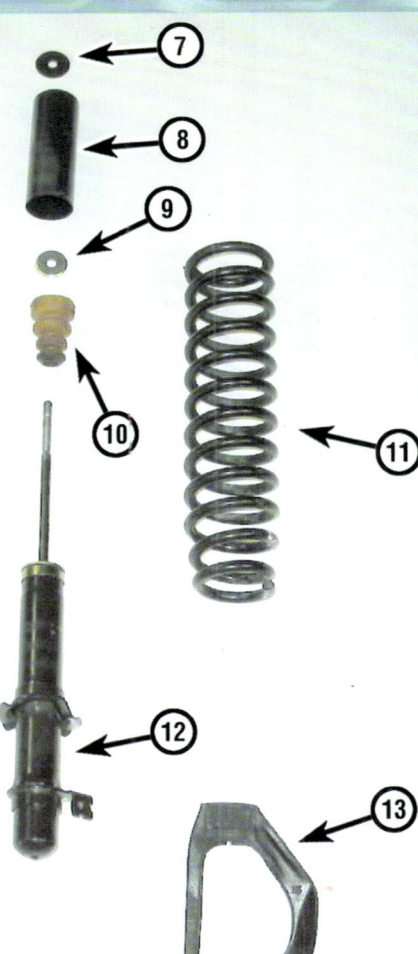

Exploded view of a shock absorber/coil spring assembly

1. Piston rod nut
2. Washer
3. Insulator
4. Upper mounting plate/spring seat
5. Collar
6. Insulator
7. Dust cover washer
8. Dust cover
9. Bump stop plate
10. Bump stop
11. Coil spring
12. Shock body
13. Damper fork

103

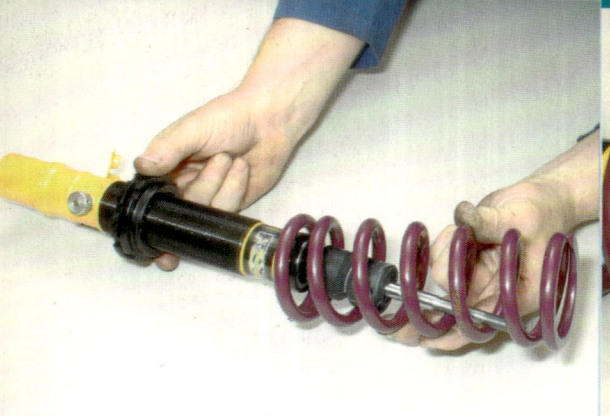

**20** If you're fortunate enough to have scored a set of matched springs and coilover shock/strut bodies, start assembling them. Make sure you put the spring on the correct way; if it isn't obvious, look for writing (or a logo) on the spring and make sure it's right side up. Also, make sure you install the front springs on the front shocks and the rear springs on the rear shocks if they're different. If you can't tell, call the manufacturer. Even if the springs all look the same, they could be different rates (stiffness).

**21** Now install the spring seat . . .

**22** . . . followed by the washer and the upper mounting plate . . .

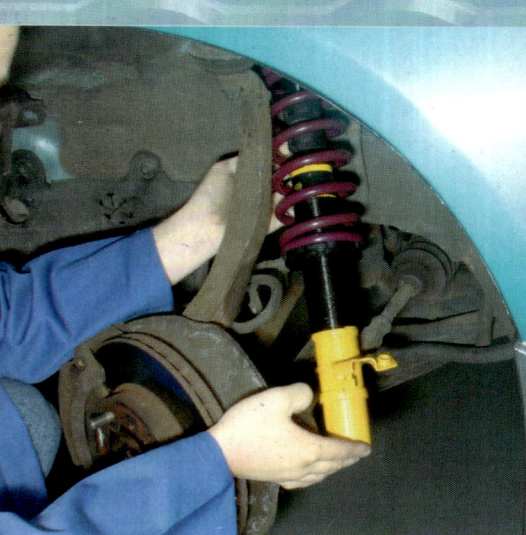

**26** On 2000 and earlier models, smear a little grease on the bottom of the shock body . . .

**27** . . . then slip on the damper fork and install the pinch bolt, tightening the bolt to the proper torque (see your *Haynes Automotive Repair Manual*)

**25** Guide the shock absorber/coil spring unit into place, then install the upper mounting nuts

104

**23** ...and the insulator and dished washer, as applicable (different kits may have slight variations). Install a new nut and tighten it securely while holding the piston rod from turning

**24** Apply some anti-seize compound to the threads on the shock/strut body, then run the lower spring seat up to the coil spring. Now pre-load the spring using the C-wrench provided with the kit. You won't really know how much pre-load will be required until you install the units on the car, but at least you'll have a starting point. Just be sure you pre-load both front shocks and both rear shocks the same amount (see the accompanying *Tip*). Once you've got the pre-load set, tighten the lock ring up against the spring seat.

**TIP** Before installing shocks or struts with coilover adjusters, set all the springs to the same height. More than likely you'll still have to do some fine tuning after they're all installed, but at least you'll know that each side will require the same amount of adjustment. Also, when adjusting coilovers, raise the vehicle and support it on jackstands before turning the lock ring and spring seat.

**28** Also on 2000 and earlier models, install the damper fork-to-lower control arm bolt and nut. This bolt and nut has to be tightened with the suspension at normal ride height, which can be simulated by raising the control arm with a floor jack or waiting until the car is back on the ground (if you tighten this with the suspension hanging free, it'll cause the bushing to "wind up" when the weight of the car is back on the suspension). Make sure you tighten it up to the proper torque

**29** Complete reassembly by reversing the appropriate disassembly sequence (Steps 1 through 10). Be sure to reconnect the brake hose to the shock body, as shown. Also connect the ABS speed sensor harness to the shock, if equipped

**30** Reinstall the wheel and lower the car, then tighten the shock absorber upper mounting nuts and the wheel lug nuts to the proper torque. Have the wheel alignment checked and, if necessary, adjusted

105

# Coilovers

If you've chosen matched shocks/struts/coil springs with "coilover" adjusters, you obviously know quality when you see it, and you're not prepared to compromise. True, quality costs, but you get what you pay for. This is an expensive option, but it offers one vital feature that others can't - true adjustability of ride height, along with proper damping rates and piston rod travel. This means you can get exactly the ride height you're looking for, but won't be bottoming-out your shock's piston rods like you would with a conversion kit.

## Coilover conversion

Another option gaining popularity is the "coilover conversion." If you must have the lowest, baddest machine and want to save some money, these could be the answer. Offering as much potential for lowering as a genuine matched set of struts or shocks/coilovers, these items could be described as a cross between coilovers and lowering springs - the standard struts or shocks are retained (which usually results in less ride quality). What you get is a new spring and a threaded sleeve with an adjustable bottom mount - the whole thing slips over your standard strut or shock body. Two problems with this solution:

- Standard struts/shocks are not designed to operate as well when lowered, so the car's ride and handling will be compromised if you lower the car very much.
- The standard struts/shocks are effectively being compressed, the lower you go. There is a limit to how far they will compress before being completely solid. Needless to say, even a partially compressed strut or shock won't be able to do much actual damping - the result could be a very harsh ride.

# Rear suspension

**01** Working in the luggage compartment, remove the trim and loosen (but don't remove) the two shock absorber upper mounting nuts. Don't loosen the one in the middle; that's the shock absorber piston rod nut, and it keeps the coil spring from flying out

**02** Loosen the rear wheel lug nuts, then raise the rear of the vehicle and support it securely on jackstands. Remove the rear wheels. In a perfect world, all you'd have to do would be to remove this shock absorber lower mounting bolt, take off the upper mounting nuts, then guide the unit down and out

**03** But in our real world, this bolt was completely seized, so we chose to remove the inner and outer control arm bolts . . .

**04** . . . and remove the shock and control arm together

107

**05** We sliced the nut off with a hacksaw and found that the bolt was also seized-up inside of the bushing

**06** So, it took a little extra effort to get it out. Here we used a vise, another bolt and a socket to push the stubborn bolt out. Depending on what happens to the bushing after this kind of surgery, you may wind up having to buy a new control arm

**07** The rear shock assembly comes apart like the front one. Here we're using a different kind of spring compressor set-up, but the idea is the same: the spring MUST be compressed before the piston rod nut is loosened! Read the **Warning** we've included here and follow any instructions that come with the spring compressor you use. If you're going to install a new spring, loosen the compressors evenly and transfer them to the new spring

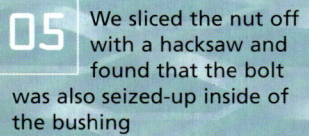

**Warning:** *Disassembling a coil-over type shock absorber is potentially dangerous! Your full attention must be directed to the job, or serious injury may result. Before disassembling the shocks, make sure you have a good spring compressor and obtain a new piston nut for each shock absorber (the nut should be replaced every time it is removed).*

**08** Assembling the rear shock is just like the ones up front. On the kit we're installing, the only old part we need is the upper mounting plate

**09** To install the shock unit, guide it up into place and install the upper mounting nuts . . .

**10** . . . and connect the lower end to the control arm. Here's another one of those fasteners that can only be tightened with the suspension at normal ride height (otherwise the bushing will "wind up" when the car is lowered). Remember, though, you can simulate normal ride height by raising the outer end of the control arm with a floor jack. Be sure to tighten it to the proper torque. When you're finished, install the wheels and lower the vehicle. Tighten the shock absorber upper mounting nuts and the wheel lug nuts to the proper torque (see your *Haynes Automotive Repair Manual*)

# Air suspension

Air suspension systems provide the ability to raise or lower the car instantly, from the driver's seat, or even from a distance on systems equipped with a remote control. Many consider this the ultimate suspension system, since you can lower the car as low as you want for shows and cruises, but still be able to easily raise the car to a reasonable ride height for your daily commute. The main components are air "springs" (which are basically strut assemblies with no coil springs) filled with compressed air. Pumping air into the air springs increases the air pressure and raises the vehicle, while releasing air from the springs lowers the vehicle. The system also has an electric air compressor, valves and air lines to deliver and release the compressed air. Air suspension systems also have a high-tech look: the compressors are often highly polished and sometimes chrome or gold plated - they can really dress up your engine compartment!

The primary disadvantage of an air suspension system, as you might have guessed, is cost: generally, they have a similar cost to coilover kits. And the ride quality and handling will never reach the level of a good, well-adjusted coilover kit - in fact, ride quality will likely be worse than with the stock suspension system. Another disadvantage is that the systems can cause damage to your vehicle's suspension and body if they are not set up and used carefully. The systems should be set up so that there will be no fender rub or metal-to-metal suspension bottoming when the air is released. Sometimes systems can leak down when the vehicle is left sitting for an extended period - you don't want to wind up with bent parts as a result.

There are a variety of air suspension systems available, and installation procedures vary. The air "springs" install basically the same way as standard struts or shocks. The air compressor is generally installed under the hood. Many owners choose to install a large separate storage tank for compressed air that allows rapid, repeated cycling of the system ("bouncing" the car up and down). When installing this equipment, refer to the manufacturer's instructions and recommendations.

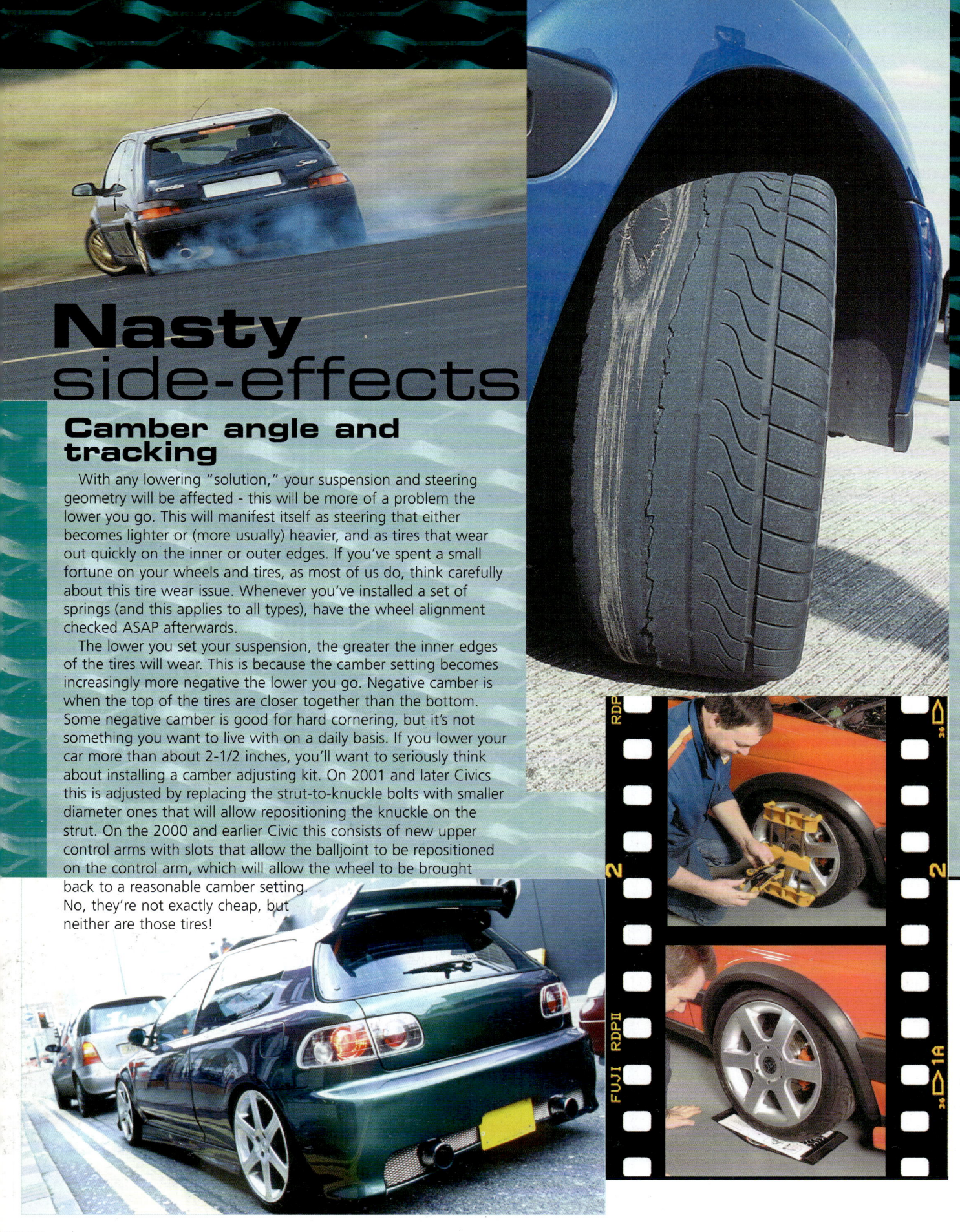

# Nasty side-effects

## Camber angle and tracking

With any lowering "solution," your suspension and steering geometry will be affected - this will be more of a problem the lower you go. This will manifest itself as steering that either becomes lighter or (more usually) heavier, and as tires that wear out quickly on the inner or outer edges. If you've spent a small fortune on your wheels and tires, as most of us do, think carefully about this tire wear issue. Whenever you've installed a set of springs (and this applies to all types), have the wheel alignment checked ASAP afterwards.

The lower you set your suspension, the greater the inner edges of the tires will wear. This is because the camber setting becomes increasingly more negative the lower you go. Negative camber is when the top of the tires are closer together than the bottom. Some negative camber is good for hard cornering, but it's not something you want to live with on a daily basis. If you lower your car more than about 2-1/2 inches, you'll want to seriously think about installing a camber adjusting kit. On 2001 and later Civics this is adjusted by replacing the strut-to-knuckle bolts with smaller diameter ones that will allow repositioning the knuckle on the strut. On the 2000 and earlier Civic this consists of new upper control arms with slots that allow the balljoint to be repositioned on the control arm, which will allow the wheel to be brought back to a reasonable camber setting.

No, they're not exactly cheap, but neither are those tires!

# Shock tower/ strut brace

When you pitch your car into a corner hard, and then start sawing the wheel back and forth as you negotiate a tricky series of left and right hand corners, the loads imposed on the front end are considerable enough to actually twist the body, which will change the relationship of the struts or upper control arms to each other. You don't want that!

If you've installed an aftermarket stabilizer bar, this problem could actually be *magnified*, because of the greater cornering forces you'll be imposing on the chassis. The camber and caster of the front wheels is established by the position of the upper ends of the control arms or struts. Allowing the upper mounting points of the control arms or struts to move means that the camber and caster are changing. A strut or shock tower brace simply ties the two towers together and prevents them from flexing. And that's a good thing!

**01** We're going to help out this '95 Civic's handling by installing a shock tower brace. On the kit we're using, the first step is to remove the shock absorber upper mounting nuts. Don't remove that nut in the center (between the shock absorber mounting nuts) - that's the piston rod nut and it keeps the coil spring from flying out!

**02** Place the mount over the shock absorber upper mounting studs, then install the nuts

**03** Tighten the nuts to the proper torque specification (see the *Haynes Automotive Repair manual* for your vehicle)

**04** The right side mount is installed the same way

**05** Measure the distance between the centers of the holes in the mounting brackets (write this figure down; you'll need it in a minute)

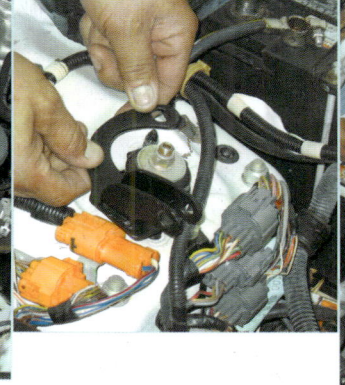

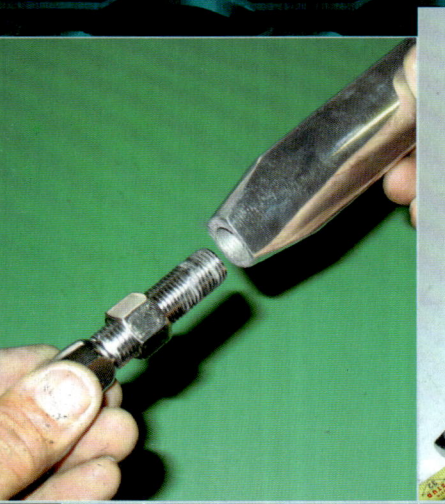
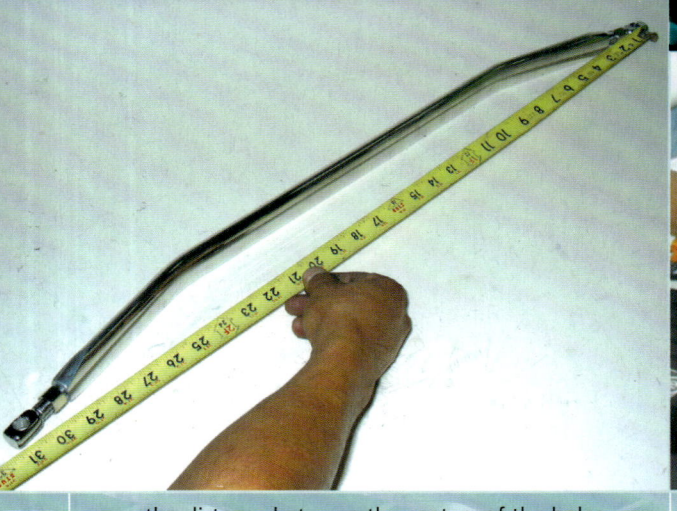

**06** Thread the locknuts onto the adjusters, then screw the adjusters into the brace . . .

**07** . . . so the distance between the centers of the holes in the adjusters is the same as the distance between the centers of the holes in the mounts

**08** Place one end of the brace into its mount and install the bolt and nut. Don't tighten the nut yet

**09** Now guide the other end into place and install the bolt and nut. Although not included in the kit, we placed a washer between each adjuster and bracket just to take out the little bit of slack that was present

**10** Now tighten the mounting nuts securely

**11** The last thing to do is tighten the locknuts on the adjusters up against the brace

**12** An installation so clean you could eat off it. Sushi, anyone?

# Installing stabilizer bars

Even with stock suspension, most sport compact cars are fun to fling around. But their handling limitations become apparent when you start flicking them into corners a little harder than usual.

Stabilizer bars reduce the tendency of the car's body to "roll" (or tilt towards the outside of a turn) when cornering. Your vehicle probably already has a stabilizer bar at the front, and maybe even one at the rear. But even if you have stabilizer bars front and rear from the factory, a good set of aftermarket performance bars will do you a world of good - you won't believe how flat your car will corner!

In the case of most front-wheel drive cars installing a rear stabilizer bar (or replacing the stock bar with a thicker aftermarket one) is all you'll really have to do to get rid of (or at least greatly reduce) the inherent "understeer" characteristics that plague this type of drivetrain platform.

Replacing the front stabilizer bar bushings with aftermarket polyurethane ones will help that bar function more efficiently.

## Installing a rear stabilizer bar

We'll show a typical install here, but make sure you follow the specific instructions that will come with the parts.

**Note:** *The kit we're installing requires the rear lower control arms to have either threaded mounting bosses or holes for the stabilizer bar links. If your rear lower control arms don't have threaded mounting bosses or holes, you'll have to replace them with factory units that do have them. Drilling holes in your existing control arms is NOT recommended.*

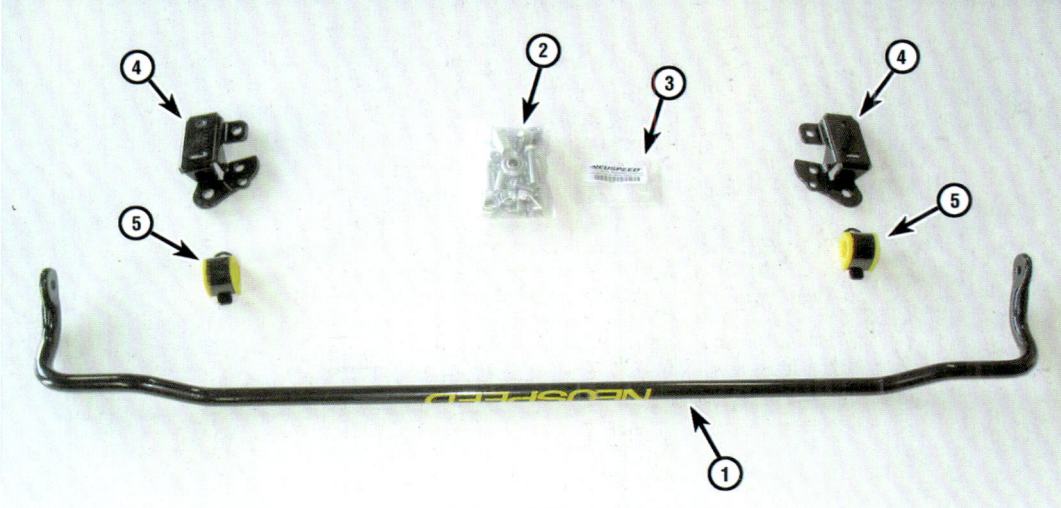

**01** Unpack your stabilizer bar kit and make sure that everything you'll need is there. This kit includes a pair of polyurethane bar clamp bushings and a pair of links (to connect the stabilizer bar to the control arms). It also includes a small bag of a special synthetic grease

1. Stabilizer bar
2. Links and mounting hardware
3. Synthetic grease (for bushings)
4. Mounting bracket
5. Clamp and bushing

**02** Raise the vehicle and place it securely on jackstands. Locate the stock link at each end of the stabilizer bar, then remove the bolt securing each link to each control arm

**03** Unbolt the mounting bracket from each side . . .

**04** . . . then remove the stabilizer bar, links and brackets as a single assembly. Better go hide this twig - it's really not the kind of thing you'd want your friends to see!

**05** If your car is equipped with ABS, unscrew the bolts and remove the bracket for the wheel speed sensor on each side

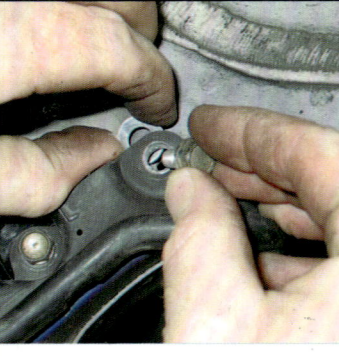

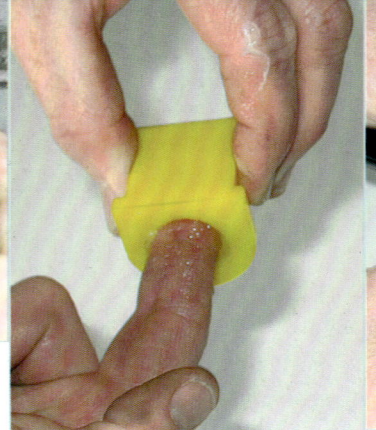

**08** Install the other two mounting bracket bolts; these you can tighten fully now (but don't tighten that lower control arm pivot bolt yet!). If your car has ABS, reinstall the speed sensor harness bracket. On our vehicle we installed the outer bolt first . . .

**09** . . . and installed a couple of washers behind the bracket, followed by the inner bolt. We did this because the new stabilizer bar mounting bracket spaced this wire harness bracket out about 1/8-inch

**10** Coat the insides of the new bushings with the special grease supplied with the kit. This is a waterproof synthetic grease and is extremely sticky and hard to wash off. Wear latex gloves if you have some

**11** Fit the lubed-up bushings to the bar, then position them all the way out to the bend

**06** Now remove the lower control arm pivot bolt from each side. You don't have to worry about spring pressure on the arm, because the spring is contained by the shock absorber. The arm might shift a little as you remove the bolt; however, we found that levering the arm outward a bit helped ease bolt removal

**07** OK, let's get on with the upgrade. Start by installing the new mounting brackets - the control arm pivot bolt goes in first. Don't fully tighten this bolt yet, for two reasons: One, it would make installation of the other bolts difficult, and Two, tightening this bolt with the suspension in full rebound will cause the bushing to "wind up" when the car is lowered (and even more when the suspension compresses when soaking up a bump). Such a condition can lead to premature failure of the bushing. We'll tighten this bolt a little later.

**12** Raise the bar into position and place the clamps over the bushings. Hook the bottom part of one clamp into the slot in its mounting bracket, then rotate the bushing and clamp into position. Install the bolt and tighten it securely, then repeat on the other side

# Understeer and oversteer

What exactly is "understeer"? And what is "oversteer"? A good understanding of oversteer and understeer is essential to anyone planning to upgrade the tires, wheels, coil springs and front and rear stabilizers.

## Understeer

Understeer is the tendency of a car to slide off the road nose end first when you pitch it into a corner too hard. You turn the steering wheel as you enter the corner, but the car turns less than it should in response to the amount of steering input you're giving it. Most modern sport compact cars, particularly front-wheel-drive vehicles, are set up by the manufacturer for some understeer because at normal cornering speeds a bit of understeer feels safer and more predictable. But if you want your car to stick in the corners, you'll have to eliminate your car's understeer tendencies. One way to do that is to install a rear stabilizer bar or, if your car is already equipped with one, a bigger rear bar.

## Oversteer

Oversteer is the tendency of a car to slide off the road tail-end first when you pitch it into a corner too hard. You turn the steering wheel as you enter the corner, but the car turns more than it should in response to the amount of steering input you're giving it. An oversteering car can be quick through the corners, but it can also be dangerous unless it's in the hands of a very skilled driver. Luckily, very few front-wheel-drive sport compact cars have an oversteer problem, because their weight distribution is invariably biased in favor of the front end.

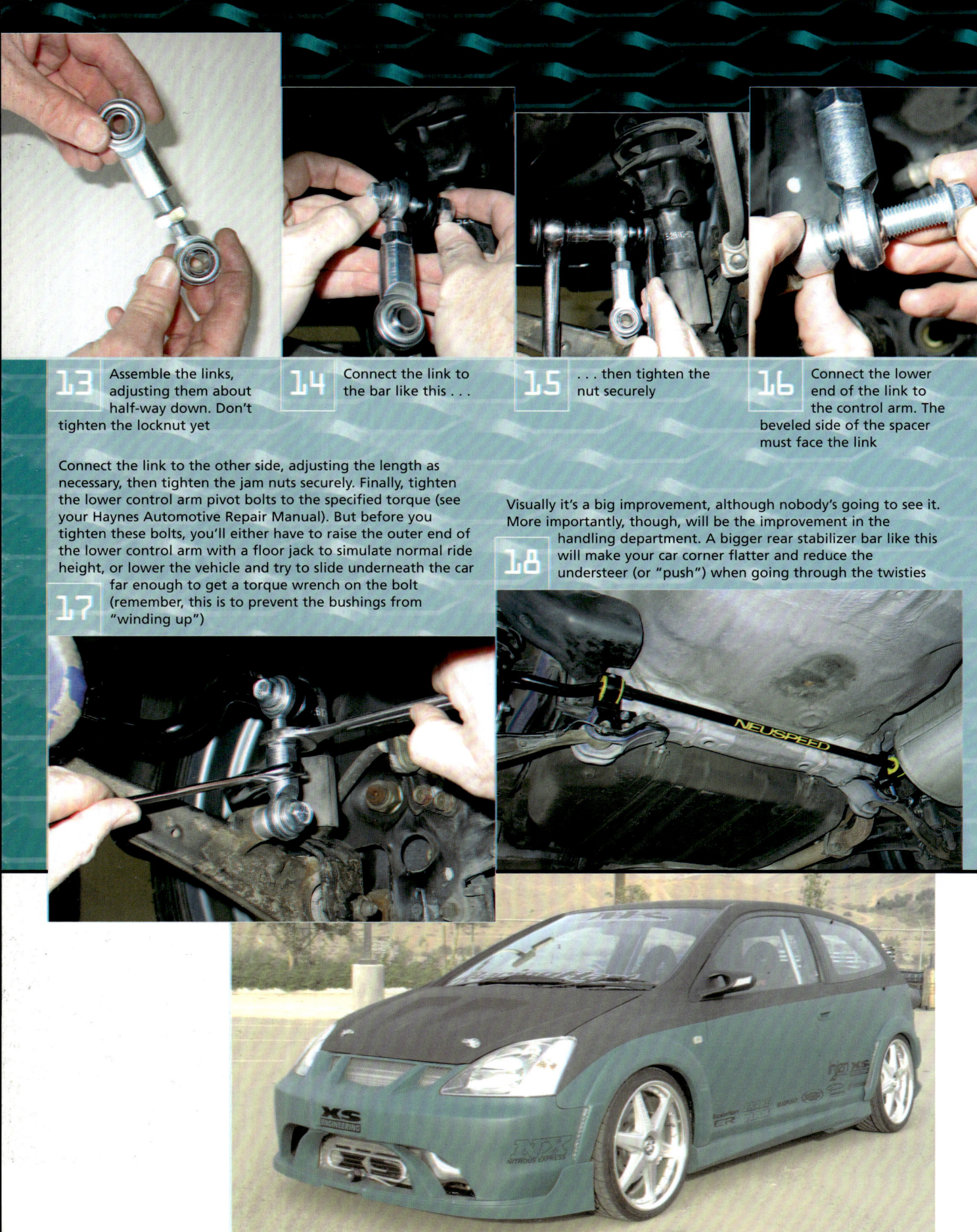

**13** Assemble the links, adjusting them about half-way down. Don't tighten the locknut yet

**14** Connect the link to the bar like this . . .

**15** . . . then tighten the nut securely

**16** Connect the lower end of the link to the control arm. The beveled side of the spacer must face the link

**17** Connect the link to the other side, adjusting the length as necessary, then tighten the jam nuts securely. Finally, tighten the lower control arm pivot bolts to the specified torque (see your Haynes Automotive Repair Manual). But before you tighten these bolts, you'll either have to raise the outer end of the lower control arm with a floor jack to simulate normal ride height, or lower the vehicle and try to slide underneath the car far enough to get a torque wrench on the bolt (remember, this is to prevent the bushings from "winding up")

**18** Visually it's a big improvement, although nobody's going to see it. More importantly, though, will be the improvement in the handling department. A bigger rear stabilizer bar like this will make your car corner flatter and reduce the understeer (or "push") when going through the twisties

# 07 Brakes

Brakes - the final frontier, or the biggest difference between a heroic high-speed charge and a humiliating high-speed crash. Here's what's what...

## Brake pedal

Where it all starts, from your point of view. The pedal itself is a mechanical lever, and has to provide enough leverage to work the brakes if the power booster fails. Manufacturers use "brake pedal ratios" to express this - a low-ratio pedal, for instance, will give quick-acting but hard-to-work brakes.

## Booster

The power brake booster on these vehicles is vacuum-operated, and it produces extra force on the pistons inside the master cylinder when the brakes are applied, reducing brake pedal effort. Most cars these days are equipped with boosters because they are also equipped with disc brakes (at least up front), and disc brakes require more force than drum brakes do (they aren't self-energizing).

## Master cylinder

Below the brake fluid reservoir is the master cylinder, which is where the brake pedal effort (force) is converted to hydraulic effort (pressure), and transmitted to each brake through the hydraulic lines and hoses.

## Brake fluid

Pressing the brake pedal moves the brake fluid through the lines to each brake, where the hydraulic pressure is converted back to mechanical force once more, as the pads and shoes move into contact with discs and drums. Fluid does not compress readily, but if air (which is compressible) gets in the system, there'll be less effort at the brakes and you'll get a fright. This is why 'bleeding' the brakes of air bubbles whenever the system has been opened is vital.

## Brake hoses

For most of the way from the master cylinder to the wheels, the fluid goes through rigid metal brake pipes. At the suspension, where movement is needed, the pipes connect to flexible hoses. The standard rubber hoses are fine when they're new, but replacing old ones with great-looking braided hoses is a good move - in theory, it improves braking, as braided hoses expand less than rubber ones, and transmit more fluid pressure.

## Calipers

These act like a clamp to force the brake pads against the discs - fluid pressure forces a piston outwards, which presses the brake pads onto the disc. Generally, the more pistons your calipers have, the more surface area the brake fluid has on which to push, providing greater clamping power. Most cars have only one or two per caliper, while exotic calipers may contain three, four or even more!

## Discs

Clamped to your wheel hubs, the discs spin around as fast as your wheels. Over 90% of braking is done by the front brakes, which is why all modern cars have front discs - they work much better than drums, because they dissipate heat better. Many base models have "solid"

discs, while higher-performance cars have "vented" ones, which have an air gap between the braking surfaces to aid cooling. The bigger the disc diameter, the greater pad area available, with greater stopping power (think of a long lever as compared to a short one).

## Pads and shoes

Both have a metal backing plate, with friction lining attached. Brake linings used to be made of an asbestos compound, which had excellent heat-resisting qualities but could cause cancer or asbestosis in people who breathed in the dust. Now they come in non-asbestos organic (stock), or for higher-performance applications, semi-metallic or carbon metallic.

## Anti-lock Brakes (ABS)

Bottom line: Two cars are cruising down the road and a hay truck pulls out from a side road. Both drivers stand on the brake pedal. The car without ABS "locks up" the wheels and starts skidding, ending up sideways in a ditch. The car with ABS is able to slow down and safely maneuver around the truck. Great stuff, and here's how it works.

ABS works by detecting when a particular wheel is about to lock. It then reduces the hydraulic pressure applied to that wheel's brake, releasing it just before the wheel locks, and then re-applies it.

The system consists of a hydraulic unit, which contains various solenoid valves and an electric fluid return pump, four wheel speed sensors, and an electronic control unit (ECU). The solenoids in the hydraulic unit are controlled by the ECU, which receives signals from the four wheel sensors.

If the ECU senses that a wheel is about to lock, it operates the relevant solenoid valve in the hydraulic unit, which isolates that brake from the master cylinder. If the wheel sensor detects that the wheel is still about to lock, the ECU switches on the fluid return pump in the hydraulic unit and pumps the fluid back from the brake to the master cylinder, releasing the brake. Once the speed of the wheel returns to normal, the return pump stops and the solenoid valve opens, allowing fluid pressure back to the brake, and so the brake is re-applied. Pretty impressive, especially when you consider all this is happening in a fraction of a second! You

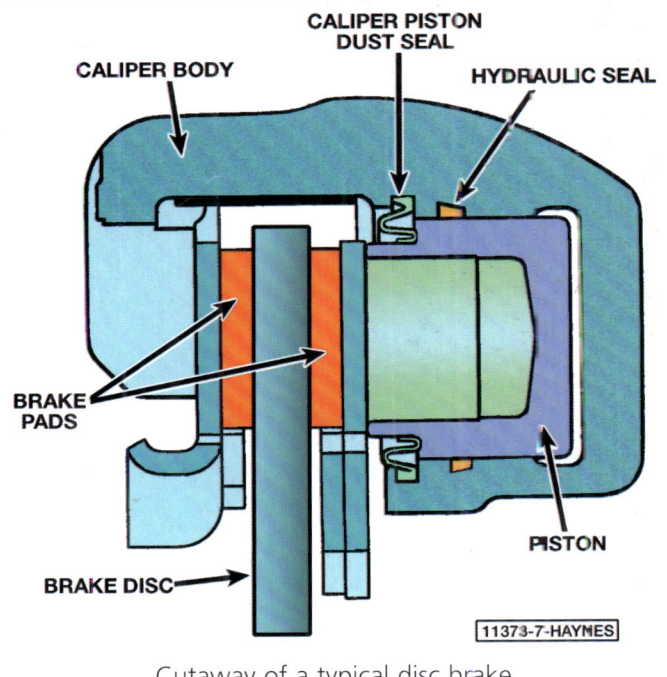

Cutaway of a typical disc brake

may feel your ABS system working in a hard braking situation. The brake pedal will "pulse" as the pressure varies. But don't let up or "pump" the pedal yourself - let the ABS do its job. The rapid variations in fluid pressure cause pulses in the hydraulic circuit, and these can be felt through the brake pedal.

The system relies totally on electrical signals. If an inaccurate signal or a battery problem is detected, the ABS is automatically shut down, and a warning light on the instrument panel will come on. Normal braking will always be available whether or not the ABS is working.

ABS cannot work miracles, and the basic laws of physics will still apply: stopping distances will always be greater on slippery surfaces. The greatest benefit of ABS is being able to brake hard in an emergency without having to worry about correcting a skid.

If you have any problems with an anti-lock brake system, always consult an authorized dealer service department or other qualified repair shop.

# Grooved
## and drilled discs

Besides the various brands of performance brake pads that go with them, the main brake upgrade is to install performance front brake discs and pads. Discs are available in two main types - grooved and cross-drilled (and combinations of both).

Grooved discs (which can be had with varying numbers of grooves) serve a dual purpose - the grooves provide a 'channel' to help the heat escape, and they also help to de-glaze the pad surface, cleaning up the pads every time they're used. Some of the discs are made from higher-friction metal than normal discs, too, and the fact that they seriously improve braking performance is well-documented.

Cross-drilled discs offer another route to heat dissipation, but one which can present some problems. Owners report that cross-drilled discs really eat brake pads, more so than the grooved types, but more serious is the fact that some of these discs can crack around the drilled holes after serious use. The trouble is that the heat 'migrates' to the drilled holes (as was intended), but the heat build-up can be extreme, and the constant heating/cooling cycle can stress the metal to the point where it will crack. Discs which have been damaged in this way are extremely dangerous to drive on, as they could break up completely at any time. Only install discs of this type from established manufacturers offering a useful guarantee of quality, and check the discs regularly.

Performance discs also have a reputation for warping (nasty vibrations felt through the pedal). Justified, or not? Well, the harder you use your brakes, the greater the heat you'll generate.

Okay, so these wicked discs are meant to be able to cope with this heat, but you can't expect miracles. Cheap discs, or ones which have been abused over thousands of miles, will warp.

Performance pads can be mated to any brake discs, including the stock ones, but are of course designed to work best with heat-dissipating discs. Unless you plan on regularly participating in your club's track day, or hit the autocross circuit frequently, don't be tempted to go much further than 'fast road' pads - anything more competition-orientated may take too long to come up to temperature on the road. Remember what the brakes on your old ten-speed bike were like in the rain? Cold competition pads feel the same, and at regular street speeds may never get up to their proper operating temperature.

Lastly, installing all the performance brake parts in the world is no use if your calipers have seized up. If, when you remove your old pads, you find that one pad's worn more than the other, or that both pads have worn more on the left wheel than the right, your caliper pistons are sticking. Sometimes you can free them up by pushing them back into the caliper, but this is a sign that you really need new calipers. If you drive around with sticking calipers, you'll eat pads and discs. You choose.

# Upgraded
## discs and pads

Upgraded discs and pads are often the first step to a high-performance brake system, a simple modification that takes a couple of hours max, and can make a huge difference. Since they do wear down over time, and are also prone to warpage, there's a chance you'll have to change your discs anyway, so why not upgrade them at the same time?

**Warning:** The dust created by the brake system is harmful to your health. Never blow it out with compressed air and don't inhale any of it. An approved filtering mask should be worn when working on the brakes. Do not, under any circumstances, use petroleum-based solvents to clean brake parts. Use brake system cleaner only!

**01** Loosen the wheel lug nuts, raise the front of the vehicle and support it securely on jackstands. First job is to remove the caliper mounting bolts . . .

**02** . . . then lift off the caliper. You won't be able to remove it completely, as it's still attached by the fluid hose - tie the caliper up with string or wire so the hose isn't stretched (don't let it hang on the hose)

**03** If all you're doing is changing the pads, this is the end of the road. Take 'em out, slap in the new ones, put it back together. But we hope you're more dedicated than that

## Some good things to know about working on brakes

- Brakes create a lot of dust from the friction linings. Although usually not made from asbestos (very bad stuff) anymore, the dust is still something you'll want to avoid. Spray everything with brake cleaner and don't blow it into the air where you'll breathe it.
- Brake fluid is nasty stuff - poisonous, highly flammable and an effective paint stripper. Mop up spills promptly and wash any splashes off paintwork with lots of water.
- Do not use petroleum-based cleaners and solvents on or around brake parts. It will eat away all the rubber parts and hoses. Use only brake cleaner.
- Most brake jobs you can do without loosening or removing the fluid hoses and lines. If you mess with these you'll let air into the system and then have to "bleed" the brakes, which can be tricky. If you finish your job and then step on the pedal and it goes all the way to the floor, or feels soft or "spongy," you've let air into the lines.
- Which brings up a good point. After working on your brakes, start the car and pump the pedal a few times to bring the pads into contact with the discs, and to make sure all is well before charging down the street.

**04** To get the disc off, the caliper mounting bracket comes off next. There's two bolts to remove, and they will be tight (they'd better be tight, anyway)

**05** Lift off the caliper mounting bracket - the disc should now be free to come off

**06** Well, "free to come off" might be a tad optimistic. There's only a couple of Phillips-head screws holding the disc on, but they're almost always rusted. Sometimes they fall out, and sometimes you need an impact driver, like us. If they are tight, find a screwdriver/bit that's a good fit before getting too brutal, or you'll wreck the screw heads and be really stuck. WD-40 might help, too

**07** Sorry, more bad news (possibly). Even if the screws come out, the disc might not just fall off for you. If it's rusted on, first try a few well-aimed blows with a blunt instrument. If that doesn't work, find two bolts that'll screw into the larger pair of holes in the disc. Tighten them equally and hard, and additional persuasion with that hammer should get the disc to come off

**08** Alright, so your disc just fell off. Lucky you. If your discs had to be beaten off, they're only fit for scrap (no point in keeping them to re-convert the car later)

**09** Any rust on the hub now has to go, along with any other crud. If the wheel hub isn't totally pristine, the new disc won't sit on quite straight, and will eat its way through the new pads in no time. So do it right and take a wire brush to the hub flange

**10** If you want to spare yourself the misery of stuck-on discs in the future, a little copper grease on the hub flange will be a big help.

**11** Like the hubs, the new discs must be clean before installing - give 'em a squirt of brake cleaner and wipe them down with a rag. Your new discs probably are not identical, and should only be installed with the grooves facing a certain way (this is the left front). Check the paperwork that came with your discs

**12** If your disc screws are useable you can go ahead and install them, but they're not really necessary; the disc is going to be sandwiched between the wheel and the hub anyway. Painting your calipers? Now would be an excellent time. Reinstall the caliper mounting bracket and tighten the bolts to the proper torque (see your *Haynes Automotive Repair Manual*).

**13** To make room for your new pads, the caliper piston must be bottomed in the caliper. If you're working on a front caliper or a rear caliper with no parking brake cable attached to it, you can pry it back in with a screwdriver and block of wood, or squeeze it back using water pump pliers (or even this, a cheap ratchet clamping tool from a local hardware store). If you're working on a rear caliper that has a parking brake cable attached to it, you'll have to rotate the piston to get it to go down; you can engage the tips of a pair of needle-nose pliers with the slots in the piston face. Watch the brake fluid level in the master cylinder reservoir - it mustn't overflow.

Smearing a film of copper grease on the pad backing plates shows you're serious about not having annoying squealing brakes (but don't overdo it). If any grease gets on the disc, get it all off with brake **14** cleaner and a rag.

Slip the new pads into position on the caliper mounting bracket (the greased backing plates face away from the disc, obviously), then install the caliper. If it won't go on, you haven't **15** pushed the piston back in enough (Step 13).

Install the caliper upper and lower mounting bolts (wiggle the caliper to get them in) and tighten them to the proper torque (see your Haynes Automotive Repair Manual). Give the brake pedal several good pumps to bring the new pads up to the new disc. Install the wheel and lug nuts and you're ready for a road test. When you've done both sides, that is. Your calipers **16** may be slightly different to this - if so, refer to the Haynes manual for details.

**Caution:** New pads of any sort need careful bedding-in (over 100 miles of normal use) before they'll work properly - when first installed, the pad surface won't exactly match the contours of the disc (even if the disc is new) so it won't actually be touching it over its full area. This will most likely result in a set of very underwhelming brakes for the first few trips, so take it easy for awhile.

# Painting calipers

Installing custom rims means that your brakes can be seen by anybody - not a problem usually, but if you've got massive wheels, you really need something good to look at behind them. So if you can't stretch to a big disc conversion or even upgraded pads and discs, why not clean up what you've got there already?

You can spray them or hand-paint them, but either way the key is in the prepping. Brakes are dirty things, so make sure they're really clean before you start.

We know you won't necessarily want to hear this, but the best way to paint the calipers is to do some disassembling first. The kits say you don't have to, but trust us - you'll get a much better result from a few minutes extra work.

**Warning:** *The dust created by the brake system is harmful to your health. Never blow it out with compressed air and don't inhale any of it. An approved filtering mask should be worn when working on the brakes. Do not, under any circumstances, use petroleum-based solvents to clean brake parts. Use brake system cleaner only!*

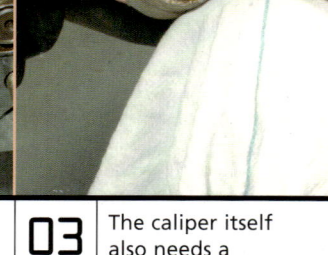

**Tricks n' tips**
*If you have trouble reassembling your brakes after painting, you probably got carried away and put on too much paint. We found that, once it was fully dry, the excess paint could be trimmed off with a knife.*

**01** Remove the caliper and its mounting bracket, but leave the disc in place. Getting stuff clean is the name of the game, and you'll do a way better job with it all apart. This is the caliper mounting bracket getting the wire-brush treatment . . .

**02** . . . and by the time we're done, it's so shiny, it's almost a shame to paint it. You can bolt this part back on now. Be sure to tighten the bolts to the proper torque (see your *Haynes Automotive Repair Manual*)

**03** The caliper itself also needs a thorough scrub with the wire brush . . .

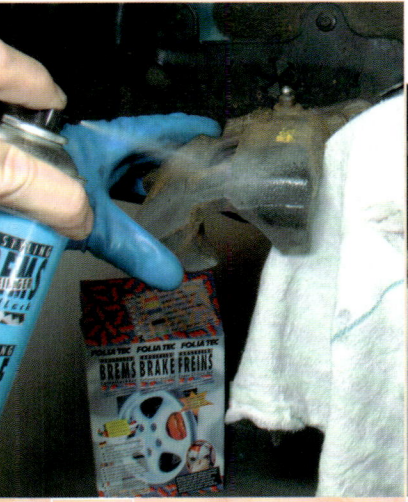   

**04** ...followed by a good squirt of the brake cleaner supplied in most kits. Don't just spray it and leave it - get wiping as soon as possible. Spraying alone will only loosen the muck. If you don't get it spotless, you'll get black streaks in the paint later, which will ruin all your hard work

**05** We found the best way to paint was to re-mount the caliper by its top bolt, and swing it up, supporting it with a piece of wire. So as not to get our new disc covered in green paint, some masking tape was applied

**06** Most caliper paint comes in two cans, which you mix together - if yours is like this, remember it sets up fast. You really should have all four brakes scrubbed and ready to paint before mixing

**07** Stick some paper under the brake to catch any drips. Remember that you only have to paint the parts you'll see when the wheels are on. Also, it's best to do more than one coat. Wait until the paint is totally dry (like overnight, or longer) before reassembling

# Painting drums

**01** At least there's no disassembling the drums - just raise the rear of the vehicle, support it securely on jackstands and remove the wheel. Now clean off the drums with brake system cleaner, the wire brush and sandpaper (to smooth the surface). After all that hit it with the brake cleaner one more time and wipe it down with a clean rag

**02** You definitely don't want any paint on the wheel studs, nor where the wheels will touch the drum. If you've got a steady hand, masking it off shouldn't be necessary. Painting the drums is much easier than the calipers. One piece of advice - for the drums, use a thicker, better-quality brush than the one you might get in a kit, as you'll get a much smoother paint finish on the drums. Again, two coats of paint seemed like a good idea.

## 08 Engine performance

# Engine performance

The sign in the old performance shop used to read "Speed costs money . . . how fast do you want to go?" and it's just as true today. More important even than cost is organizing your modifications as a "package" of planned mods that work efficiently together.

Remember also that speed can cost you in other ways. An engine built to make 600 horsepower at the racetrack is not going to idle smoothly, get good gas mileage or go 200,000 miles between overhauls. Performance modifications are frequently called "upgrades," but we need to keep in mind that the performance end of the operational spectrum is what's being upgraded, and often you'll have to give up some of the smooth, reliable and economical operation that sport-compact cars are famous for.

So it's best to have a plan for your project, even if you don't have all the money to do everything right away. Don't plan on having a 9-second car that you can still loan to your mom on grocery day - neither one of you will be happy. Most of us will want to build a car that is a compromise: a car that is fast enough to race on the weekend, but is still practical to drive to work every day. Many upgrades, such as an exhaust header, cat-back

## Mistake number one

Ya gotta have a plan! The most common mistake when young enthusiasts start to modify their sport compact cars is getting dazzled by cars seen at shows or in magazines. This leaves the temptation to just start "throwing parts" at your car in an effort to be as cool or fast as those show cars. Every level of performance for your car should be a coordinated effort. Let's say there are several "phases" in your path to performance. In Phase One, you make several modifications that are all at the same "strength" of improvement. A "Phase Four" camshaft designed for very high rpms will do what it's designed for, but only when used along with a number of other modifications suited to that level.

Don't mix parts designed for different levels of performance! Have a performance goal in mind that is a realistic compromise for your driving needs and budget. If you really demand maximum horsepower and you're willing to upgrade your drivetrain and lose a lot of driveability, then make your plan to use only Phase Four components. If a realistic plan for you is modifying your engine only to Phase Two, then only make those mods, nothing further.

Many enthusiasts start out buying parts that really don't help their engine at the performance level they're seeking. For instance, an aftermarket ignition system will add nothing to your relatively-stock engine except looks. The stock ignition works fine for most purposes, so unless you're building to a high level, you don't need the hot coil and amplifier. However, when you get to the higher stages, that performance ignition system will be *required* in order to fire the engine at high rpm with the increased cylinder pressure of a power adder like nitrous or a turbo. The other side of that coin is that a Phase Four camshaft on a Phase Two engine may give you less-desirable performance.

Planning ahead means you won't have a garage full of expensive parts you bought and then later took off when you changed to higher or lower-Phase parts because things didn't perform the way you expected.

system, and air-intake tube give "free" horsepower, with the only compromise being more noise (or as we like to call it, "engine music"). These upgrades are also relatively inexpensive and are "no-brainers" for any sport-compact build-up.

When you get into nitrous, turbos and superchargers, you'll be spending more money and also getting into more risk of engine damage. Camshafts and cylinder head work will reduce your car's low-speed driveability and frequently decrease your gas mileage. Often, when these modifications are designed to increase high-rpm horsepower, you'll actually lose some low-rpm power.

**Before** The stock engine compartment is not really something you'd want to show off

# Engine compartment dress-up

Open the hood on a Honda Civic and what do you see? Black plastic air filter housing, black air intake duct, black battery, black radiator and heater hoses, black vacuum hoses, black fuse box, black electrical harnesses, black accelerator and cruise control cables, black valve cover (with, of course, a black oil filler cap), black . . . well, black everything. Black, black, black everywhere! A sea of black! It's as if the engine compartment was dressed for a funeral or some other somber occasion.

Show-car engine compartments don't look like midnight in a coal mine, so why should yours? Look how we transformed the engine compartment shown on next page - this only took a few hundred bucks and a couple of weekends.

After

**Before**

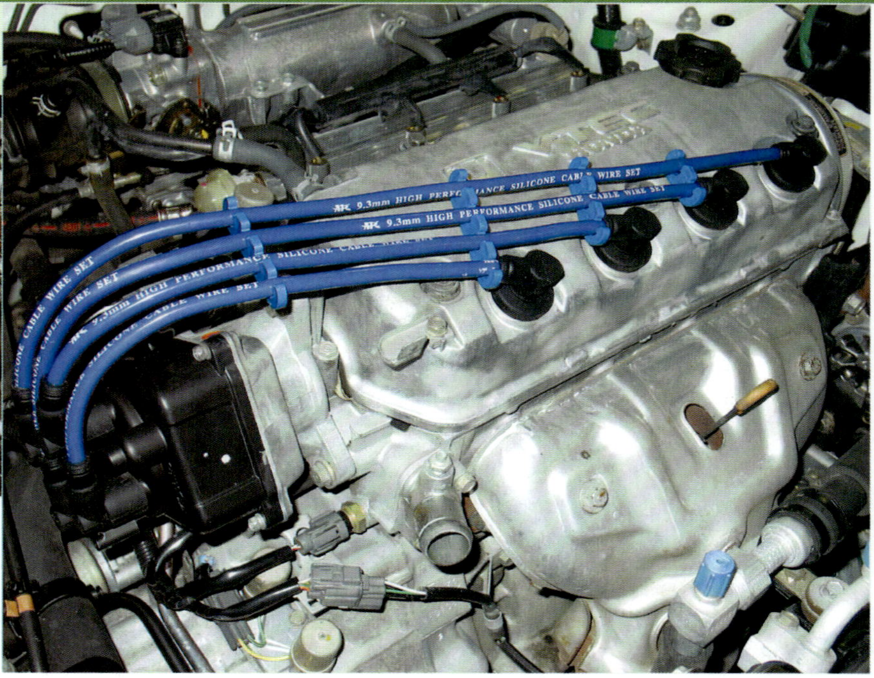

**After**

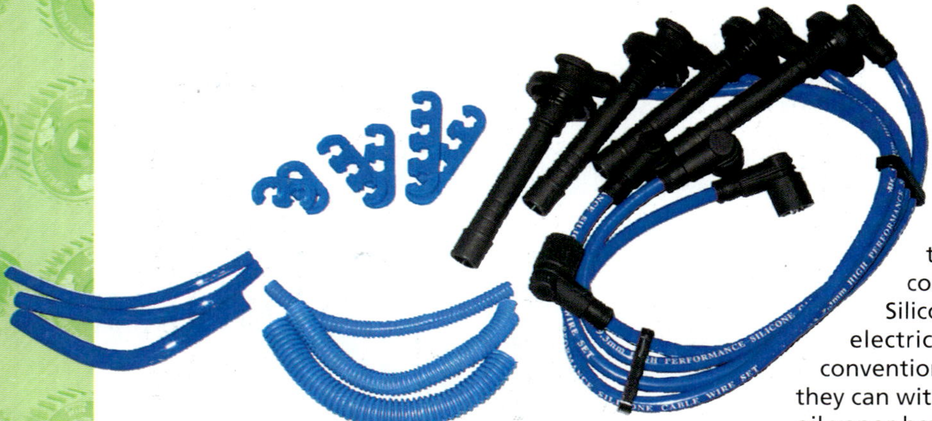

# Silicone spark plug wires

Want better looking spark plug wires? Silicone spark plug wires and plug wire boots look better than those boring black plug wire sets, because they're available in a wide variety of colors. You say you want functionality too? Silicone plug wires and boots have better electrical insulating capabilities than conventional rubber plug wires and boots! And they can withstand heat, cold, vibration and fuel and oil vapor better than rubber insulated wires.

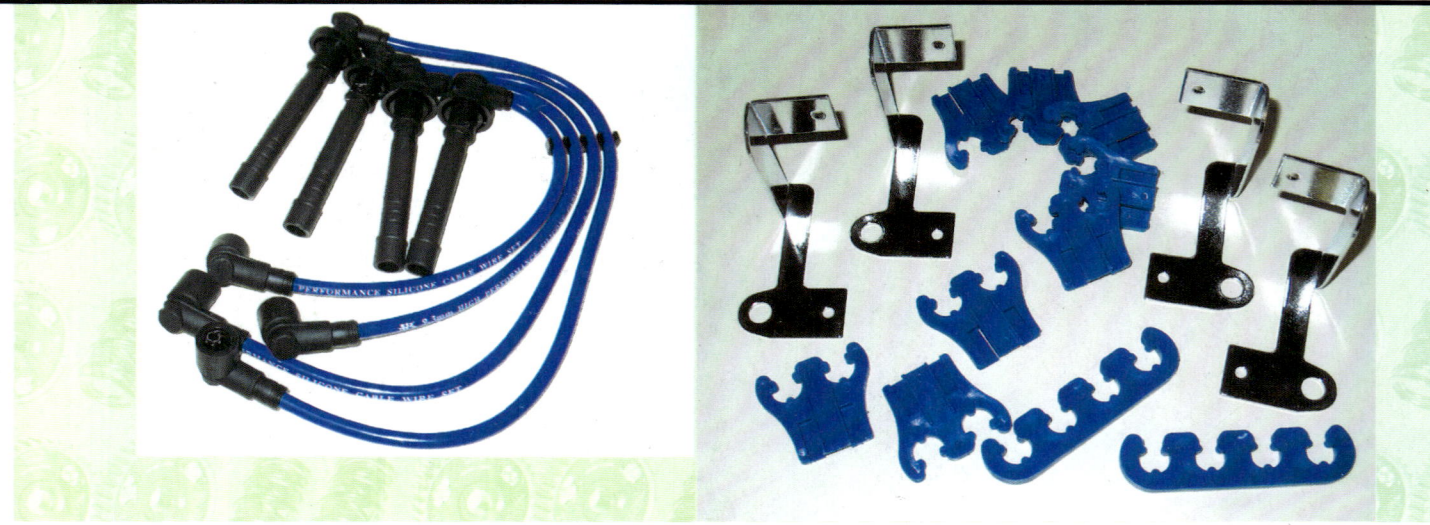

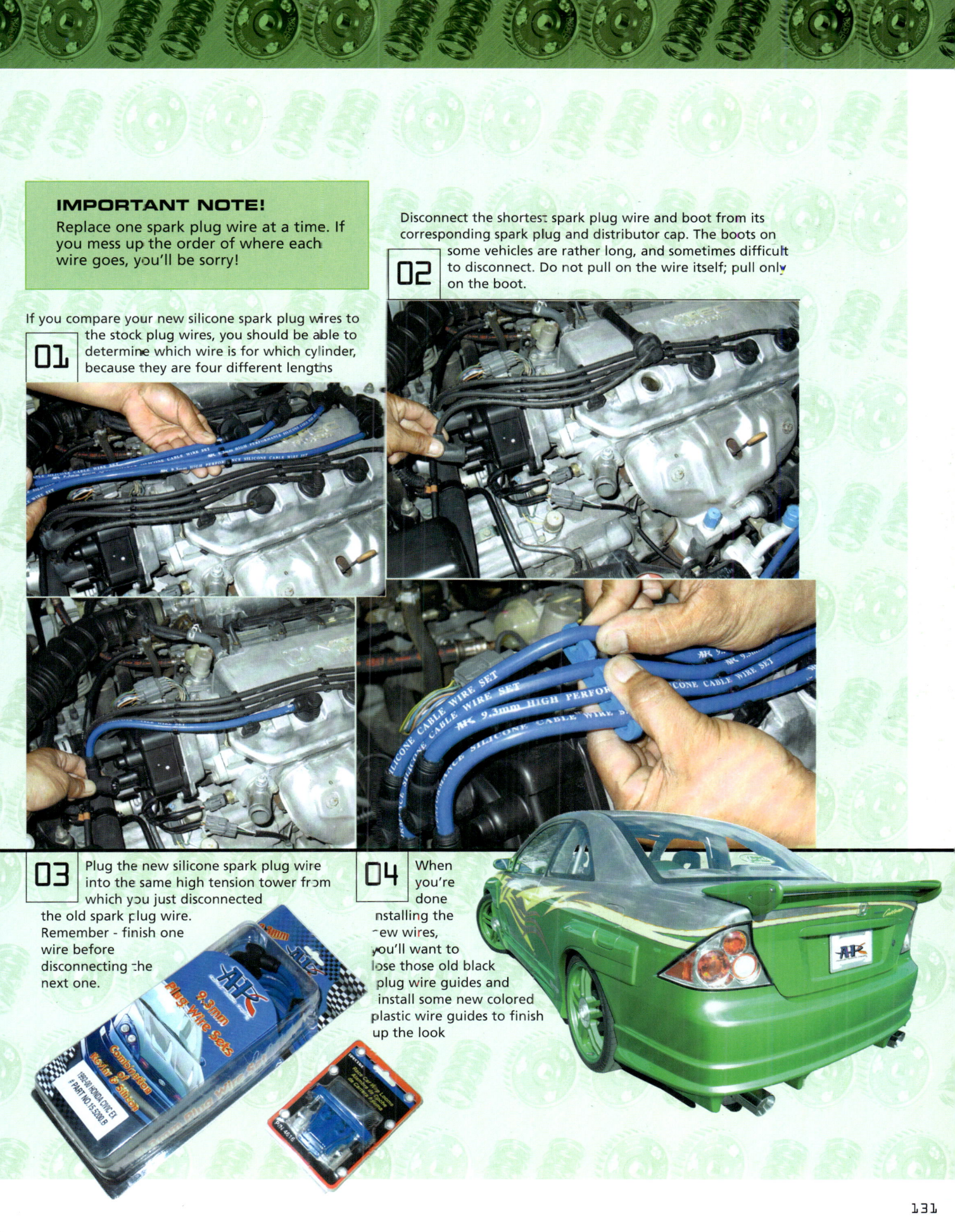

**IMPORTANT NOTE!**
Replace one spark plug wire at a time. If you mess up the order of where each wire goes, you'll be sorry!

**01** If you compare your new silicone spark plug wires to the stock plug wires, you should be able to determine which wire is for which cylinder, because they are four different lengths

**02** Disconnect the shortest spark plug wire and boot from its corresponding spark plug and distributor cap. The boots on some vehicles are rather long, and sometimes difficult to disconnect. Do not pull on the wire itself; pull only on the boot.

**03** Plug the new silicone spark plug wire into the same high tension tower from which you just disconnected the old spark plug wire. Remember - finish one wire before disconnecting the next one.

**04** When you're done installing the new wires, you'll want to lose those old black plug wire guides and install some new colored plastic wire guides to finish up the look

131

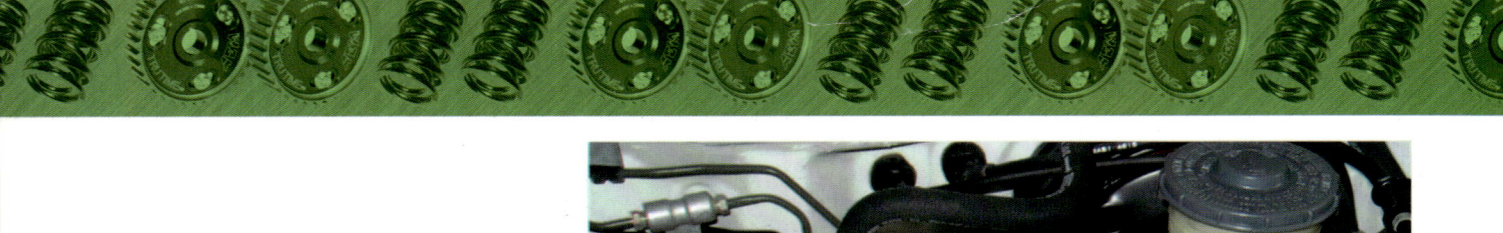

**Before**

**After**

## Silicone vacuum hoses

Remember when you could have any color vacuum hose you wanted . . . as long as it was black? That's not a problem with silicone vacuum hoses. They come in a dozen colors, so you can go with an all-red or all-yellow theme, or you can use an assortment of colors to denote various functions (red spark plug wires, yellow vacuum lines, blue coolant hoses, etc.). The possibilities are endless! Silicone vacuum hoses are available in all three common diameters (4 mm, 6 mm and 8 mm). You can buy starter kits that include an assortment of diameters, or you can buy lines individually, by the foot.

**01** After finding a candidate for your hose swap, disconnect the stock hose. If it's really stuck, you may have to carefully slice it with a knife.

**02** Cut the new hose to length and you're set. Just make sure the hose is a nice snug fit (the correct inside-diameter). If it's loose, you'll have a leak and your engine won't run right.

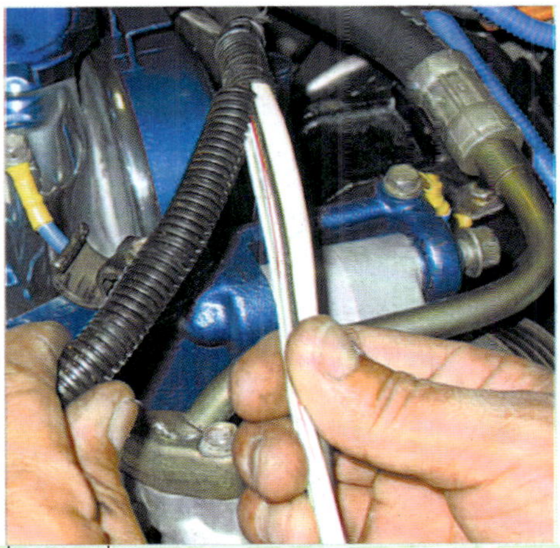

## Split loom wire harnesses

Plastic split-loom is easy to install and looks great. It will help protect your wiring and is easy to remove for servicing. You'll never realize how many wires you have until you have to cover them - but don't worry, this one's easy!

**01** If the harness is already covered by the old black plastic stuff, remove it first

**02** Install the new split loom over the harness and tape the end (the end that you're not going to cut) with matching electrical tape

**03** Where wires go off in different directions, make a clean Y and tape

133

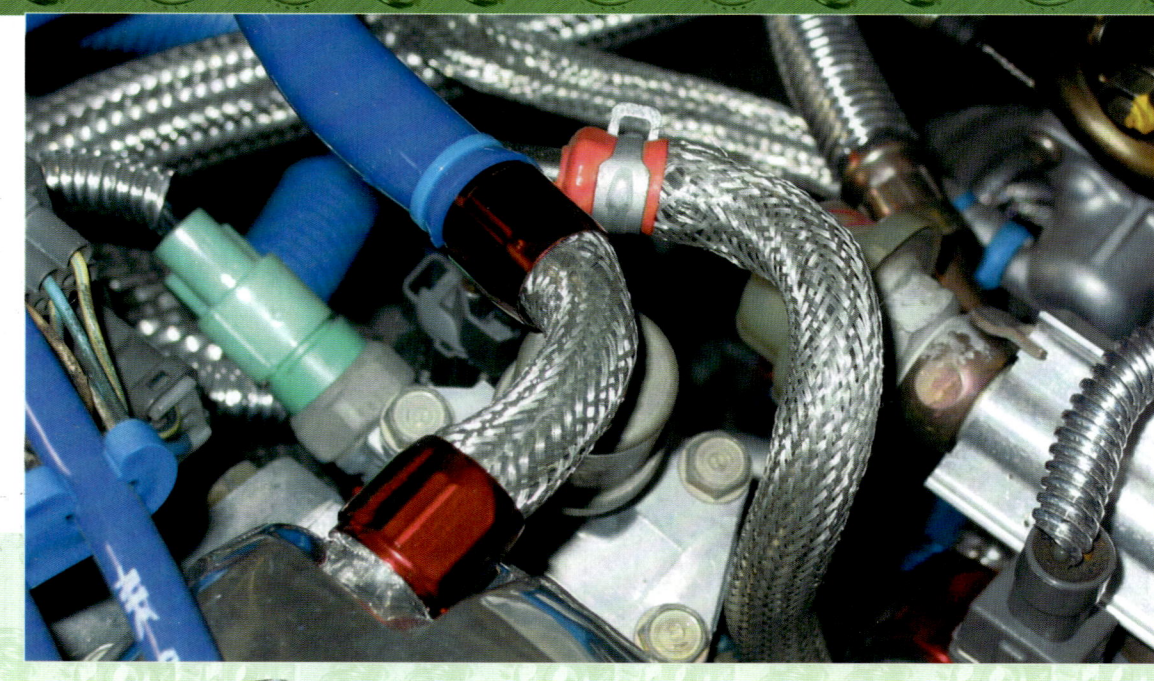

## Braided metal hose covers

Braided covers are available from automotive retailers in a variety of lengths and diameters. Typical cover kits include six feet of material for vacuum lines, fuel hoses or heater hoses. Radiator hose covers are available in three or six foot lengths, each of which is available in 1-1/2 inch or 1-3/4 inch diameters.

Most aftermarket manufacturers of stainless-look braided cover kits also include anodized aluminum "clamps" which look just like the more expensive fittings used on race car plumbing. Except that they're just aluminum rings, machined to look like big nuts, which fit over a standard hose clamp (which you can easily hide by putting it on the side of the hose that nobody will ever see).

**01** To cover a radiator hose, first wait until the engine cools off completely. Drain the engine coolant (refer to your Haynes manual if necessary), then loosen the hose clamps, slide them back and disconnect the hose

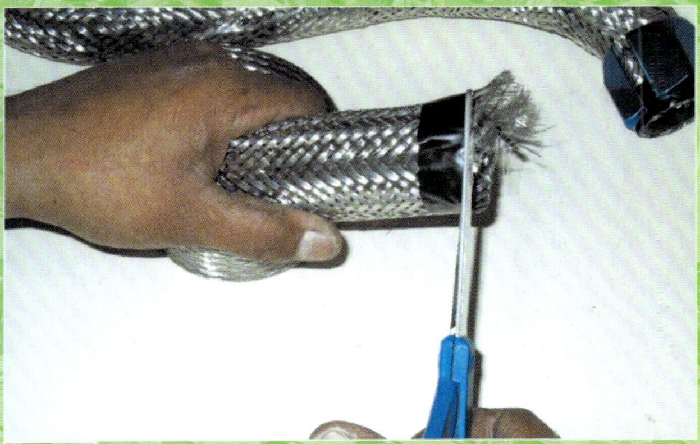

**02** Insert a short section of PVC pipe (usually included in your kit) into one end of the braided cover to hold the cover in a rigid tubular shape, then wrap the end of the cover with electrical tape, remove the PVC pipe and cut off the frayed ends of the cover

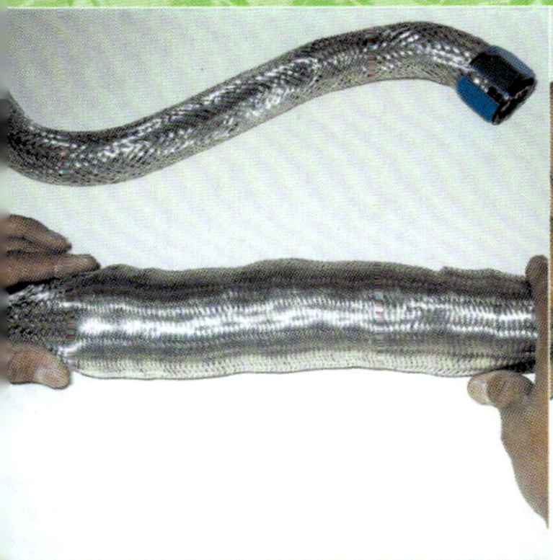

**03** Now run the upper radiator hose through the braided cover

**04** Install a hose clamp and clamp cover on each end of the radiator hose

**05** Install the hose and then tighten the hose clamps at both ends.

## Installation on the PCV hose

**06** The PCV vent hose is another good choice for a braided metal cover. Loosen the hose clamp and disconnect the PCV hose from the valve cover.

**07** The kit will come with a "shrink sleeve" to use at each end of the hose. Use a heat gun to form a solid, clean end for the metal covering

**08** Use a new clamp over the shrink sleeve for a good-looking and secure fit

**09** The finished PCV hose, now covered in braided metal

135

## A little fresh paint

No matter how pretty your engine compartment might look by now, all those black cast-iron and stamped steel brackets for the engine, transaxle, radiator and other big or heavy components are always going to be an eyesore. Why not simply paint some of the more prominent pieces to match your engine compartment color scheme?

## Painting brackets

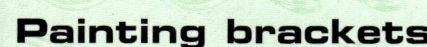

We chose the radiator brackets for some color-matched paintwork.

**01** Begin by removing the brackets, along with the rubber insulators

**02** After thoroughly cleaning the parts, give them a couple light coats of spray paint

**03** Install the bracket mounting bolts and tighten securely

**04** If you haven't installed a good-looking exhaust header yet, that big ugly heat shield could be helped by a coat of fresh paint. Let it cool before removing it from the engine

**05** Remove all grease and oil with a good solvent or degreaser. Then sand off all rust and any bugs or crud that's baked onto the shield. You're not trying to remove all the original paint, you're just trying to create a nice, roughed up surface so that the paint will adhere to it

## Painting an exhaust manifold heat shield

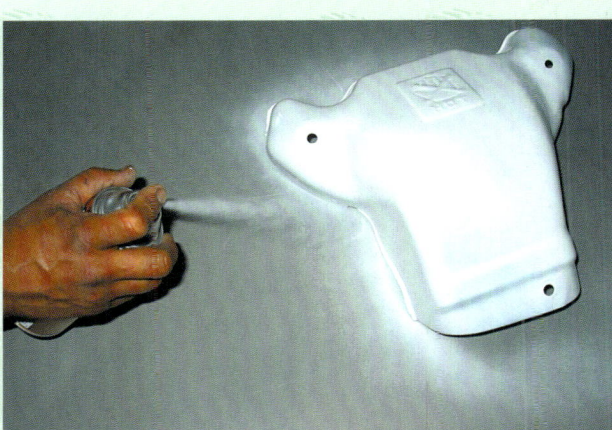

**06** The surface of the heat shield can get *really* hot, so make sure that you use a high-temperature paint. Apply the high-temperature paint evenly to the heat shield surface.

**07** Securely tighten the heat shield fasteners. Looks better, doesn't it?

## Polished valve covers

The engine valve cover is a fairly large and noticeable covering on your engine. And there's no sense in customizing the rest of your engine compartment and leaving this ugly stock valve cover at the center of it all.

You really have a couple of choices. You can simply remove it, paint it and put it back. You can go to your local parts store or tuner and buy an aftermarket one for your model. Or you can polish your stock cover to a nice shine as we've done here.

### Polishing the valve cover

**01** Removing the valve cover involves a good bit of engine disassembly. If you don't have a Haynes manual for your car, get one and follow the step-by-step instructions to get the valve cover off

**02** Remove the old neoprene seals from the spark plug holes. Discard the old neoprene gasket and spark plug seals. Be sure to install a new gasket and new seals before you install the valve cover again

**03** Give the valve cover a good scrubbing with soap and water before you get started polishing it

**04** After sanding with 300 grit, followed by 600 grit sandpaper, switch to a 3M, cutting pad and then remove any scratches caused by the grinding discs

**05** Polish the valve cover with polishing compound and a buffing pad

A big buffing wheel on a bench grinder will give you more polishing power (polishing power is like horsepower: you can't have too much of it!). At this point, you might consider subbing out the valve cover to a professional polishing shop, which can buff it to a mirror-like sheen. A polishing shop will also be able to clean the finished valve cover better than you can because it will soak it in a hot parts-cleaner solution, then steam clean it to remove any residue from the holes

**06**

**07** Reinstall the valve cover using your Haynes manual for reference

139

# Modifying exhaust

Of all the "bolt-on" modifications you can make, improving the exhaust system is one that pays off in many ways.

When you assemble the right package of exhaust components that allow your engine to really breathe, the car's going to sound as good as it performs. It bears repeating here that the exhaust system is one of the few aspects of modifying that gives you the performance you want without any of the drawbacks or compromises that usually come with engine mods. On the contrary, the exhaust work should have no effect on your idling or smooth driveability, and your fuel economy will actually go up, not down! The cool sound is a bonus, too.

Header design is an inexact science, most of what we know is through trial and error, but basically the idea is to have the correct size and length pipes and arrange them so each pipe complements the others in terms of timing - this example is a popular 4-2-1 design where four pipes become two, then two pipes become one to connect to the system

In race-only applications, there's room to build an exhaust without compromises - most designs use larger tubes because they're only concerned with high-rpm operation, and equal-length pipes and collector length are also important when the header is all there is to the exhaust system.

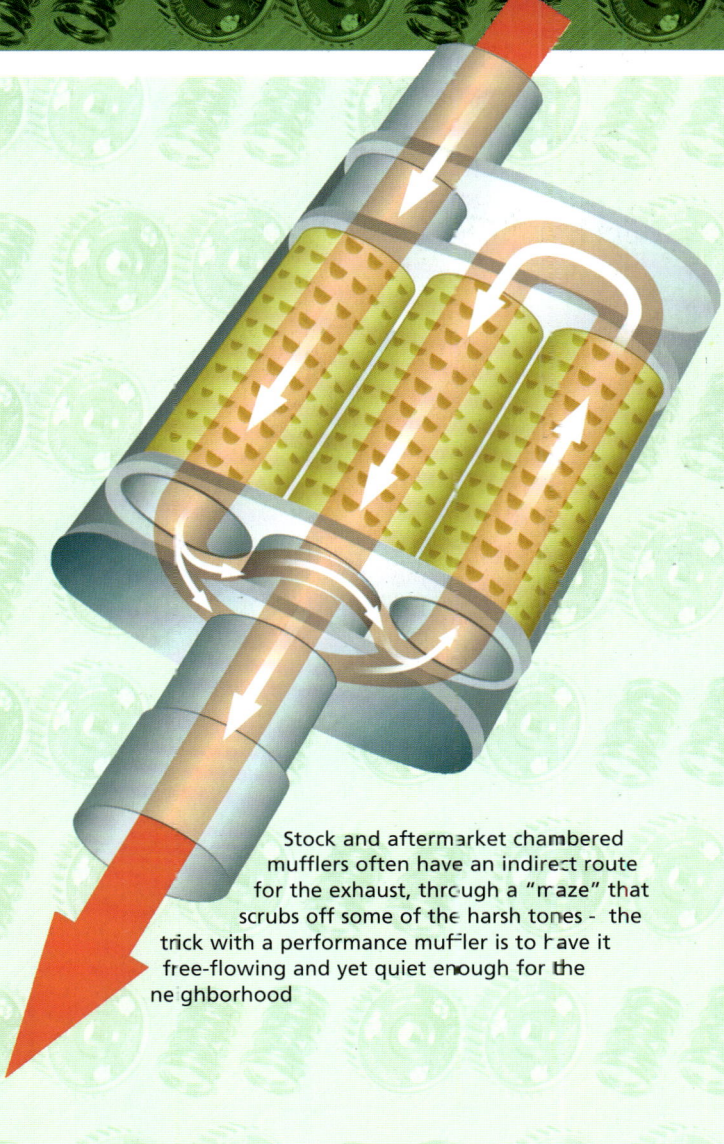

Stock and aftermarket chambered mufflers often have an indirect route for the exhaust, through a "maze" that scrubs off some of the harsh tones – the trick with a performance muffler is to have it free-flowing and yet quiet enough for the neighborhood

## Backpressure and flow

Even a stock engine that operates mostly at lower speeds has to get rid of the byproducts of combustion. If it takes fuel and air in, it has to expel those gasses after the reciprocating components have turned the cylinder pressures into work. The exhaust system needs to allow swift exit of those gasses, and any delay or obstruction to that flow can cause engine efficiency to suffer. If there is an exhaust flow problem somewhere in the system, the pressure waves coming out with the gasses can "back up," which can cause the cylinders to work harder to complete their four-stroke cycle. In exhaust terms, this is called backpressure, and getting rid of it is the chief aim of performance exhaust system designers.

We know that the right-sized length of straight pipe, with no catalytic converter and no muffler, would probably offer the least backpressure to the engine, but it's not very practical (or legal) for a street-driven machine. For our purposes, we have two main components between the exhaust valves and the tip of the tailpipe: the header, and everything from the catalytic converter back (which includes the converter, exhaust pipe, silencer, tailpipe and muffler). If we can improve flow both ahead of and behind the converter (which we must keep to be legal), we'll have the best street exhaust system possible.

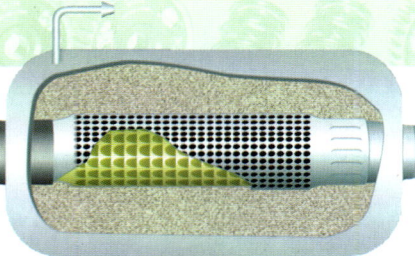

The classic performance muffler is a straight-through design, in which there is a perforated core surrounded by fiberglass sound-dampening material – they used to be called simply "glasspacks" and have always been noted for their performance sound

If you have lowered your car quite a bit, you might consider using a system with an oval-shaped muffler rather than round – the oval muffler and oval tip doesn't hang down as low as a large round muffler, giving you clearance to still get up the steep driveways or over speed bumps without scraping

**01** Start with a car that has cooled down - spray the bolts with penetrating oil, let them sit, then remove the bolts securing the factory heat shield over the exhaust manifold – then soak the exhaust manifold nuts and remove them

**02** Soak, then remove the nuts/bolts at the collector-to-catalytic converter flange, disconnect the electrical connector and remove the oxygen sensor using a special socket for this purpose - also remove the two bolts at the exhaust manifold-to-engine bracket

## Headers

The first major component of your performance exhaust system is the header, a tubular replacement for your stock cast-iron exhaust manifold. In most OEM Civic applications the stock exhaust manifold isn't too bad, at least for the needs of your stock economy engine. The exhaust flow needs of an engine go up exponentially with the state of performance "tune." The flow and backpressure needs of a stock engine aren't excessive, especially when the engine spends the bulk of its driving life under 4000 rpm. But what happens when you modify the engine and then take advantage of those modifications by using the high end of the rpm scale? The exhaust system that was once adequate is now restrictive to a great degree.

How much power you make with just the header depends on several factors. On a car with a really restrictive stock exhaust system, particularly an exhaust manifold full of tight bends and twists, the header will make a bigger improvement than on a car with a decent system to start with. What's behind the header can make a big difference as well. If the

**03** Slowly work the exhaust manifold down and out of the car (take care not to damage the radiator in the process) – on some vehicles like this Civic with an engine swap, the strut-rod crossmember must be removed for clearance, then replaced with a bolt-on aftermarket crossmember and strut rods – a 4-2-1 header could also solve the clearance problem

**04** For comparison, you can see the restrictive stock manifold (left) and the new DC Sports 4-1 header – the DC header is much lighter and maintains good exhaust velocity all the way to the collector

**05** Remove the hard gasket ring from the old collector and install it on the end of the header's collector - with the crossmember removed, there is plenty of room to install the new high-temp-coated header

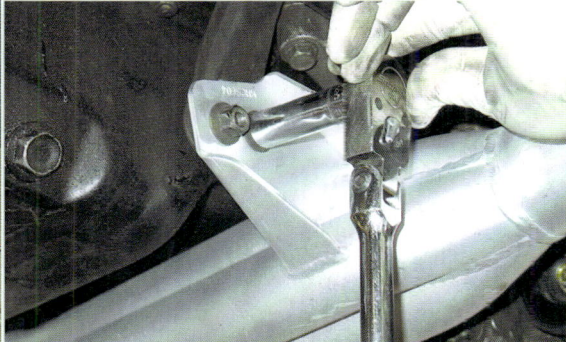

**06** Attach the two bolts at the rear header-to-engine bracket, but leave them loose at this time

stock exhaust system includes restrictive converter and muffler designs, small-diameter exhaust pipes and lots of "wrinkle bends" to boot, the header isn't going to have much chance of making a big improvement in performance. A good header on a typical Civic engine with few other modifications can be expected to make only 3-5 horsepower, depending on how good or bad the stock manifold had been. That's with a stock exhaust system from the header back.

That sounds disappointing, but if we take a case where the engine has numerous modifications yet still has a stock exhaust manifold, the same aftermarket header could gain 10 horsepower. Any of the big "power-adder" modifications, including nitrous oxide and supercharging virtually "require" a header and free-flowing exhaust system to take advantage of their power potential.

Installation of a performance header is quite easy. Most aftermarket headers are made to use all the factory mounting points and braces. In fact, beware of one that doesn't because the header may sound "tinny" when installed if the proper braces aren't connected. Make sure before buying a header that you give the shop your exact year, model and if it's an engine swap or not, especially if it's an imported, used Japanese engine you have swapped in. Most headers we've seen do not have provisions for bolting on the factory tin heat shield over the header, but we're pretty sure you want to show off your new pipes anyway

**07** If your application uses a header gasket, install a new one and bolt the header to the cylinder head with all of the original nuts – note the welded tag that shows the DC header has a CARB E.O. number that means this is a street-legal header

**08** Tighten the bolts at the header collector-to-converter flange and the header is completely installed, but don't forget to install and connect the oxygen sensor, using a little anti-seize on the threads

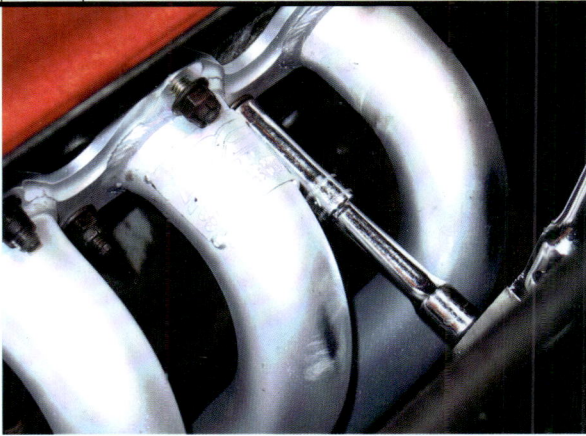

  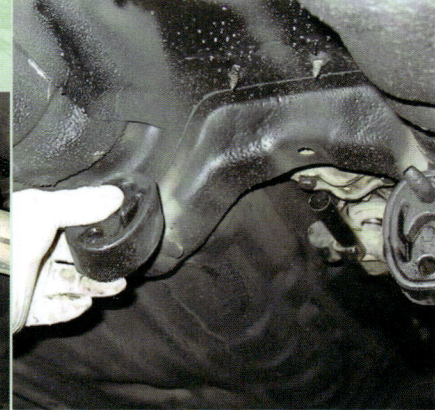

**01** After dousing all the rusted fasteners with penetrating oil, let it soak, then use a long ratchet and six-point socket to loosen the nuts/bolts at the rear of the catalytic converter – If they're original, they may just break off rather than come loose, but new fasteners are included with the exhaust – then disconnect the joint at the rear of the system

**02** Use a pointed prybar to get the rubber exhaust hanger "donuts" off the body mounts – be gentle because these are going to be reused – take off the donuts all along the system front-to-back

**03** Clean the exhaust donuts of grime, then reinstall them on the car – any broken ones must be replaced

## Cat-back system

Once the exhaust gasses leave your efficient new header, they must travel a ways to get out from under your car, and our goal is to make it more of a freeway than a mountain road. First off, there is the catalytic converter, usually bolted right there to the collector of your header. For most of us, this is not an optional component because we have to have it to pass emissions tests. That's fine, because the converter does do a great job of cleaning up engine emissions, and the designs of current converters are more free-flowing than older ones, so the converter isn't something to whine about too much.

Most of the aftermarket exhaust systems are called "cat-back," because they include everything from the converter back. The system may be in several pieces to simplify packaging, shipping and installation, but it should bolt right up to the back flange of your converter and include whatever silencer(s) and muffler(s) are needed. Many of the cat-back systems include the muffler, which on most sport compacts is a part of the car that's very visible, especially when it's a really big one mounted right at the rear bumper.

The muffler you choose has a proportionately large share of both the sound level and backpressure of your total exhaust

**04** Here laid out on the shop floor, you can see how the shiny new stainless-steel Tanabe system compares to the stock exhaust (upper in photo) just removed – it fits just the same but is much more free-flowing

**05** Before putting the new components on the car, apply a little white grease to the holes where the exhaust hangers have to squeeze into the donuts

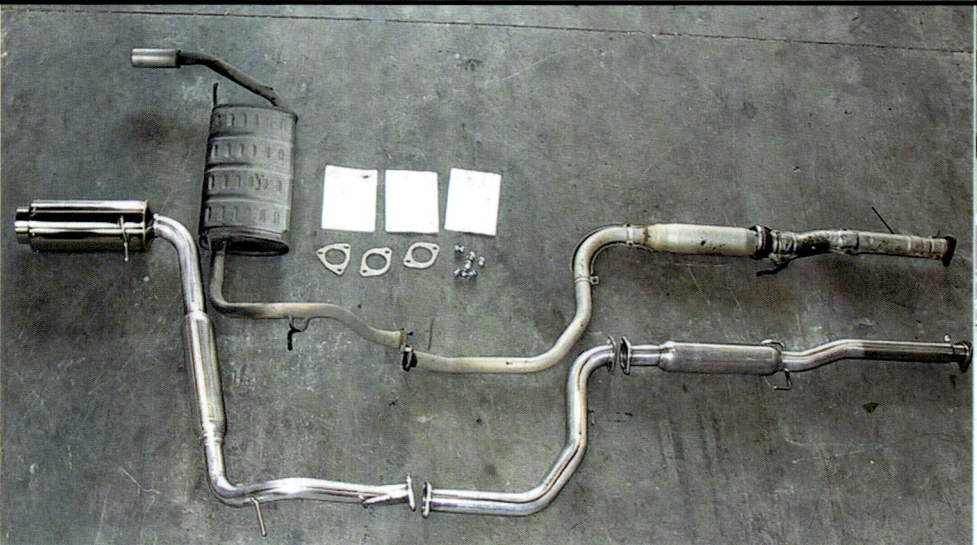 

**06** Clean the threads on the studs at the converter flange, then put the new gasket in place and bring the front section of the new exhaust up and onto the studs at the converter flange – attach the new stainless fasteners loosely and use anti-seize on the threads

**07** The rear section of the exhaust includes the large muffler/silencer – hang this section on the rubber donuts at the front and rear – this holds the pipes so you can bolt them up

system. We all like a "good" growl or purr, but a really free-flowing muffler may be loud to the point of annoying. Maybe what we want is like the sound of a Ferrari: purrs at idle; draws attention when accelerating; and at full song its like music. Some muffler companies actually have their mufflers divided into "classes," with one group having the "most aggressive" sound, another a little more subdued, and one that's described as "mellow." The perfect sound is such a subjective thing; you may want to just listen around when you're at events with a lot of sport compacts. When you hear a car whose tone suits you, check for a name on the muffler or ask the owner.

Changing the exhaust of your vehicle for a performance system is one of the modifications with more perks than almost any other. You get increased power, improved fuel economy, the sound that will complement your performance profile, and parts that make your ride look better, too. All that, and there's no real downside or sacrifice as with most engine mods.

**08** The system is in three pieces and we have the front and rear hanging there, so now position the middle pipe to the back of the front section, using the new gasket, and start the nuts in place by hand – you still have to support the rear of this piece while doing the front, so you may want a helper

**09** When you bolt up the rear of the middle section with a new gasket and bolts, the whole system starts to line up and become more solid – tighten the bolts at both ends of the middle section now

**10** The Tanabe muffler at the rear has a "coffee-can" size tip, but it comes with this bolt-in insert – this system has a great sound, not raspy, but with the insert bolted in (one bolt) it gets even more civilized – the owner opted to leave the insert off for now – here's a tip, clean all fingerprints off the stainless with rubbing alcohol or the smudges could become permanent

Seen here installed is a GReddy turbo kit that illustrates how all these components fit into the larger picture of a turbo setup: 1, the exhaust-driven turbocharger; 2, the exhaust downpipe from the turbine to the exhaust system; 3, the compressor side of the turbo; 4, the piping to duct the forced air to the intake manifold; and 5, the intake pipe that feeds air into the compressor

# Turbochargers

Of the three major "power adders" (nitrous oxide, superchargers, and turbochargers), the turbocharger offers the biggest power potential of all. Its durability and practicality has been proven many times over on production cars and trucks worldwide, whenever extra power was needed without the trouble and expense of fitting the vehicle with a bigger engine.

All the elements of a turbo system without the distraction of a car – here's a complete, installed turbo on a SOHC Civic motor with intercooler, air intake, turbo and all the hardware and plumbing

Consider the turbocharger like the six-gun "equalizer" of the old west - the SOHC applications are a good candidate for boost because it allows them to compete in performance with the more-talked-about DOHC VTEC motor.

## How it works

There are basically three main elements to a turbocharger: the exhaust turbine, the intake air compressor, and the housing/shaft/bearing assembly that ties the two pressure-related sections together. The job of the turbine is to spin the shaft of the turbocharger. The turbine is composed of an iron housing in which rotates a wheel covered with curved fans or blades. These blades fit precisely within the turbine housing. When the turbine housing is mounted to an engine's exhaust manifold, the escaping hot exhaust gasses must flow through the housing and over the vanes, causing the shaft to spin rapidly. After the exhaust has passed through the turbine it exits through a large pipe, called a downpipe, to the rest of the vehicle's exhaust system.

Within the compressor housing is another wheel with vanes. Since both wheels are connected to a common shaft, the intake wheel spins at the same speed as the turbine, so the compressor draws intake air in and the rapidly spinning wheel blows the air into the engine's intake side. The more load there is on the engine, the more the turbocharger works to give the engine horsepower. As the engine goes faster, it makes more exhaust, which drives the turbocharger faster, which makes the engine produce more power.

The unit in the center of this turbo "sandwich" has the important function of reliably passing the power between the two housings.

## Advantages and disadvantages of the turbocharger

Compared to the supercharger, the turbo is smaller, lighter, quieter, and puts less direct load on the engine. The "not at all times" boost of the turbocharger is an advantage for fuel economy, operating noise level and driveability, but in some cases may be a drawback when compared to the mechanical supercharger. While a supercharger adds boost in relation to rpm (i.e. the faster the engine goes, the faster the blower pumps) it runs up against physical limitations eventually and can't pump any more. In order to make any more boost with a supercharger, you have to change the pulleys or gearing that drives it.

The limitation for the blower-equipped cars in top end performance, and this is where the turbocharger has the distinct advantage. The turbocharger is much more customizable, with various wheels and housings available to suit whatever the intended engine or purpose. Boost can be made to come in early, or come in later at a higher boost level.

The same basic turbocharger can be used for street use or modified to make more boost than your engine can live with! Such customizing, called sizing, should be done by an experienced turbo shop that can select the exact right components for your engine size and power requirements.

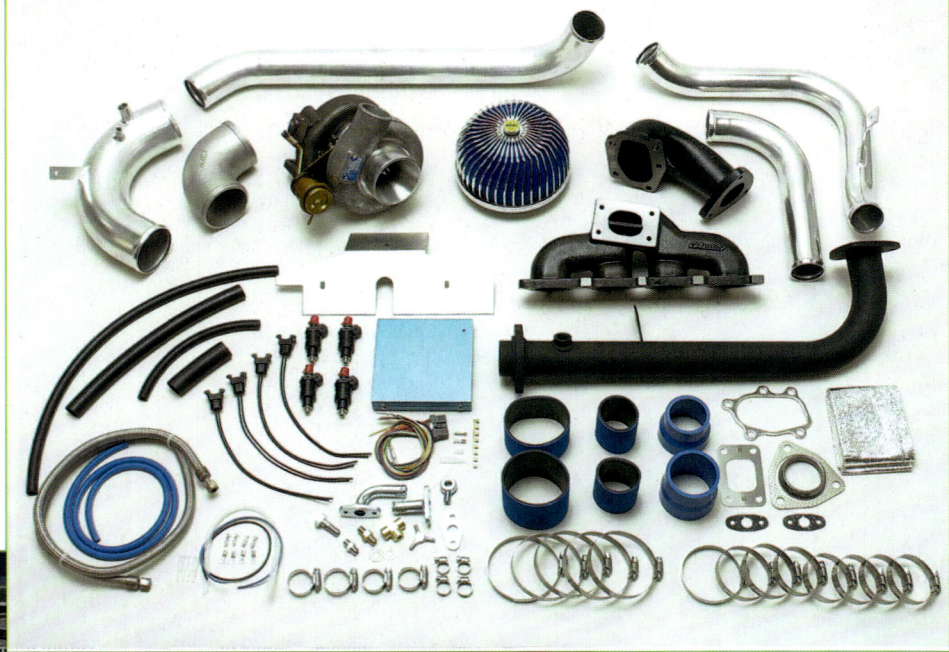

This typical complete turbocharger kit (GReddy for Civic SI) has all the good stuff, plus a set of performance fuel injectors and a computer upgrade, and . . .

. . . this is what that same kit looks like after installation on a Civic SI in the real world

# Intercoolers

One of the serious disadvantages of the turbocharger is the heat it will put into the intake air charge, which is why most successful turbo systems utilize an intercooler to combat this. Air coming from the turbocharger tends to be hot because it's compressed and also because of its close proximity to the exhaust.

The most effective and common method of dealing with intake air temperature on a turbocharged car is an intercooler. This is a honeycomb affair much like a radiator, usually mounted out in front of the vehicle's radiator in an opening below the bumper where cooler air is found. The boosted air from the compressor is ducted through pipes and into the intercooler, and then to the intake of the engine. Thus, the cooler is between the compressor and the engine, so it's called an inter-cooler. Since cooler air is more dense and produces more power, intercoolers are very popular.

# Turbocharging kits

A complete turbocharging kit from most reputable aftermarket companies will include virtually everything you need for your application, with a cost from $2500 to $4500 for everything. If the price of a good turbo kit sounds expensive, just compare turbocharging to other methods of upping your horsepower. A turbo could be your best horsepower-per-dollar investment. Installation will vary widely between different model cars and turbo kits.

Left: An efficiently-designed cast-iron manifold, here with a Turbonetics wastegate directly mounted, is ideal for street applications that see constant heating and cooling cycles, but regular "high-temp" header paint will come off in no time - temperatures here get into the red-hot range under a full load

Below: The main boost control device on a turbocharger is an exhaust wastegate – this is a selection of GReddy wastegates, the more the turbo system is designed to flow, the bigger the wastegate must be to be effective – the wastegate keeps the turbo from overspeeding (and the engine from blowing) by releasing some exhaust before it reaches the turbine portion of the turbocharger

## Durability with a turbo

Problems with turbo installations usually crop up because of detonation caused by too much boost, or not enough fuel under boosted conditions. A turbocharged performance car can be both reliable and pleasurable to drive, even on a daily basis, if you keep in mind the limitations.

The low-octane of today's pump gas will be the biggest limiting factor on street-driven (non race-gas) machines. With a reasonable boost level of 5-10 PSI and the proper precautions, you can run pump gas. With an electronic timing controller, you can switch from one timing program to another depending on the octane rating of the gas you have available.

Proper fuel mixture is very important. One lean-out and you'll fry at least one piston or valve! Keep checking your spark plugs and have a good programmable piggyback fuel controller. A fuel pressure regulator that can handle boosted conditions, a boost-capable MAP sensor, and a fuel system that can deliver extra pressure under boost should keep things under control.

We can't address every aspect of turbocharging here, but other steps to improving durability include keeping the engine cool with the use of a good radiator and fan, external engine oil cooler, and of course an intercooler. If you consistently run high boosts, internal engine upgrades will have to be made, such as forged, low-compression pistons, forged aftermarket rods, improved-flow oil pump, and a blueprinted rotating assembly. You'll find yourself addicted to the whoosh under acceleration and the snarl when you shift and your blow-off valve dumps the excess pressure so that everybody knows you're under boost!

A blow-off valve is like a wastegate for the intake side of the system – it prevents pressure surges in the intake tract when the throttle is suddenly closed (like when shifting) – most enthusiasts have their blow-off vented to the atmosphere so it makes a head-turning noise when it operates during shifting

There's nothing like a big Vortech supercharger, hot ignition, pumped fuel system and some nice shiny parts to make a Civic come alive! - research all your options and plan other mods to work with your new supercharger

# Superchargers

Your engine is in a constant state of combustion when running. It sucks in air and fuel, burns it to make the pistons go, then expels what's left. With a supercharger, instead of having to use its own energy to suck in the mixture, your engine is force-fed, and the difference can be worth 50% and more in horsepower. Boost is good!

A turbocharger is similar in function to the supercharger, but differs in that the turbo is driven by exhaust gasses, rather than by mechanical means. A supercharger (also called a blower) is driven by the engine, either with gears, chains or belts, so there is direct correlation between the engine speed and the boost produced by the supercharger.

While the turbocharger may have the upper hand when you're talking about all-out high-rpm performance on the track, the supercharger shines at improving street performance almost from idle speed on up. Low-rpm power is very helpful for "across-the-intersection" performance, where a turbocharger is probably just "spinning up" and not yet able to provide much power.

Packaging a supercharger kit for an already "compact" car engine compartment can be a challenge - this Jackson Racing kit puts the blower right where it needs to be by using a long-belt drive system - as long as the supercharger turns with the engine it makes boost regardless of location or belt length

The well-thought out installation that takes maximum advantage of the supercharger will include other modifications - in addition to the JR blower, this showy Honda has an intake pipe, header, high-output ignition and a revamped fuel system with custom fuel rail, FMU, fuel pressure gauge and big fuel filter

## Boost

Boost is any pressure beyond 14.7 psi (normal atmospheric pressure). So, if you have a turbo or supercharger that is making 14.7 psi of boost, then you have effectively doubled normal atmospheric pressure or added another "atmosphere" of pressure. Twice that amount of boost and you've added two atmospheres, and you command the bridge of a rocket ship!

However, we must be realistic about boost levels. There is a finite limit to the boost your blower can make, and probably a much lower limit of how much boost your engine can take, regardless of how the boost was generated. You'll find most street supercharger kits are limited to 5-7 psi, to make some power while working well on a basically stock engine that sips pump gasoline.

Some kits on the market have optional pulleys that will spin the blower faster for more boost, but, as with any power adder, you can only go so far in increasing cylinder pressure before you have to make serious modifications to strengthen the engine (forged pistons, aftermarket connecting rods, etc.).

Your engine's existing compression ratio is a factor in how much boost you can run. Ratios are high in most Honda applications, especially imported JDM engines. To make lots of boost (over 10 psi) your static compression ratio shouldn't be higher than about 9:1. Racers with on-the-edge turbo or supercharger setups start with 7:1 compression.

## Heat and detonation

Knock, ping, pre-ignition and detonation are all terms that describe abnormal combustion in an engine - they also describe big trouble. An increase in boost also increases the combustion chamber temperature and pressure, often leading to these problems that can destroy pistons, valves, rods and crankshafts.

The two main factors in detonation and its control are heat and timing. Ignition timing does offer some ways to deal with detonation. Supercharged engines generally "like" more timing, especially initial advance, but once you are making full boost and the vehicle is under load, too much ignition advance can bring on the "death rattle" of detonation that you don't want to hear. How much advance your application can handle is a trial-error-experience thing, but if you are using a production blower kit from a known manufacturer, these tests have already been made and some kind of timing control program should be included.

Anything you can do to control engine temperature and intake air temperature in particular will help stave off detonation also. Better oil circulation, a better radiator, an intercooler and an engine oil cooler are proven modifications to control excess heat that can contribute to detonation.

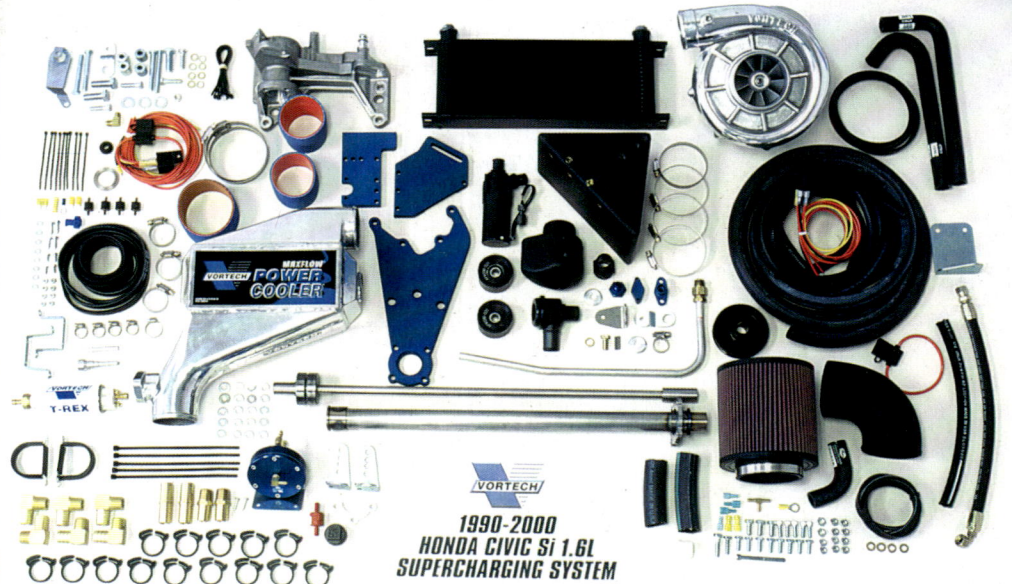

This very complete package includes wiring, hoses, fuel pump, FMU, supercharger and drive, and the compete water system for the Maxiflow Power Cooler, which works to add power by keeping intake temperatures down

## Blower kits

There are several types of small superchargers used in kits designed for Honda engines. The two main types of supercharger design you will see are the Roots type or "positive displacement," and the centrifugal design.

The Roots-type mechanical blower uses a pair of rotors that turn inside a housing. As the rotors turn, they capture a certain amount of air and propel it to the inner circumference of the case and out to the intake manifold. Each time they turn around, they capture air, hence the "positive" description. The benefit of this type is that it starts making boost at very low rpm.

A variation of this type of blower is the screw-type. These have two rotors with helically-wound vanes that, as the name implies, look like two giant screws. When the two screws mesh together, the air is actually compressed between the screws.

The other major type of bolt-on supercharger is the centrifugal design. From a quick examination, the centrifugal blower looks just like the compressor half of a turbocharger, being a multi-vaned wheel within a scroll-type housing. Unlike a turbocharger, this type of blower isn't driven by exhaust but by a mechanical drive from the engine, usually a belt. These types of blowers are not "positive-displacement," and thus do not necessarily make their boost down on the low end, but have plenty of air-movement potential when they are spinning rapidly.

Most reputable blower kits have everything you need to install the system and use it reliably. Contents include the blower, intake manifold (if needed), belt, mounting hardware, instructions and some type of electronic gear to control fuel delivery and/or ignition timing. Some kits use a larger-than-stock fuel pump that replaces your in-tank pump, and a special fuel pressure regulator that may be boost-sensitive.

Other included components could be hoses, wire harnesses, air intake, a new MAP sensor that can tolerate pressure as well as vacuum, an intercooler, and parts that relocate items in the engine compartment to provide room for the blower.

Good for any forced induction application, Holley makes this boost-compensating adjustable fuel pressure regulator - adjustment range is from 20 to 75 psi and it will raise fuel pressure four psi for each psi of boost the engine sees

If you need to have a stronger head gasket to handle boost, this GReddy metal-reinforced piece is what your need - some are available in a thick version to reduce static compression so you can apply more boost

# Nitrous Oxide

Nitrous oxide as a horsepower source can appear to be a miracle or a curse, depending on your experience. It's a fact that nitrous oxide (N2O) is the simplest, quickest and cheapest way to gain a large horsepower boost in your car. It's often referred to as the "liquid supercharger." But, just like in children's fairy tales, you court disaster if you don't follow the rules that come with the magic potion.

Nitrous oxide is an odorless, colorless gas that doesn't actually burn. It carries oxygen that allows your engine to burn extra fuel. When you inject nitrous oxide and gasoline at the same time in the proper proportions at full throttle, you'll get a kick in the butt as if you were instantly driving a car with an engine twice as big!

Done right, a nitrous kit is one of the best horsepower-per-dollar investments you can make, and is the most popular power-adder for small engines. Kits are available that add from 50 hp to 300 hp, because the more nitrous and fuel you add, the more power the engine makes … RIGHT UP TO THE POINT WHERE THE ENGINE COMES APART. In the end, it is the durability of the engine itself that determines how much nitrous you can run. As tempting as it is to just keep putting bigger nitrous jets in your engine for more power, you need to do your research first to find the limits of your engine and what can be done to protect against damage done by a little too much nitrous fun.

The serious drag racers have done everything possible to their engines to strengthen them to handle big loads of nitrous. At a very minimum, you'll need to assure adequate fuel flow (of high-octane fuel) and probably retard the ignition timing. Many racers use electronic retard boxes that allow you to retard the ignition timing from the driver's seat. Usually, you'll need to put in a more capable ignition system than the stock one (with colder spark plugs), and it's wise to add a low-fuel-pressure shut-off switch - this device will save your engine if your fuel pressure ever drops too low while you're "on the bottle."

> **Warning:**
> *Nitrous oxide is an oxidizer stored under pressure, and therefore potentially flammable and dangerous. Make sure the bottle is in a safe place and that all connections are secure, conforming to all applicable safety standards. Check with the manufacturer of your nitrous kit for more information. Also check with local authorities concerning any applicable laws.*

Your nitrous is generally stored in a 10-pound metal bottle mounted in the trunk - it should be kept out of direct sun and mounted with the knob end forward, the label up and the bottle tilted slightly up at the front as shown here

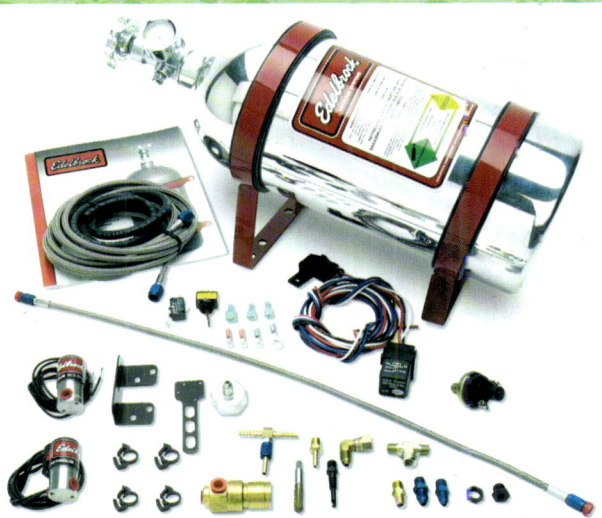

Typical of complete nitrous kits available for Hondas is this 40-60 hp Edelbrock setup with polished bottle, "dry" nozzle, hardware, lines, solenoids and an interface with the factory fuel system to increase flow at WOT during nitrous usage

153

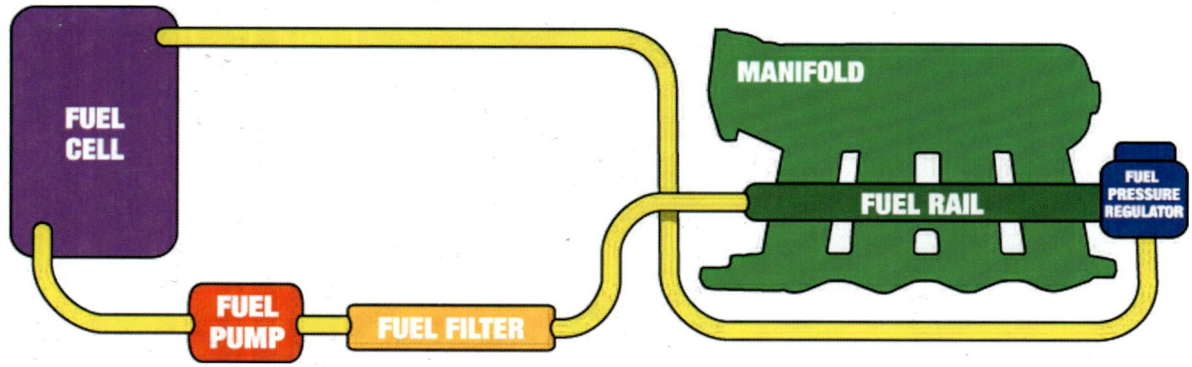

**Typical EFI fuel system, as used with a "dry" nitrous system** (Courtesy of Edelbrock Corp.)

## No laughing matter

Nitrous can be intoxicating, but confine your high to the feeling you get from gobs of extra horsepower, not from inhaling the nitrous. Yes, it was once called "laughing gas" and used by dentists as an anaesthetic, but that is medical-grade nitrous, which is a controlled substance. What you're going to buy at your local tuner or speed shop is industrial-grade nitrous, which has a serious irritant added to it. If you try to inhale this stuff, you'll be sorry. Your engine, on the other hand, will love it.

If you're going to push much past a 60-horsepower system, and certainly if you're into the 100 horsepower-and-up category, you'll need to consider internal engine upgrades to handle the additional horsepower. Generally, forged pistons are used with these higher-horsepower kits, and most stock engines generally do not have performance-style forged pistons. So, if you're planning to have your engine live very long at these high-horsepower levels, you'll need to spend some money upgrading the "bottom end" of the engine.

## Nitrous kits

The basic street-use nitrous kit consists of: a nitrous bottle, usually one that holds 10 pounds of liquid nitrous oxide; bottle mounting brackets and hardware; fuel and nitrous jets; high pressure lines, usually braided-stainless-covered AN-type with a Teflon inner liner for the high nitrous pressure; nitrous filter; solenoids, switch and electrical connectors. Kits are always sold without the nitrous in the bottle; you'll have to go to a local speed shop to have the bottle filled.

There are two basic types of nitrous kits that differ in how the nitrous and fuel are delivered: the "dry" system and the "wet" system. The "dry" system has a nozzle and solenoid only for the nitrous, and this nozzle may be almost anywhere in the intake system; behind the MAF (Mass Air Flow) sensor (if equipped) and ahead of the throttle body is typical. The dry systems are designed for factory fuel-injected engines. To deliver the extra fuel to go with

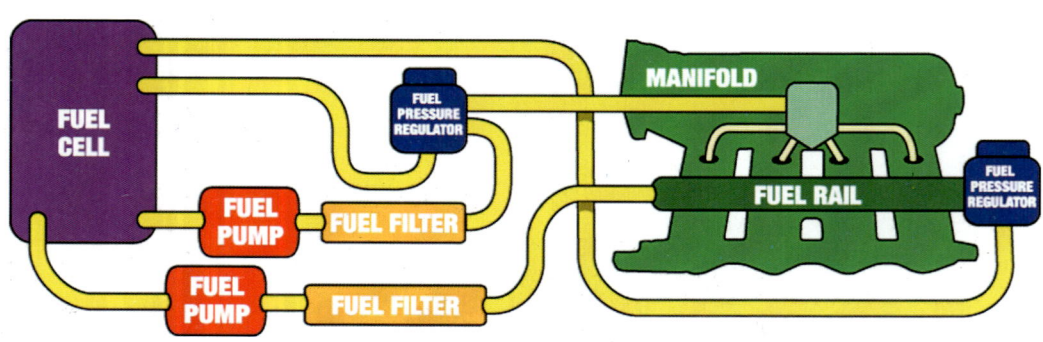

**Typical EFI fuel system, as used with the "wet" nitrous setup** (Courtesy of Edelbrock Corp.)

In "wet" systems, the nitrous nozzle (arrow) can mix and spray both gasoline and nitrous into the intake - separate solenoids control the flow of each power-adding half of the mix

The N2O solenoids and controls should be mounted in the engine compartment, close to the intake system - this Zex installation is "dry" meaning that only nitrous is injected through the nozzle on the intake. The extra fuel comes through the stock injectors based on an altered vacuum signal to the fuel pressure regulator under "juice"

the nitrous, the stock system fuel pressure is raised during the WOT (wide-open throttle) period of nitrous usage, and reverts back to the stock fuel pressure in all other driving conditions.

The "wet" nitrous systems have solenoids for both nitrous and fuel, both of which are turned on when the nitrous system is activated. The fuel and nitrous in a simple system are plumbed into a single injector that merges the two, the gasoline and its oxidizer, as they enter the engine. More sophisticated wet systems may have a nitrous nozzle for each cylinder of the engine, and one or more fuel nozzles mounted separately. In high-output racing applications, individually feeding each cylinder allows for tuning each cylinder separately for fine control. The extra nozzles also mean there is ample supply of nitrous and fuel for very high-horsepower installations.

There are all sorts of "bells and whistles" available as extra features on most of the nitrous kits on the market today. There are varying designs of nozzles, different electronic controls that work with your factory computer to control timing and fuel delivery, optional bottle covers, bottle warmers, remote shut-off valves for the bottle, PCM piggybacks that pull back the ignition timing under nitrous use, and "staged" nitrous kits that deliver a certain amount during launch, then a little more, and the full blast for the top end.

## How does it work?

In basic terms for a simple nitrous system, the tank or bottle of nitrous oxide is mounted in the trunk and plumbed up to the engine compartment with a high-pressure line. This is connected to an electric solenoid, from which nitrous (still a liquid at this point) can flow to the nozzle attached to your intake system. If you turn on an "arming" switch in the car, battery voltage is available to another switch that is located on your throttle linkage such that it is switched only when your right foot gets to "wide open throttle". Nitrous must only be injected at wide-open throttle.

Flip the arming switch and when you're hard on the throttle the solenoid releases nitrous oxide, which passes through a sized jet or orifice and turns into a vapor, to mix with your vaporized fuel in the engine. The extra fuel admitted at the same time as the N2O is easily oxidized and creates enough cylinder pressure to add 50, 75, 100 or more horsepower in an instant. So, do some research, talk to some tuners and then decide if going on the bottle is the right choice for you.

There are a variety of aftermarket ignition and fuel "modules" designed to electronically alter the spark and fuel curves under conditions such as boost or nitrous - for drag racing, this NOS controller can be programmed for several stages of nitrous application - the big shot comes only after the vehicle has full traction on the strip

The most universal sport compact kit from Nitrous Express is this one that is adjustable from 35-50-75 horsepower levels - this wet-style kit needs no electronics for timing retard and uses the stock fuel pump

The typical Civic engine compartment has had some modifications - usually to the "in-and-out" sides like a performance exhaust header and a cold ram-air intake for improved sound, looks and breathing power

# Induction systems

Performance air intakes are available in two basic forms: the "short ram" and the "cold-air" intake. In each case the idea is to get more - and colder - air into your engine. Looks are important, too, and nobody opens their hood unless they at least have a short ram.

The least expensive and easiest intakes to install are the short ram types. You'll spend longer getting the stock air filter box and inlet tube out than installing the short ram. If you have any doubts about removing the stock components, consult the Haynes repair manual for your car. Short-ram intakes place the new filter relatively close to the engine, and modifications to the engine or body are rarely necessary. Most short ram installations take only a half-hour to install and may be good for 4 to 8 horsepower, depending on the application. And of course, they look and sound really nice. The more free-flowing they are, the more intake noise you'll hear in the car, but that's OK with us, right?

For purposes of performance, the colder the air the more power you make. Cold-air intake systems are one of the most-widely-installed bolt-on performance improvements in the sport compact world. They are usually the first modification made to an import engine, and have become so common that people want one on their car whether it makes any more power or not. The long-ram intakes pick up air from down below the car's bumper or in the fenderwell, where the air is coolest (not so affected by engine heat), hence the long-ram kits are usually called CAI's for Cold Air Intake.

If there's a drawback to the longer CAI, its the possibility that the filter end of the tube could pick up water when driving in the rain, which could seriously damage your engine. Some companies offer rain hoods for the air pickup, and a relief valve can also be used to prevent water getting all the way through the intake system.

Aftermarket cold air intake systems can be worth 8 to 20 horsepower, depending on the design and how modified the engine is. A stock engine doesn't need to gulp huge quantities of air, but a modified engine does. Obviously, a cold air intake is going to need some bends in order to reach the cold air, but if there are too many bends or bends made too sharp, the horsepower gain from the colder air could be offset by a reduction in airflow.

The rest of your induction system will be fine unless you're making bigger engine modifications, such as hotter cam(s), cylinder head work, increased compression and/or power adders like a blower or nitrous oxide. When you're really going for all you can get from your Civic engine, you can add a bigger throttle body and a high-flowing aftermarket intake manifold to really perform at high rpm. Just remember that modifying your engine to run its best at high rpm means it isn't going to be so hot anymore at low, around-town speeds, and throttle response can get seriously "doggy" unless you're constantly blipping the right foot pedal.

The simplest modification you can make to your stock air induction system is to open the factory airbox, lift out the OEM paper air filter, and replace it with a high-flow aftermarket filter with a pleated-cotton lifetime filter - these can be reused over and over by washing them, then treating them with a special oil

A typical aftermarket bolt-on induction mod is to install a short ram, which is a new, large diameter pipe with an aftermarket filter - these flow much better than stock, though they do make the engine noisier

For a little more power than the short rams offer, you can install a long ram like this AEM unit that picks up air below the fender on a Civic

To protect your engine against ingesting rainwater, the AEM bypass valve pulls air through an external diaphragm to keep dry air flowing, even if the filter is clogged with water - such valves can generally be used only on normally-aspirated (not supercharged or turbocharged) applications

This aftermarket Honda intake manifold from Edelbrock (Performer-X model for SOHC D16Y8 VTEC engines) is said to be good for the 3,000 to 7,500 rpm range, and has a larger plenum, nine-inch-long passages, extra injector bosses and 50-state legality

When you're ready for improved induction for a thoroughly-modified engine, you'll probably want a larger throttle body - this Holley billet-aluminum throttle body for Hondas accepts all the stock wiring and plumbing and is available in 62mm and 58mm bores, said to be good for 5-10 hp

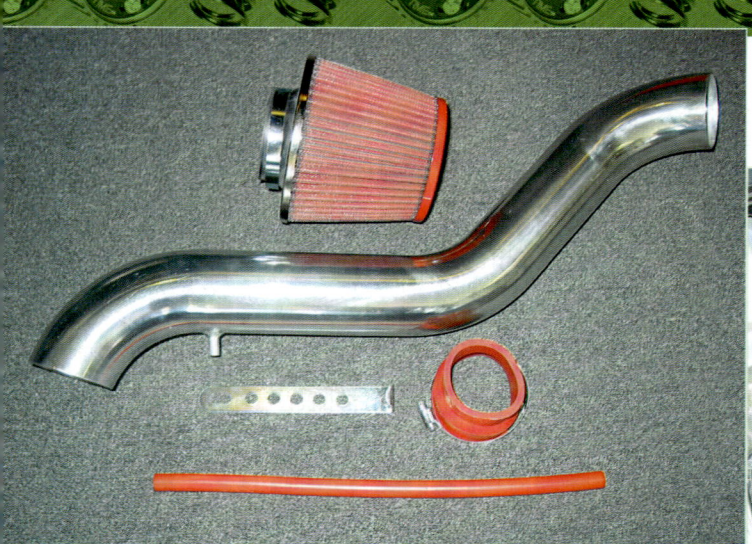

**01** Our kit came with all the necessary hardware for installation

## Short ram intake installation

**02** Remove the stock air filter housing. On most vehicles the housing is bolted to the body from the inside. If you can't figure out how to remove it, check the Haynes manual for your vehicle

**03** Disconnect the breather hose from the valve cover and loosen the clamp securing the intake hose to the throttle body

**04** Remove the intake hose and air filter housing from the vehicle. Keep the duct and housing just in case you intend to sell the vehicle in the future (in stock form)

**05** Install the silicone step hose and hose clamps onto the throttle body

**06** Install the intake hose to the silicone step hose

**07** Connect the supplied breather hose and hose clamp to the valve cover

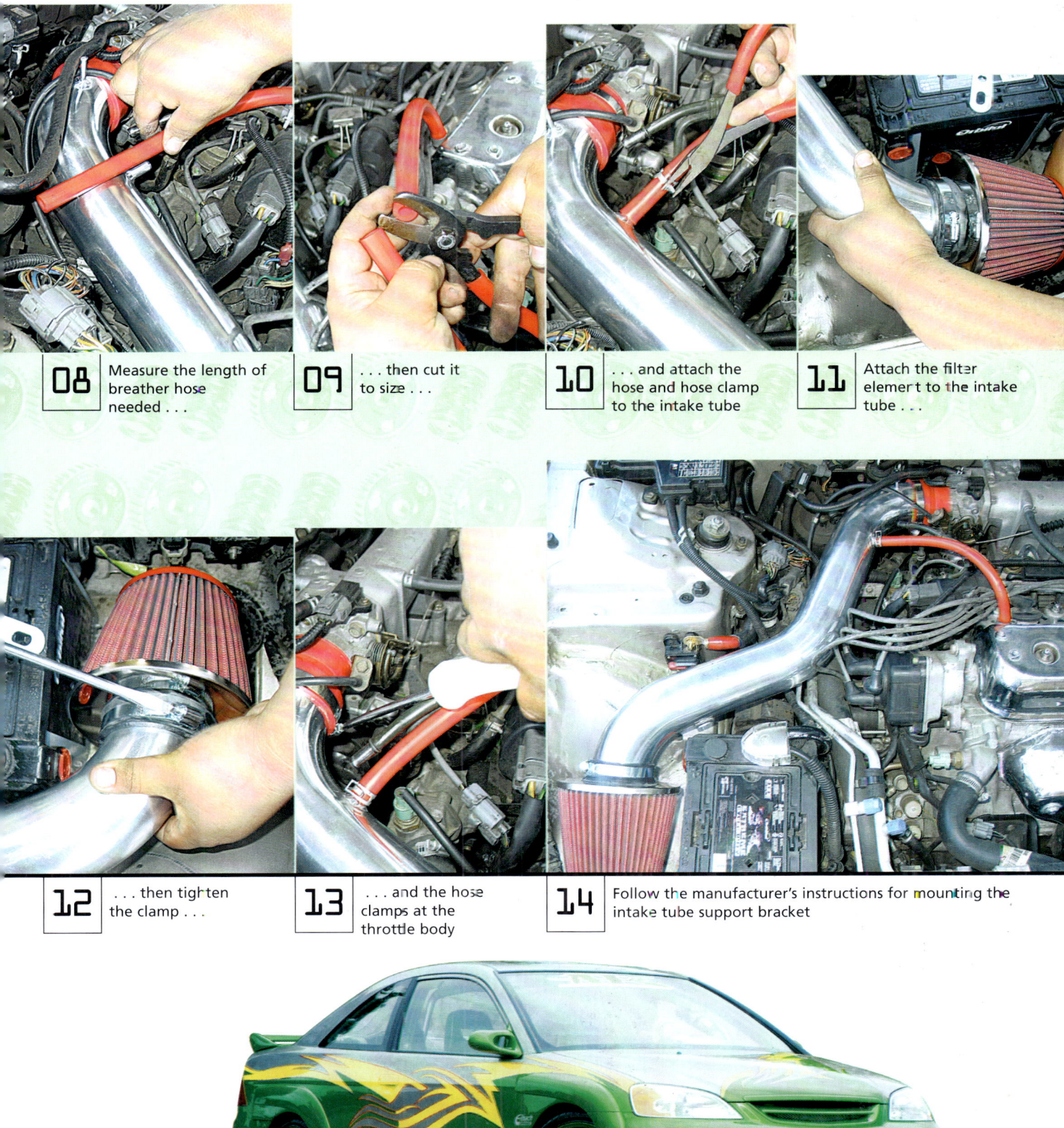

**08** Measure the length of breather hose needed . . .

**09** . . . then cut it to size . . .

**10** . . . and attach the hose and hose clamp to the intake tube

**11** Attach the filter element to the intake tube . . .

**12** . . . then tighten the clamp . . .

**13** . . . and the hose clamps at the throttle body

**14** Follow the manufacturer's instructions for mounting the intake tube support bracket

# Computers and chips

The engine computers in our modern vehicles were developed to make cars more fuel-efficient and emissions clean, using computer-controlled electronic fuel injection.
The side benefit for performance enthusiasts is that engine control modifications to the fuel and ignition systems are relatively easy.

## Engine management basics

Automotive computer systems consist of an onboard computer, referred to by the factory as the Powertrain Control Module (PCM) or Engine Control Module (ECM), and information sensors, which monitor various functions of the engine and send data to the PCM. Based on the data and the information programmed into the computer's memory, the PCM generates output signals to control various engine functions via control relays, solenoids and other output actuators.

The PCM is the "brain" of the electronically controlled fuel and emissions system, and is specifically calibrated to optimize the performance, emissions, fuel economy and driveability of one specific vehicle/engine/transaxle/accessories package in one make/model/year of vehicle.

For a minimal outlay of cash and trouble, a simple chip upgrade for your ECU can improve engine response by altering the fuel flow and ignition curve "maps" - to go along with this, you may have to upgrade the octane of your fuel to premium, especially if your engine has high compression

Not all ECU's have a customer-serviceable chip, but computer upgrade work can be done by mail - Jet Performance Products can do upgrades for most sport compact ECU's and ship it back to you in 24 hours, all with the special packaging they will supply you

"Non-serviceable" chips must be carefully unsoldered from the board, which is why this is usually done by a specialized company or tuning shop with the proper tools and reprogramming equipment

## Computer codes keep track

You may have heard of the term OBD or OBD-I. This means On-Board Diagnostics and refers to the ability to retrieve information from the PCM about the performance characteristics and running condition of all the sensors and actuators in the engine management system. This is invaluable information in diagnosing engine problems. The PCM will illuminate the CHECK ENGINE light (also called the Malfunction Indicator Light) on the dash if it recognizes a component fault.

So, if your dashboard warning light comes on you know the computer has spotted something it doesn't like. To then figure out what it has found, you (or your mechanic) need to access the diagnostic code that the computer has stored in its memory for that fault. On some vehicles, getting these codes is an easy in-the-driveway job. On others, it takes an expensive "scan tool." Your Haynes repair manual will give specific information for your make and model.

## Add-on chips and computers

For improved performance, many enthusiasts upgrade their computer chips, or replace their entire computer. The advantages are increased fuel flow, an improved ignition advance curve and higher revving capability. While replacing computer components can provide substantial performance gains when combined with other engine upgrades, they also have their downside. Perhaps most importantly, replacing any original-equipment computer components can void your warranty or cause you to fail an emissions inspection. Nevertheless, if you are seriously into modifying your engine, at some point you will have to consider dealing with the computer.

The factory programming in your car's ECU is a highly developed, extensively-tested system that works perfectly for your engine in stock condition. Remember that the goal of the factory engineers is maximum fuel economy, driveability, longevity and efficiency. Our goals as

The upgrade technicians will take into account the engine modifications you have made and "burn" the correct programming into your stock chip

If you have a number of engine mods and plan more over time, the S200 from Hondata can be installed in conjunction with your Honda ECU - it retains factory idle quality and code retrieval but allows a Hondata dealer to tune for each mod you make any time, including control of VTEC function

Engine performance

enthusiasts are more in the high-performance sphere and our programming needs are slightly different. The average person driving a Honda will never see 6000 rpm in the car's lifetime, but the average enthusiast wants to see the upper power band as often as possible.

Where the factory ECU programming needs some "help" for performance use is in the ignition timing and fuel curves. Virtually all new cars are designed to run on the lowest grade of unleaded pump gas, with an 87-octane rating. To get more performance, the ignition curve can be given more timing and the fuel curve adjusted for more fuel at higher rpms, but the octane rating of the gas now becomes a problem. When more timing is added, the engine may have more tendency to exhibit detonation or ping, signs of improper burning in the combustion chamber and potentially dangerous to the lifespan of the engine. Thus, if you want to alter the timing "map" in your computer for more power, you'll probably have to up the grade of gasoline you buy. In fact, the more serious engine modifications you make, the more you will probably have to "reprogram" your ECU.

While most bolt-on engine modifications will work well with increased timing, the serious "power adders" like nitrous oxide, superchargers, turbochargers and even just high-compression pistons will require less ignition advance. The big gains in horsepower come from modifications that increase the cylinder

## Accessing the Civic ECU

**01** After disconnecting the battery, use a trim tool to pry up the plastic trim at the doorsill

**02** Under the right side of the dashboard, use a screwdriver to twist the large carpet retaining screws loose

**03** Pull back the carpeting, with the plastic trim still attached, to expose the ECU in the kickpanel area

pressure in the engine, the force pushing the pistons down. Increases in cylinder pressure really raise the octane requirement in a hurry. The best you can get at most gas stations won't be enough to stave off detonation, unless you're lucky enough to live near one of the few stations that sells 100-octane unleaded "racing" gas, and that gets pricey.

So, over the process of modifying your sport compact's engine, your programming needs may change. As you make more and different changes, different tweaks need to be applied to the "brain." Hopefully, you have located a trustworthy "tuning" shop near you. They'll be able to help you with computer upgrades.

In many new cars, the programming that affects the areas we want to modify is part of a "chip" on the motherboard of the ECU. The chip is a very small piece of silicon semiconductor material carrying many integrated circuits. These are usually called PROM chips, for Programmable Read Only Memory. In some cases, the chip is a "plug-in" which can be easily removed from the ECU and replaced with a custom chip. Other chips are factory-soldered to the board. Cars with plug-in chips are the easiest to modify, but many imports do not have replaceable chips.

It isn't recommended to remove a soldered chip from the motherboard at home. Your factory ECU is very expensive to replace and just a tiny mistake with the solder or the heat source could ruin it. Aftermarket companies offer reprogramming services for these kinds of ECU's, and some tuning shops also have equipment to do this. In most cases you remove your ECU and send it to the company by overnight mail, they modify it and overnight-mail it back to you.

Based on the information you have given them about your vehicle, driving needs, and modifications you have made to the engine, they will custom-program the timing, fuel and even the transmission shifting information on vehicles with ECU-controlled electronic automatic transaxles. On vehicles so equipped, they can even change the factory-set rev limiter. On most applications, your car will require a better grade of gas than before, so factor the increased fuel cost in your budget.

 **04** Remove the three bolts and one nut to remove the ECU

 **05** Carefully pull the ECU down without stretching the wiring, then squeeze the two green plastic clips to release the cover over the electrical connectors

 **06** Disconnect the electrical connectors, being careful not to bend any of the delicate pins - now you can ship your ECU off for performance "brainwashing"

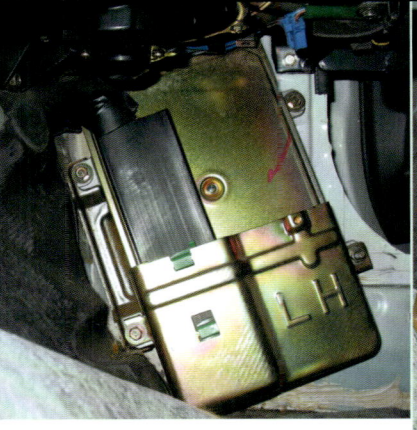
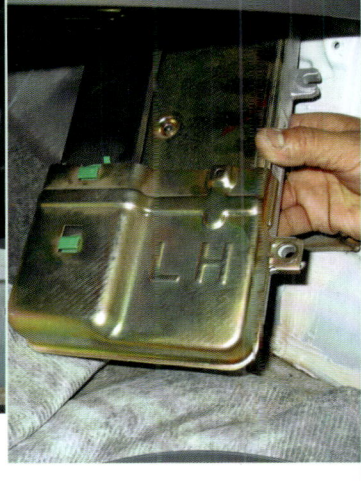

*Engine performance*

# Ignition system

Higher engine speeds put an increased load on stock ignition systems, but modifications that lead to increased cylinder pressure can really put out the fire. If you install higher-compression pistons - always a good move for increased engine performance - the spark plugs need a lot more zap to light off a mixture that is packed tighter than ever. The denser the mixture, the harder it is for a spark to jump the plug's electrodes, like swimming through wet concrete. Other major power-adders such as nitrous oxide, supercharging or turbocharging also create much higher cylinder pressures and require ignition improvements to handle this.

## Aftermarket ignition coils

The typical aftermarket coil is capable of making more secondary voltage than the stock coil, so the spark can jump the gap even at extreme cylinder pressures.

An aftermarket coil won't add any horsepower, but it could eliminate some misfire problems in the upper rpm range.

On Civics with distributors, the coil is mounted inside the distributor. Simple kits are available to add a more powerful, external aftermarket coil to replace the distributor mounted unit.

When shopping for a performance coil, look for a model that has good separation (distance) between the primary (12v) and secondary (fat wire to distributor) terminals. This prevents high voltage from shorting to the primary terminals before ever getting to the spark plugs.

An aftermarket coil with more windings and a heavy-duty case can up your secondary voltage to the spark plugs considerably – important if you plan to run high cylinder pressures in your engine

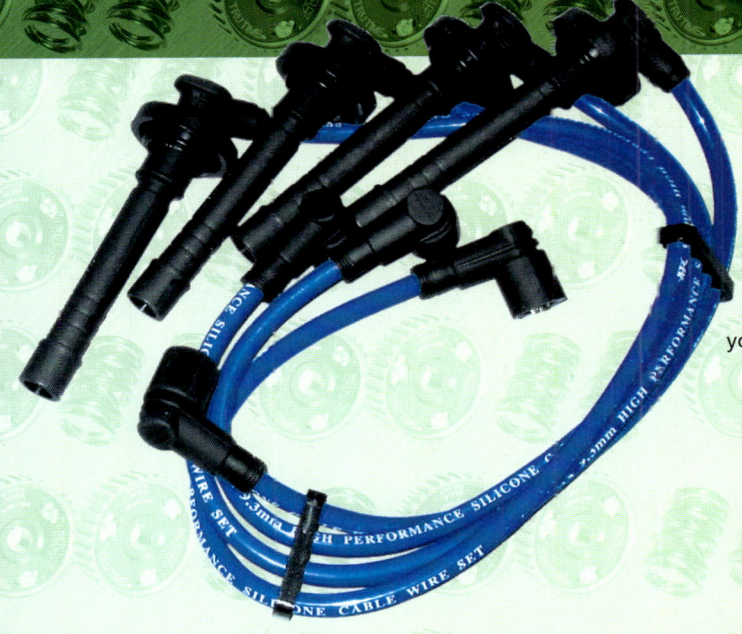

> **Warning:**
> Carbon-conductor wires have a very fragile core. Never try to bend them sharply or pull on them.

Your Civic is probably already in need of new plug wires, so go for a set of fatter and more colorful performance wires that look good and can handle your high rpm usage without voltage leaks

## Plug Wires

Aside from making your engine compartment look cool, high performance spark plug wires serve a very useful purpose. If you install a high-voltage coil and keep your stock wires, you are asking for voltage to leak from the wires under load, at high engine speeds, or boosted (blown or turbocharged) conditions. Voltage will try to seek the "path of least resistance" and that could be any engine ground that is close to one of your plug wires.

The typical factory plug wire has a core of carbon-impregnated material surrounded by fiberglass and rubber insulation, which is fine for stock engines.

Most aftermarket performance wires use a very fine spiral wire wound around a magnetic core and wrapped in silicone jacketing, and are available in thicker-than-stock diameters to handle more current flow. Some import cars have stock plug wires as skinny as 5 or 6mm, while aftermarket wires are offered in 8mm, 8.5mm and even 9mm for racing applications. Good aftermarket wires also come with thicker boots, which is important, since the boot-to-plug contact area is a frequent source of voltage leaking to ground. Wires in the 8mm range are big enough to handle the spark of most street-modified cars, and the bigger wires are good for racing, but there's no such thing as having too much insulation on your plug wires.

## Timing controls

Once you start modifying the engine, you have changed the ignition parameters and you now need to adjust the timing with something other than the factory ECU. Installing a chip or reprogramming your ECU will advance the timing, but can't increase the energy level of the spark. For that you need a CD (Capacitive Discharge) aftermarket ignition system.

The CD ignition usually consists of an electronic box you mount in the engine compartment, and the wiring harness to connect to your vehicle. Your ECU still does the triggering and controls the advance, but in the CD box is a large capacitor, which is an electronic storage device. These ignition systems have been used in performance applications for years and are well proven. Juice usually comes into the coil or coilpack as battery voltage (12V) and is bumped up from there to 5,000, 10,000 or 40,000 volts of secondary current. In the CD ignition, the capacitor stores incoming juice until there is more like 450 volts to go to the coil. Now the coil has a much easier time of quickly building up to the required voltage for good spark, regardless of the rpm.

 **Caution:**
When removing spark plug wires, pull only on the boot. Never pull on the plug wire itself. The plug wire's core is fragile and can be broken by careless stretching.

An electronic ignition control box can provide multi-fire capability as well as user-settable control of rev-limit, plus retard control for boosted engines and nitrous applications

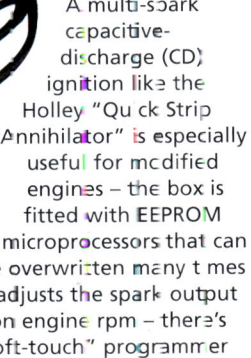

A multi-spark capacitive-discharge (CD) ignition like the Holley "Quick Strip Annihilator" is especially useful for modified engines – the box is fitted with EEPROM microprocessors that can be overwritten many times and adjusts the spark output based on engine rpm – there's even a "soft-touch" programmer keypad for racing

# Spark plugs

The final links in the ignition system's chain-of-command are the spark plugs, the front-line combat troops. We may have mentioned this before but, as with other ignition modifications, don't expect to make big gains in power or mileage by switching spark plugs. Despite the wild claims dreamed up by advertising copywriters over the last fifty years, the only time spark plugs will make much difference on a street-driven engine is when the engine is really in need of a tune-up and you install fresh plugs.

Nonetheless, there are a wide variety of spark plugs out there to choose from. If your engine is only mildly modified, stick with the factory recommended spark plugs, gapped to factory specs. Most engines with above-average level of modifications can utilize a plug that is one heat range colder than stock.

## Required Reading. . . your spark plugs!

Without a lot of complicated and expensive test equipment, you can tell a great deal about the operating conditions inside your engine just by examining its spark plugs.

This may seem like a primitive tuning tool, but watch the pit activity at any professional-level race and you'll see the top mechanics looking at spark plugs with a magnifying glass. When a spark plug tells a story, it can save you an entire engine by giving early warning signs of detonation. The color, uniformity, cleanliness and even smell of a freshly-pulled spark plug can tell you reams, if you know what to look for. In the back of the Haynes repair manual for your vehicle (you do have one, don't you?) you'll find a large chart of various spark plug conditions, close-up and in color.

When you pull the plugs on your street-driven machine, you're looking at long-term conditions - the plugs can tell you if the engine is too rich, too lean, if it's burning oil, if the electrodes are worn from too many miles, etc. At the race track conditions are quite different than everyday driving. When you're ready to make a run at the drags, install a fresh set of plugs and make your run, but just as you go through the lights, shut off the engine "clean" and put the trans in neutral at the same time (make sure you don't turn your ignition key to the LOCK position, or you won't be able to steer).

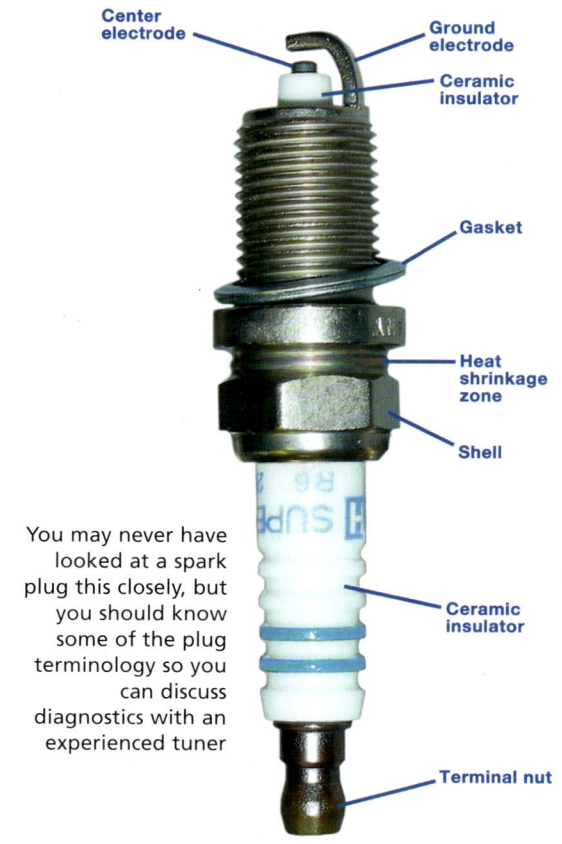

You may never have looked at a spark plug this closely, but you should know some of the plug terminology so you can discuss diagnostics with an experienced tuner

Coast back to the pits or have a friend tow you. Pull these plugs and you'll see only what plug conditions are the result of hard running *on that run only*. You must shut off clean, or the deceleration and pit driving could show a false richness or oil symptoms. If your plug is free of the signs of detonation, like pits or the presence of aluminum specks on the porcelain, then you're good to run hard.

Whenever you make important changes on your state of tune, like adding more performance equipment, doublecheck the part's influence by doing a plug check like this. Too rich, and you'll just go too slow. Too lean and you'll toast the engine if you're not careful. The simple plug check tells you if you're safe or not!

The condition of your spark plugs is a good indicator of conditions inside your engine – check your plugs after each new modification to see if you need to change fuel and/or timing calibrations

A really good close-up magnifying glass will let you see every tiny detail - compare the results to a Haynes color spark plug chart

# Treat your Civic to a hot external coil

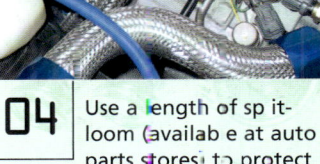

**01** After removing the distributor cap and rotor (see your Haynes Automotive Repair Manual, if necessary), remove the screws securing the coil primary wires and the coil mounting screws, then remove the old coil

**02** Take two lengths of new 16 gauge wire, crimp terminals on them, then connect them to the stock wires – keep track of which color is positive and which is negative

**03** Use a hacksaw and carefully cut a small slot (make two cuts close together) in the mounting flange of the new MSD cap – cut a rubber grommet in half and glue one half in the slot you've made – this will secure the two new coil primary wires. Push the wires and grommet into the slot in the cap, then install the cap

**04** Use a length of split-loom (available at auto parts stores) to protect the new primary wires and make a neat appearance – just open the split part and press in the wires as you go

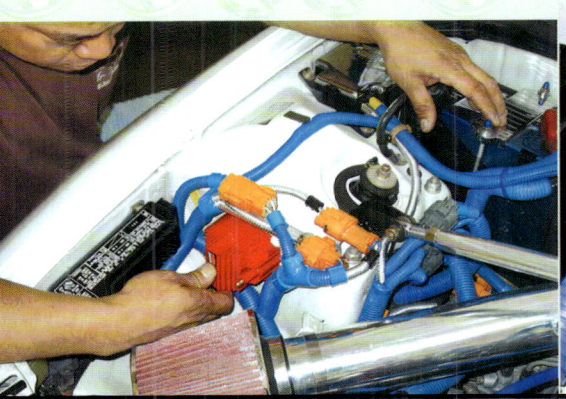

**05** Now you can swap the spark plug wires to the new cap, one at a time so you keep the correct firing order – attach the factory-finished end of your MSD coil wire to the cap also, the MSD instructions give precise directions on how to cut and crimp the new secondary terminal to the other end of the coil wire

**06** We found a perfect spot for the new MSD external coil at the front of the right shock tower. All we had to do was drill a couple of holes and mount the coil using the supplied hardware and rubber mounts

**07** Here's the new external coil all mounted and wired up – our project Civic will now have the electrical fortitude to handle whatever power-adders we install later on

# Valvetrain Modifications

*Engine performance*

When you run fast, you breathe harder - so does your engine. To make more power, an engine must "inhale" more air and "exhale" more exhaust. To make this happen, you can open the valves more, leave them open longer and/or enlarge the "ports" (passages in the cylinder head where the air and exhaust flow). These cylinder head and valvetrain modifications can seem complicated, but understanding them is essential. Mistakes here can cost you power or even an engine overhaul.

The modifications discussed here usually come after all the other bolt-ons have not gained you the power you're after. Most of these modifications require going inside the engine, which is not a place an amateur should go alone. You'll need to find a reputable tuner and machine shop who know your particular engine inside and out.

If you make no other mod to your valvetrain, at least install quality performance valve springs and lightweight retainers like these from Crane – they could save your engine when you spend time at high revs

What happens when you override your factory rev-limiter at 8000 rpm with weak valve springs? – This valvehead imbedded in a Civic piston is the typical result of valve float

## Cam sprockets

A cam gear or gears (more properly, sprockets) swap is a very popular modification on Overhead Cam (OHC) engines. They not only look great, they can actually provide a few extra horsepower when set up properly. While dialing in the degrees on the sprockets is relatively easy, you will need to know the precise number of degrees to advance or retard each cam in your particular application. The correct "degreeing in" specifications are determined by the engine type, level of modification and type of power you're after (low-rpm or high-rpm). Because of this complexity, it's best to ask a tuner who's familiar with your type of engine, or go by the recommendations that come with the gears.

Installing cam gears means you'll have to remove, then reinstall the timing belt. This procedure is best left to a qualified technician, since any slight error could cause you to bend your valves from valve-to-piston contact. At the very least, get the Haynes repair manual for your particular vehicle and follow the procedure carefully. Be sure to rotate the engine through two turns by hand after the belt is back on and double-check that all the timing marks are still aligned - this way you'll identify any problems before turning the key to the sound of grinding metal if you make a mistake.

Top: The adjustable gear is two-piece, so the bolts can be loosened and the relationship between the inner section on the camshaft and the outer section connected to the timing belt can be advanced or retarded – Good ones like this AEM "Tru-Time" gear are machined of billet aluminum and feature very clearly engraved timing marks

Left: You'll find that cam gears are one of the most popular engine modifications there is – adjustable cam timing gears like these from AEM allow you to adjust camshaft timing to suit the other tuning modifications you have made or plan to – SOHC engines would use one gear, DOHC'ers use a pair

Left: With their three-lobe arrangement, cams for VTEC engines are expensive, but if you have the experience and a Haynes repair manual or Haynes Extreme Sport Compact Performance book, an upgrade to new cams like these from Crane can give you a good boost in the mid-range and top end

## Camshafts

Installing camshafts is an expensive and precise task. The most important work comes before any tools come out. You, consulting with your tuner, need to pick out the best cam for your car and driving style.

Stock camshafts are designed as a compromise to consider economy, emissions, low-end torque and good idling and driveability. The performance camshaft lifts the valves higher (lift), keeps them open longer (duration) and is designed mainly to produce more horsepower. A performance camshaft usually makes its gains at mid-to-higher rpm and sacrifices some low-rpm torque. The hotter the cam, the more pronounced these attributes become. A cam design that is advertised for power between 3000 and 8000 rpm won't start feeling really good until that rpm "band" is reached.

Aftermarket cams are usually offered in "Stages" of performance. A typical Stage 1 cam might have a little higher lift than stock and a little longer duration. It would still keep an excellent idle and work from idle or 1000 rpm up. A Stage II cam would be hotter in all specs (with a band from 3000 to 7000 rpm) and have a slightly rough idle (maybe 750 rpm). A Stage III cam would feature serious lift, duration and overlap and make its power from 5000 to 8000 rpm. The hotter the cam specs the worse the idle, low-end performance and fuel economy is going to be, but the more top-end horsepower you'll make.

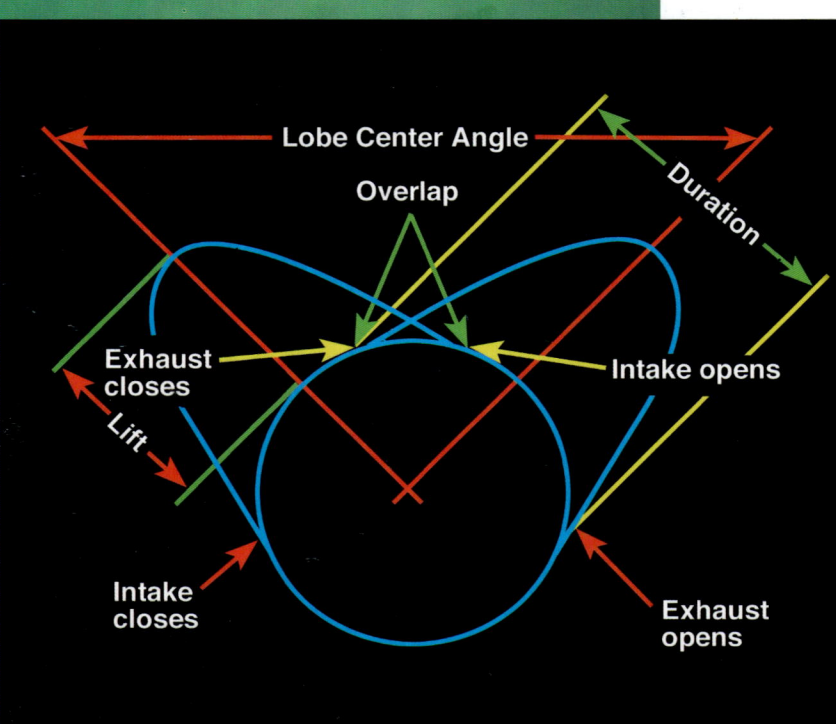

The relationship between camshaft intake and exhaust lobes is complicated and the right cam design can do wonders, especially on street-driven cars that retain the VTEC function, which acts like a street cam up to 5500 rpm and a hot cam after that

## Valve springs

When you install a "bigger" camshaft, you'll usually want to install better valve springs. High-performance valve springs allow the valves to open further without the springs binding and also are stronger to prevent valve "float." Valve float occurs when the engine is at very high rpm and the inertia of the valve is too much for the spring to handle. So the valves actually lose contact with the lifter or cam follower and can make contact with the piston, bending the valve and/or damaging the piston.

For this reason, high-performance valve springs are recommended whenever you change the camshaft or make other modifications to extend the rpm range beyond stock. Your stock springs will not last long at repeated high-rpm operation, and when springs fail, the valves usually hit the pistons with results that are major-league bad.

Once you start altering the stock Civic ECU or add an aftermarket controller that allows you to change the factory rev limit, it's only a matter of time before the stock valve springs in that 100,000-mile Civic you're starting with are going to fail.

The piston makes up half of the combustion chamber in a cylinder, and there are a number of choices when rebuilding an engine for performance – at left is a forged replacement piston with stock compression ratio, at center is a forging with very high compression for racing (note the high dome), and at right is the opposite end of the piston spectrum, a forged 8:1 dished piston for high-boost turbocharged applications

When you are rebuilding your cylinder head, if you discover some bad valves, why not replace the whole set with performance valves like these from REV that are lightweight and made of high-temp alloys to handle boosted and nitrous-equipped applications

## Cylinder head work

The most basic of cylinder head work is a valve job, which will assure the valve faces, seats and guides are in good condition. This is very important for an engine running at high rpm, and is essential if your engine has very many miles on it. If you're planning to install performance camshafts with new valve springs and lightweight retainers, make sure you get a good valve job at the same time, preferably a three-angle valve job from a performance machine shop. You won't see much performance gain from this work; it's insurance against damage on an engine that will be pushed to the limits.

Cylinder head porting is a specialized art and science that is practiced by performance machine shops. Novices can damage the cylinder head or actually reduce airflow. A performance machine shop has all the right equipment for the job, including a flow-bench. With the aid of a flow-bench, the performance machine shop can "open up" your heads for maximum performance. Be sure to find a shop that specializes in your type of engine.

Sometimes swapping cylinder heads is the path to more power – the most common swap in Honda circles is the E16 VTEC head onto a larger-displacement non-VTEC block - when pros prepare the head, some holes in the head have to be modified by TIG-welding, then the head is surfaced

To replace valve springs and retainers on a Honda engine with the head in place, you need a special valve spring compressor that you can rent at tool shops - compressed air is pumped into the cylinder to keep the valves from falling in while you swap the components for the good stuff

Engine performance

A Civic with lots of engine mods needs a steady supply of fuel – here equipped with the full gamut of aftermarket fuel system components

# Fuel system

Your engine burns fuel and air. When you increase the amount of air it's using, you have to up the fuel, too. The more you modify your engine, the more fuel system modifications you may have to perform.

Your stock engine management system will adapt to an increase in airflow such as an aftermarket intake pipe and free-flowing air filter, but the physical limitations of the stock fuel delivery system under wide-open throttle (WOT) conditions can hold back the engine's potential when more aggressive mods are made. Since you are modifying the engine to go faster, i.e. spending more time at WOT, you are sort of on your own to develop the fuel combination that works best for your engine and the modifications you've made. The major mods you might make, such as power-adders, cams or head work, have been done by many others before you, and the manufacturer of the components should have plenty of data on what fuel system upgrades go along with their equipment.

An adjustable fuel pressure regulator is probably the first modification for your fuel system. The aftermarket units are a direct bolt-on replacement for the stock regulator, with the same vacuum connection, but feature an adjuster screw on top that changes the fuel system pressure. Once you start playing with your fuel system, you must have a reliable way to measure the fuel pressure, which usually means

A performance-type adjustable fuel pressure regulator will be adequate for all your pressure control needs for now and with any future engine add-ons

An aftermarket high-pressure fuel pump will be needed when you have serious power mods – some, like this one, replace your in-tank pump; other types can be added to the system somewhere near the fuel tank

Left: You have to know what kind of fuel pressure you have, so a gauge can simply be added to the fitting on top of your stock Honda fuel filter at the firewall

Right: Replace your stock Honda fuel filter with this take-apart unit from AEM, and you can use throwaway filters inside the cool, anodized filter housing

installing a quality fuel pressure gauge.

When you increase the fuel pressure in your FI system, you are putting a greater load on the injectors themselves. Experts tell us that for street cars with mild bolt-on modifications, you shouldn't raise the factory fuel pressure much more than 10% over stock. Engines built for all-out racing will require a completely aftermarket fuel system that delivers much higher pressure and volume, with special injectors, fuel pump, regulator, fuel rail and stand-alone engine management.

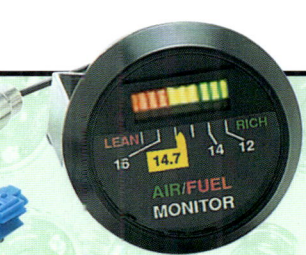

Tuning to find the correct air-fuel ratio when you're doing engine mods is a lot easier if you have a wide-band aftermarket oxygen sensor and gauge like this one from K&N that features ten LED lights in different colors that correspond to different A/F ratios

FWD traction is always limited, but especially so on regular streets – at the track, you've got all the hookup you can handle and you get some real competition – you don't have to get your times announced if you don't want that

# Race and Live !

## The basics

Street racing has been around a long time – today's legitimate organized drag racing was begun in the early 1950's as a reaction to hot rods racing on public streets.

But times have changed over the years. Now we have a huge increase in the number of very modified imports running around and at the same time, the number of deserted streets once deemed "safe enough" to race on have been eliminated by urban sprawl. Worse yet, the urban sprawl has led to the demise of many of the nation's race tracks.

The things that haven't changed about street racing is that the participants still get a thrill, racers and spectators still bet on the outcome of the matches and unfortunately, sometimes people get hurt or killed.

Even if no one is killed or hurt, there are serious negatives to street racing. Right now, the biggest weapon in the establishment's arsenal is vehicle confiscation. That means you lose your car forever. After all the hard work, investment and wrenching you've put into your modified sport compact, is this how you want it to end up?

In a number of areas where there is a legitimate race course or NHRA dragstrip, what local organizers have done is institute "street-legal" drags. On a Wednesday night, a Friday or some other day where the track doesn't have their professional program, the street racers come in for a nominal fee and make all the runs they want.

Such events have become very popular where they have been instituted. Racers and spectators can relax without fear of arrest, and the racers have the benefit of superior traction, guardrails, ambulance and firetruck on premises, and the chance to show off in front of much larger crowds of their peers. Like with the sports or music businesses, those who are good can advance up the ranks, make a name, build a true race car, and maybe one day be a sponsored touring professional drag racer like one of their heroes.

# Race safe

There's no "bravery" in racing stupid - that is, without the basic safety items that can save your life or limbs. The good news is that any race-oriented safety device you add to your street-driven car only increases its cool factor, whether you race or not.

First off, you should really have a serious set of seat belts. Your factory shoulder belt is only OK. A wide-belt, racing harness is way better, both for safety and looks. Every time you strap in, you'll feel like one of the pro import racers! In most cases, such belts are installed in conjunction with an aftermarket seat, which is lighter and more rigid to keep you in place, especially if you ever decide to try some slalom or other road-course racing.

In the back seat area, carry around a legitimate (i.e. approved by NHRA or other sanctioning body) helmet. Have your name and blood type lettered on it just like the real racers do, and strap it to the back seat with a seat belt. It's always a conversation starter, and some tracks will make you get a helmet anyway.

The ultimate in safety and points-gathering is probably a roll-bar. You can buy bolt-on kits for a simple roll-bar for most popular imports, or have one bent and welded into the car at a race shop. It's not as expensive as you might think, and is way more impressive than neon lights under your car or a pod-mounted tach.

There are many more safety items of a technical nature that you can add to your ride, but we don't have space to detail all of them. Get yourself an NHRA rulebook, and do some research on the net. Most racetracks have a website with information on when they have street-legal drags or "grudge" nights. Also, look up *nhra.com*, *RaceLegal.com* (a San Diego group organizing events to get racers off the streets), and *racersagainststreetracing.com*. That last one is a coalition of aftermarket manufacturers, pro racers, car magazines and race sanctioning bodies dedicated to providing alternatives to street racing.

Try some real racing at a dragstrip, even if you go as a spectator the first time – at the import drags/street legal drags and other such grassroots events, you'll find lots of your peers having fun going fast and safe

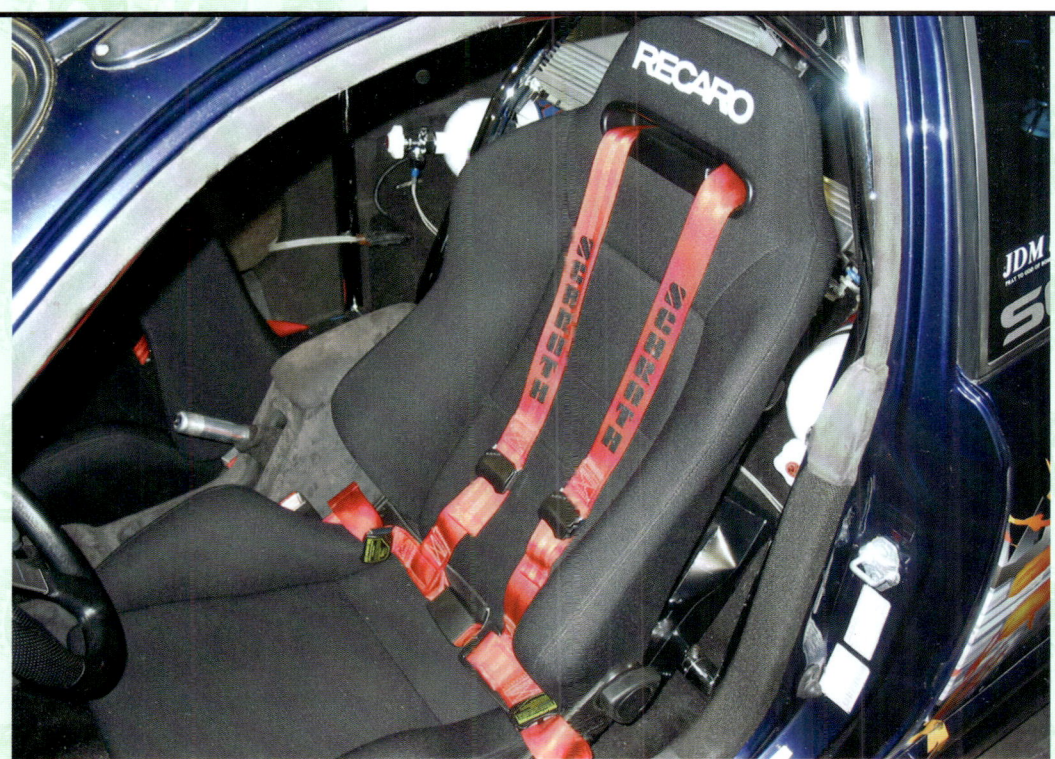

A helmet, a set of firm racing seats and a racing harness will put some safety into your racing, plus look cool at any time - the chromed rollbar here just ups the safety/wow factor

## 09

In-car entertainment

# In-car entertainment

**DVD, Satellite radio, video screens in every headrest... isn't this a great world!**

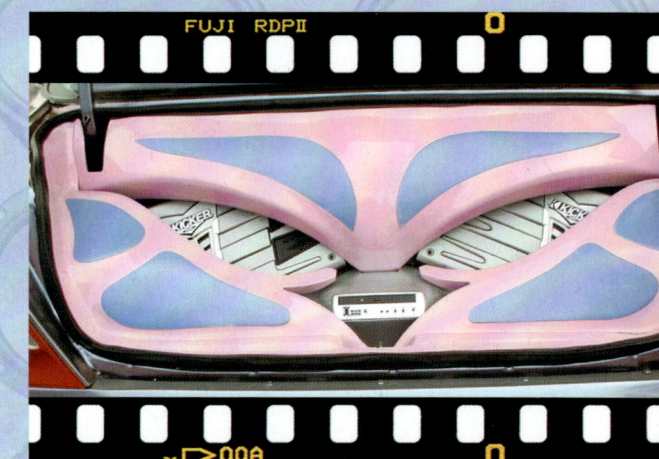

# In-dash receivers & players

To give your Honda Civic's audio system a decent start, you need a good head unit to provide the signal that an amp will beef up, and that the speakers will replay.

If an upgrade of the sound system is what you have in mind, there are plenty of decent head units out there to choose from. Don't be afraid to consult with an expert on which features matter most. The head unit is an important part of a good sound system - always go for the best you can afford.

Our Eclipse head unit is typical of the current single-CD state of the art - nice appearance, good sound, plenty of features. The peak of in-car entertainment, so to speak.

**01** First the old set's got to go. Resist the urge to just crowbar the thing out of the dash (refer to the Haynes manual for your vehicle). On our late model Civic we needed to remove the dashboard lower center cover . . .

**07** . . . then got to work on the wiring. In this case we needed to solder a connector to the radio's wiring harness (which will plug into the existing connector in the vehicle's dash). Don't panic - just follow the instructions that will come with your head unit and if you don't feel comfortable soldering, use easy crimp connectors

**08** The cage for the new head unit is placed into the center panel . . .

**09** . . . then the mounting tangs are bent to keep it in place

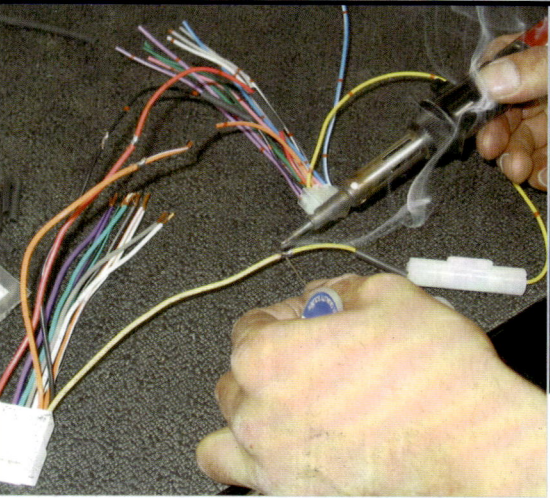
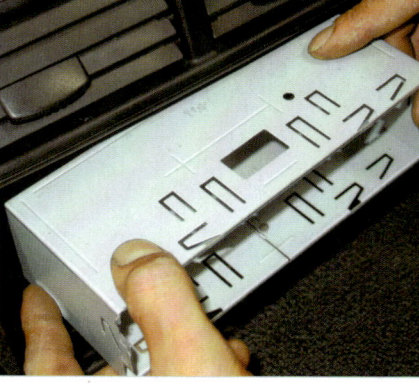
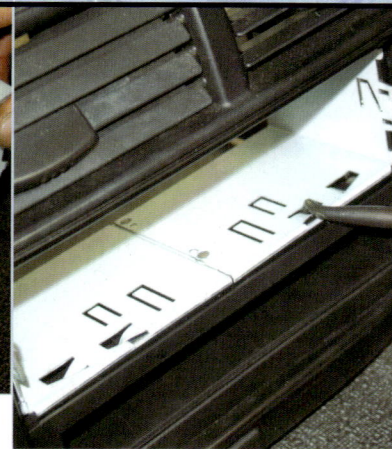

**02** ...then we removed the center panel mounting bolts

**03** Out comes the center panel, just enough to disconnect the radio's wiring

**04** After removing a couple connectors and mounting bolts...

**05** ...the radio can be removed from the center panel

**06** To make the head unit fit perfectly in the dash, Scosche supplied us with a vehicle-specific installation kit. After reading the instructions, we trimmed a few of the mounting tabs...

**10** Now it's just a matter of sliding home the radio...

**11** ...connecting the harness and reinstalling the center panel

**12** Now get out the instruction manual and set those levels properly

**13** Nice job!

# Speakers

Most Civic factory speakers are low on power and made with nasty paper cones that disintegrate after a few years - installing any aftermarket speakers would be considered an upgrade. But we're going top-shelf with some really first-class speakers courtesy of our friends at Focal.

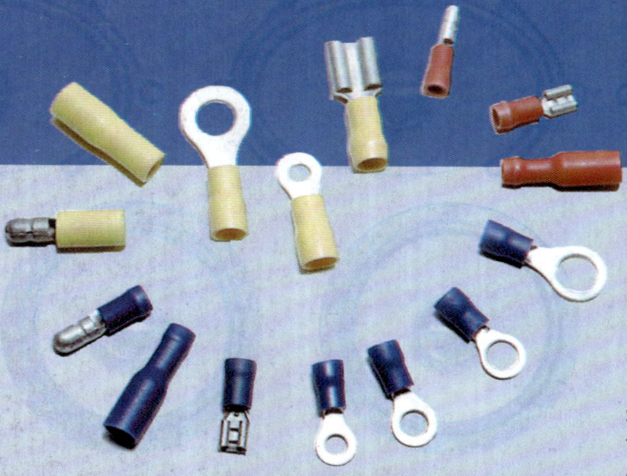

# Crimp connectors

There is a wide variety of crimp-type connectors available at auto parts stores, which will allow you to make virtually any type of connection you need to make. To make the connections properly, you'll need to use a special crimping tool (available at most auto parts stores). Try to get a good-quality tool that presses an indentation into the connector. Some of the cheaper tools simply flatten the connector, which gives an inferior connection. Also, be sure you're using the correct connector type for the gauge of wire you're connecting.

If you don't know the wire gauge, you can figure it out using your crimping tool by inserting the end of the wire into each of the stripping holes in your crimper until you find the one that strips off the wire's insulation.

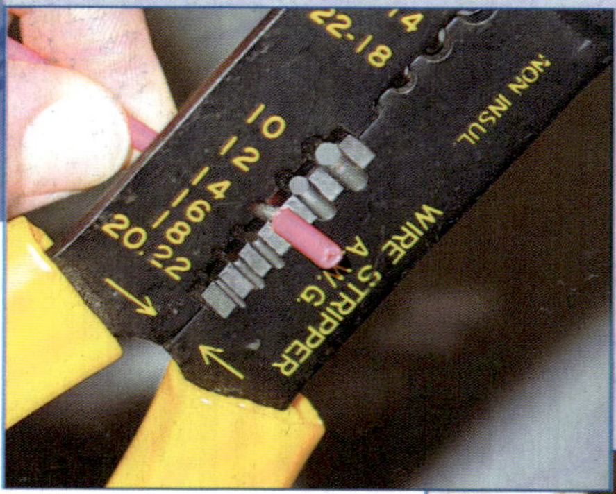

### Note:
*When installing spade or bullet connectors, always crimp the female side of the connector to the feed wire. This way, if the connector comes unplugged, the "hot" wire won't short out if it touches a ground (it'll be shielded by the insulation surrounding the female side of the connector).*

Crimp connectors are quick and easy to install - simply strip off about 1/4-inch of insulation using the proper-gauge hole on your stripping tool . . .

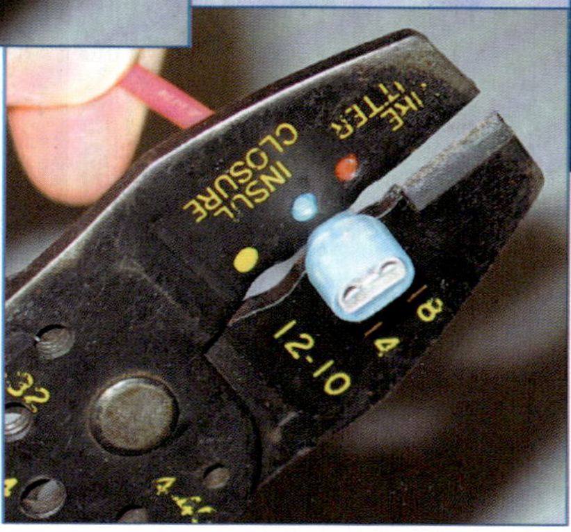

. . . insert the stripped wire and crimp the connector firmly onto it using the correct crimping jaws of the tool

| Wire gauge | Industry standard color on crimp connector |
|---|---|
| 22 to 18 | Red |
| 16 to 14 | Blue |
| 12 to 10 | Yellow |

# Front speakers

**01** The most convenient place for the front components is in the doors. Lucky for us the factory installed speakers and tweeters were already separate components, so a swap wasn't bad at all. Off came the speaker . . .

**02** . . . then came the door panel. Don't just rip the panel off, be sure you've got all the screws out. Most door panels are also secured by push-in plastic fasteners around the perimeter of the panel (if necessary, refer to the *Haynes Automotive Repair Manual* for your vehicle)

**03** With the door panel removed, the factory tweeter can be disconnected. We saved the factory tweeter mounting panel to use with our new tweeters

**04** Run the new tweeter and speaker wire through the rubber sleeve. You only need to run enough wire to just go under the dash, where the crossover is going to be mounted

**05** This is one of the two front crossovers being wired with the amp input lead and the outputs to the tweeter and speaker. The crossover can then be mounted under the dash when it's finished

**06** Next we installed the new tweeter into its mounting panel, then soldered the crossover's tweeter output wire to the short lead wire coming from the tweeter

**07** After the door panel was installed, a minor trim was necessary to fit the new speaker's magnet

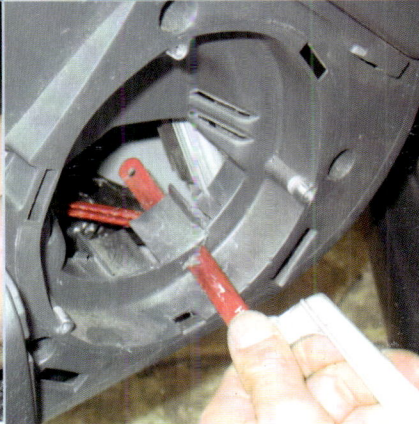

# Front speakers (continued)

**08** We soldered the crossover speaker output wire to the speaker

**09** Our new Focal Polyglass speaker was then mounted carefully to the door

**10** We stared at the speaker for a moment, admiring our work, just before we reinstalled the factory cover

# Crossovers

Crossovers separate different frequency bands and redirect them to the proper drivers. Without some type of crossover, these ranges of sound can't be separated, resulting in an audio system that sounds "flat" and/or distorted. So, they're incorporated into the system to send the high frequencies to the tweeters, mid-range frequencies to the mid-range speakers, low frequencies to the woofers, and ultra-low frequencies to the subwoofer(s), if used. Some are adjustable and can be set to separate these ranges at certain frequencies, thereby eliminating the frequencies that the speaker can't use (or that would cause it to operate inefficiently). Others aren't adjustable, and some are built right into a component (like a triaxial speaker).

There are two types of crossovers: active and passive. Active crossovers are placed into the signal chain before the amplifier, and require a separate DC voltage input to operate. Some amplifiers have built-in active crossovers.

Passive crossovers are placed into the signal chain between the amplifier and the speakers. They don't require DC voltage to operate. And, since they are connected just before the speakers, one amplifier can drive a number of speakers correctly.

# Rear speakers

**01** Out with the package tray. Don't just rip the panel off! Most package trays are secured by push-in plastic fasteners around the perimeter of the panel (if necessary refer to the *Haynes Automotive Repair Manual* for your vehicle)

**02** Off with the wiring plug, out with the screws - not much grief to be found acios-ing the factory speakers

**03** Our new set of Focal Polyglass 6X9's are a perfect fit, no need for fabrication

**04** That looks so much better - let's hope they sound as good as they look

**05** The only thing left is wiring 'em up. A little double-sided tape and we found the perfect mounting spot for our crossover

**06** A few wires from the amp, and a few wires to the speaker...

**07** ...and a job well done

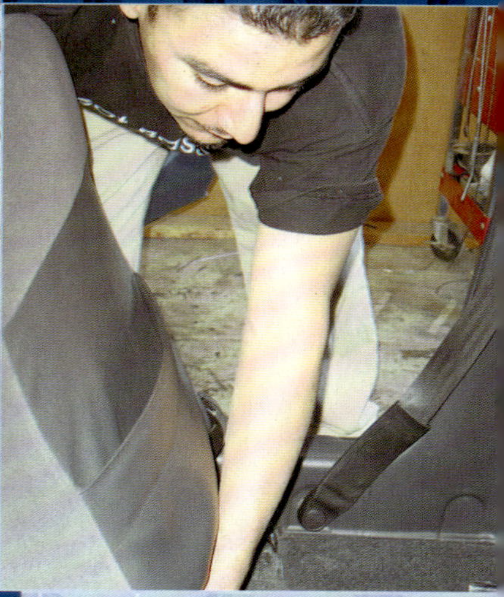

# Amplifiers

If you really want your sound system to crank, there's no substitute for power. And that means adding an amp.

**TIP** *Decide where you'll mount the amp carefully. Amps must be adequately cooled - don't cover it up so there's no airflow, and don't hang it upside down. We found ourselves a nice mounting platform under the front passenger's seat.*

**01** First we removed the front seat. A simple matter of removing the four bolts securing the seat to the floorpan and lifting the seat from the vehicle. You may also have to disconnect an electrical connector or two. If your vehicle is equipped with side-impact airbags, you'll have to disable the airbag system (refer to the Haynes Automotive Repair Manual for your vehicle)

**06** The amplifier's remote turn on wire and signal patch cable need to be connected at the back of the stereo head. Marking the signal cables left side/right side will assure correct connection at the amplifier

**07** Cut a short length of wire for the ground and crimp a ring terminal on one end then find a spot and mount it to the vehicle chassis. Be sure to sand off any paint so that the connection is made directly to metal.

**08** Read the amp's instruction book carefully when connecting any wires, or you might regret it. Identify your speaker positive and negative/ left side and right side wires, then make the connections

**09** With the installation complete it's time to install the fuse and test the amplifier. Carefully follow the manufacturer's instructions for powering up the amp and making any necessary adjustments

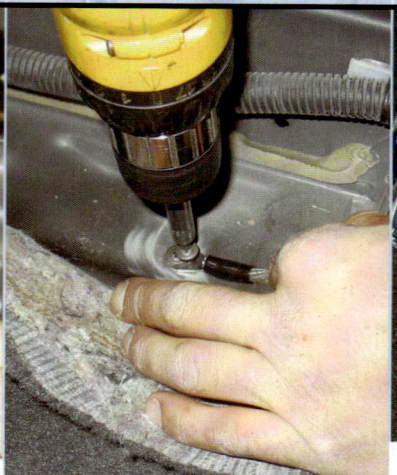

**02** An amplifier wiring kit like this one from Scosche supplies us with all our amplifier wiring needs

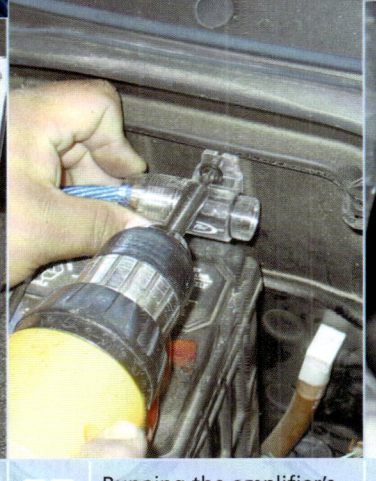

**03** Running the amplifier's power wire starts at the battery. The main power wire needs to have a waterproof fuse holder mounted as close to the battery as possible.

**04** The power wire needs to be routed to the passenger compartment. How to get the wire through the firewall doesn't have to be a dilemma, just find an existing hole like this one, then remove the grommet, cut a small hole in it and feed the power wire through grommet and firewall. Be sure to refit the grommet to the firewall to prevent water leaks and to protect the wire

**05** Connecting the power wire at the terminal is ok, just be sure NOT to install a fuse and complete the power connection until you finish the entire installation

**Note:** Always follow the manufacturer's recommendations for mounting the amplifier. Properly securing an amp is very important so that it's not sliding around. A sliding amplifier that's not properly mounted can damage the unit, or worse, be dangerous in an accident.

# Choosing the right amp

The first step is to determine the needs of your system. If you're just adding an amp to improve your original equipment system, you may need only minimal amplification. Therefore, a small inexpensive amp will suffice. On the other hand, if you're planning on running multiple subwoofers and component speakers, you'll most likely need multiple amplifiers.

Next, you have to figure out if you need an amplifier with a built-in crossover or an amp that is dedicated to playing a full-range signal. A built-in crossover can cross over different frequencies dedicated to a particular speaker, whereas a 12-inch subwoofer will sound best playing 100Hz and down. This will maximize the life of the speaker playing in this frequency range.

How powerful of an amp does your system need? Well, that depends what kind and how many speakers it has to drive. The amp should be capable of putting out 1-1/2 to two times the power (continuous, or RMS power in watts) that the lowest-frequency speaker that it'll be driving is rated. The specifications you'll find when shopping for an amp will indicate how many watts-per-channel the amp is able to produce continuously. This sounds weird, but an underpowered amp can actually damage your speakers when the volume is turned way up. The waveform it puts out changes from a nice curvy sine wave into more of a square wave, which speakers don't like; this is called clipping, because the top and bottom of the wave gets "clipped" off. The speakers can handle the extra power better than they can this ugly square wave.

Finally, how many channels must the amplifier have in order to interface with the stereo system? Say, for example, you're running four speakers and you want to add amplifiers to enhance the sound. You must decide if you want to retain the use of the fader. If you do, you will need to purchase a four-channel amplifier with four independent RCA inputs. A four-channel amplifier can run four speakers in a stereo fashion without losing fading capability.

# Subwoofer

### Want to actually *feel* the music pumping through your system?

Subwoofers are usually sold as a stand-alone item, but in just about all applications they will have to be mounted in some type of enclosure. These are big, heavy speakers that just can't be tossed into a door panel or under the dash. There are many types of enclosures, designed to manipulate the acoustics of the subwoofer(s) depending on the type of vehicle in which it is being installed or the type of music that will be listened to. The physics behind these various designs is not easy to understand and is way beyond the scope of this manual, so we won't go there. However, your basic choices are a ready-made cabinet, an enclosure that has been designed to replace a center console or side panel specifically for your model car, or a custom built enclosure you build yourself.

## Ready-made cabinet

**01** The wiring was already connected to the terminal cup that was fitted on the box, so the ends just needed stripping back and terminating with the correct fittings to join onto the subwoofer. The cable is coded with plus and minus symbols for easy connection. As long as you get the feed wire into the box the right way, everything will be fine

**02** After carefully positioning the subwoofer to get the center logo straight, the eight mounting holes were drilled with pilot holes, and then the screws were tightened steadily by hand. You can use a power screwdriver, but be careful not to go too tight and ruin the pilot hole you've just drilled or you'll have to put your speaker in at a funny angle once you've drilled some more holes

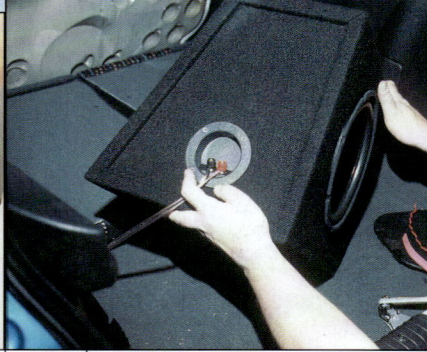

**03** The sub cable from the amplifier was clamped tightly under these screw terminals. Like the rest of the wiring, the cable was stripped back and then the ends protected with a short piece of heatshrink tube. This neatens the cable ends and makes it more difficult to short out the wiring. Just be sure to leave enough bare cable to connect to the terminal, eh?

## Model specific enclosures

A slick option for adding a subwoofer is one of these ready-made vehicle-specific enclosures. Most are designed for easy-installation and to blend with the vehicle's interior for a factory look. But the sound will be anything but factory!

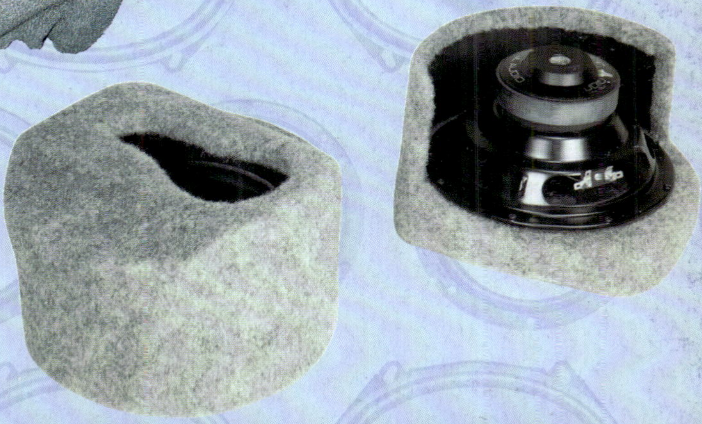

## Building a sealed enclosure

**01** Using 3/4-inch Medium Density Fiberboard (MDF) for the enclosure, mark the enclosure's measurements and carefully cut the boards

**02** Use the template supplied with the subwoofer or the subwoofer mounting ring to mark the positions of the holes, then cut out the holes with a jigsaw

**03** When putting the box together, run a bead of glue along the edges of the adjoining seams, then use screws to secure the panels to each other

**04** To prevent any air leaks, seal all the seams inside the box with a silicone sealant

**Warning:** Wear a filtering mask before cutting: MDF gives off an extremely fine dust which can be harmful to your health

**05** Using spray glue, cover the box with carpet that'll match your interior, then carefully cut out the holes. You'll also have to drill a hole for the speaker wires

**06** Follow the manufacturer's instructions for connecting the subwoofer wiring, then place them into the enclosure and mount them, also according to the manufacturer's instructions

**07** Be sure to bolt the sub box down so it doesn't roll around. A loose enclosure can be dangerous, particularly in a crash. The last thing you want during an accident is half a ton of unhappy speaker and box come hurtling in the passenger compartment to remind you they weren't bolted down!

**01** The trunk area was stripped of the spare tire to make room for the enclosure, and a support frame was constructed of 3/4-inch Medium Density Fiberboard (MDF)

**02** We fabricated rings to hold the subwoofers. The rings are tied in the center by a piece of MDF glued to the bottom, then secured by screws through the top

**03** We stretched speaker fabric over the top of the box, secured it with staples, then cut out the holes. Then we brushed a coat of fiberglass resin on both sides

**04** After the resin completely dried . . .

# Building a custom fiberglass enclosure

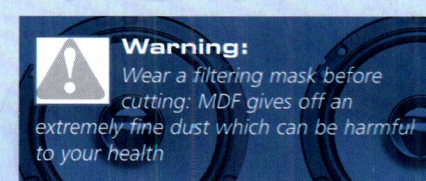

**Warning:** Wear a filtering mask before cutting: MDF gives off an extremely fine dust which can be harmful to your health

**05** . . . we reinforced the inside of the box with steel mesh and body filler

**06** We also applied a coat of body filler to the exterior to fill in any imperfections . . .

**07** . . . then sanded, primered and sanded again for a smooth surface that's ready for the paint shop

**08** After returning from the paint shop the box is placed in its final resting spot, then the subs are wired up and mounted

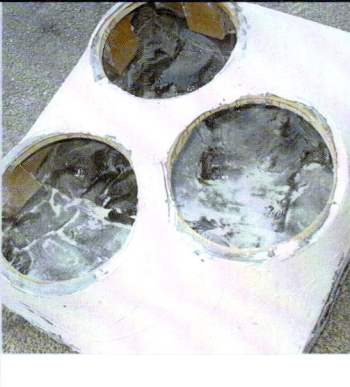
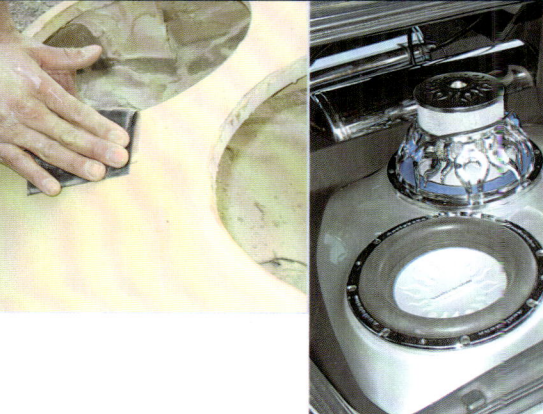

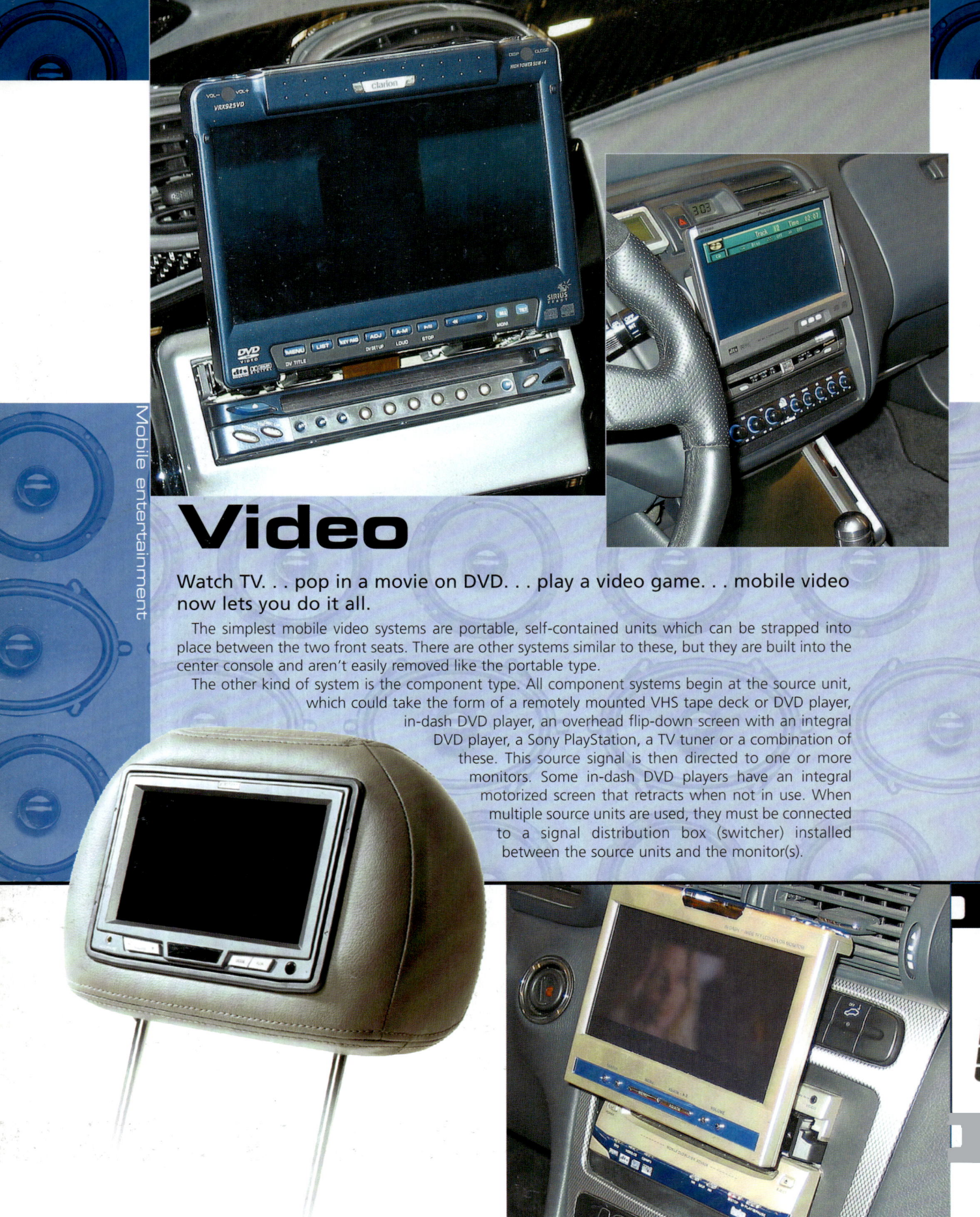

Mobile entertainment

# Video

Watch TV... pop in a movie on DVD... play a video game... mobile video now lets you do it all.

The simplest mobile video systems are portable, self-contained units which can be strapped into place between the two front seats. There are other systems similar to these, but they are built into the center console and aren't easily removed like the portable type.

The other kind of system is the component type. All component systems begin at the source unit, which could take the form of a remotely mounted VHS tape deck or DVD player, in-dash DVD player, an overhead flip-down screen with an integral DVD player, a Sony PlayStation, a TV tuner or a combination of these. This source signal is then directed to one or more monitors. Some in-dash DVD players have an integral motorized screen that retracts when not in use. When multiple source units are used, they must be connected to a signal distribution box (switcher) installed between the source units and the monitor(s).

Monitor types include the already-mentioned in-dash motorized screen, sunshade monitors, headrest monitors, flip-down overhead console monitors, center console monitors, and monitors that can be mounted on a pedestal or bracket just about anywhere in the vehicle that there's enough room. Just keep in mind that no screen visible to the driver can be operational when the vehicle is in motion.

Video game consoles can be integrated into the system by the use of a signal distribution box and a power inverter that converts 12 volts DC into 110 volts AC. And, with the use of the proper switchbox, a video game can be played on one monitor while a movie is watched on another.

Another neat option that's available with some systems are infrared headphones that allow passengers to listen to the movie or game audio track without the hassle of cords that could get in the way. The infrared signal on these systems is broadcast from transmitters embedded in the monitor housings or from a remote transmitter, usually mounted on the headliner or at the rear of the overhead console where the line-of-sight between the transmitter and headphone will be uninterrupted.

Audio can also be piped through the vehicle's existing speakers. If you've upgraded your audio system with a surround sound system, your passengers will be able to enjoy a near-theatre experience. Just don't let them spill their drinks on the floor, throw bon-bons at the screen or stick their chewing gum to the underside of the seats!

# Security

## 10

## Avoiding trouble

Those shiny wheels and flashy paint are like a billboard to car thieves and bandits looking for expensive sound system components to sell on the black market. And you've got to be careful when and where you choose to show off your car's mobile entertainment, and to whom. Be especially discreet the nearer you get to home - turn your system down before you get near home, for instance, or you might draw unwelcome attention to where that car with the loud stereo's parked at night.

If you're going out, think about where you're parking - somewhere well-lit and reasonably well-populated is the best bet.

If you're lucky enough to have a garage, use it. And always use all the security you have, whenever you leave the car, even if it's a tedious chore to put on that steering wheel lock. Just do it.

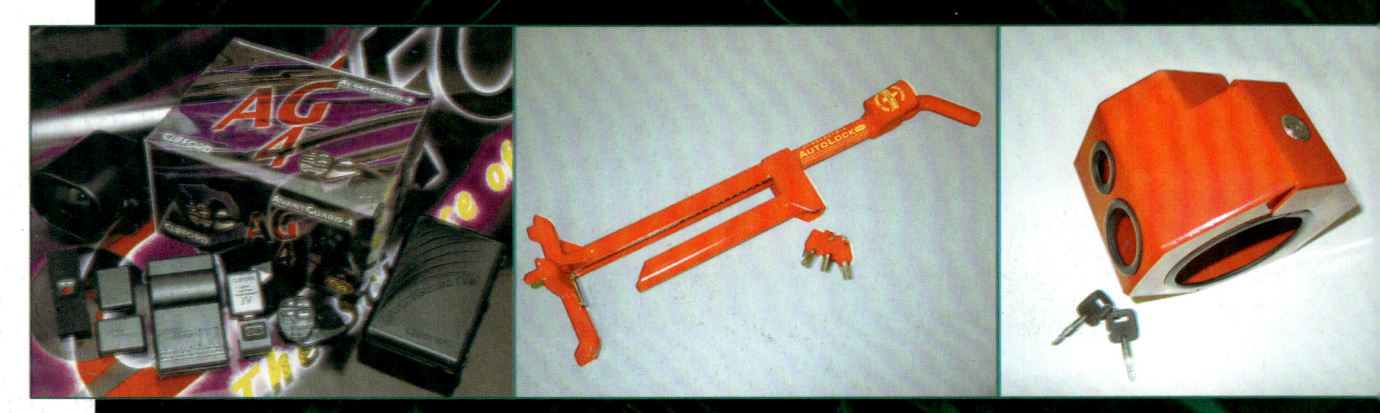

# Alarms

Alarm systems are available in many different packages depending on cost and complexity. Here are just a few examples of types of alarm system sensors designed for different types of protection.

A more sophisticated alarm will feature shock sensing (which could be set off by a thief attempting to steal your tires); this type of sensor monitors the impact/vibration level.

Ultrasonic sensors monitor an enclosed space inside of a vehicle (such as the passenger compartment) with

# Anti-theft devices

Other types of anti-theft devices are available as less expensive alternative to alarms.

An automobile equipped with a steering wheel lock or a removable steering wheel could make your car a less likely target for a thief. Also available are locking covers for the steering column which can help prevent a thief from being able to access the ignition lock, and devices that prevent the brake or clutch pedal from being depressed. Whatever your choice may be, now every time you park, at least you can relax a little. Remember, though, there's no guarantee that installing an alarm or security device will make any difference to a determined thief or mindless vandal.

If your vehicle is equipped with an alarm system or an anti-theft device, you may be eligible for discounted insurance premiums. Certain companies offer a higher percentage discount for vehicles that have more sophisticated alarm system packages. Each insurance company will have their own guidelines and insurance discounts. Contact your insurance representative for all the specific details.

# Wiring basics

## Security

ultrasonic sound waves. If the sensor detects a change in the sound waves the alarm will sound.

Field Disturbance Sensors protect an area with an energy shield. Similar to ultrasonic sensors, FDS sensors monitor the space inside of a vehicle. They are often used to protect the passenger compartment of a convertible with the top down.

Pin switches typically monitor the doors, hoods or trunks by completing the circuit and activating the alarm when one of these has been opened.

Many suppliers have designed security systems not only to protect a vehicle; some are designed to give added convenience with packages that allow you to add onto the alarm network, such as keyless entry, power window control or remote starting capability. When purchasing an alarm, be sure to take the time and study each kit and their advantages and shortcomings.

With your wires identified, how to tap into them? The three best options are:

**a** **Soldering** - *avoids cutting through your chosen wire - strip away a short section of insulation, wrap your new wire around the bared section, then apply solder to secure it. If you're a bit new to soldering, practice on a few spare pieces of wire first.*

**b** **Bullet connectors** - *cut and strip the end of your chosen wire, wrap your new one to it, push both into one half of the bullet. Connect the other end of your victim wire to the other bullet, and connect together. Always use the "female" half on any live feed - it'll be safer if you disconnect it than a male bullet, which could touch bare metal and send your car up in smoke.*

**c** **Block connectors** - *easy to use. Just remember that the wires can come adrift if the screws aren't really tight, and don't get too ambitious about how many wires you can stuff in one hole (block connectors, like bullets, are available in several sizes).*

With any of these options, always insulate around your connection - especially when soldering, or you'll be leaving bare metal exposed. Remember that you'll probably be shoving all the wires up into the dark recesses of the under-dash area - by the time the wires are nice and kinked/squashed together, that tiny bit of protruding wire might just touch that bit of metal bodywork.

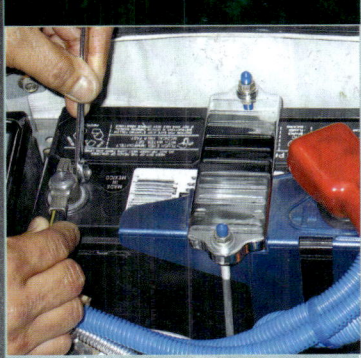
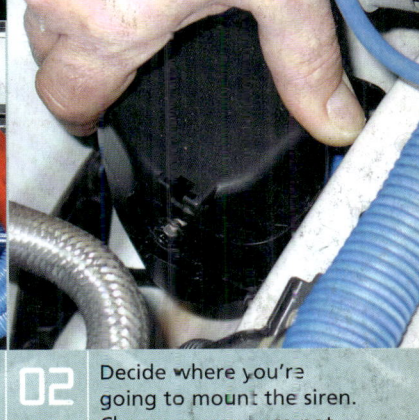

**01** Disconnect the cable from the negative battery terminal, and move the cable away from the battery. This will probably wipe out your stereo settings, but it's better than having sparks flying and your new alarm chirping during installation

**02** Decide where you're going to mount the siren. Choose somewhere not easily reached from underneath. Try the siren in position before deciding. It's also best to pick a location away from where you'll be adding fluids to the window washer reservoir, oil to the engine or coolant to the radiator. Loosely fit the alarm to the bracket, to help you decide how well it'll fit in your chosen spot, then take the alarm away

# Alarm installation

Installing an alarm system can be one of the best investments you make in your car. Most alarms are fairly easy to install. We'll run through a typical installation here, but you should follow the specific instructions that will come with the alarm you chose.

**Warning:** Whenever working on a vehicle equipped with an airbag (or airbags), be sure to disable the airbag system before working in the vicinity of any airbag system components. This is especially important when working around the instrument panel and center console. Consult the Haynes Automotive Repair Manual for your vehicle for the airbag disabling procedure. If no manual exists, consult a dealer service department or other qualified repair shop to obtain the information. Also, NEVER splice or tap into any wiring for the airbag system, and never use a test light or multimeter on airbag system wiring. On most vehicles the wiring for the airbag system is yellow, or is covered by yellow conduit, or at the very least will have yellow electrical connectors.

Mark the position of the mounting holes, then carefully drill the holes (make sure there's nothing behind the panel you're drilling). Once you've got the bracket where you want it, install and tighten the mounting bracket screws

The next stage is to sort your wiring. The amount of wiring, and where you'll want to run it, will depend on your alarm. If, like us, you've got wires coming from the siren which should be fed into the car, you'll need to feed them through somehow. We chose a cover on the firewall, which we removed, then drilled a hole big enough for the wires to pass through

Clean up any rough edges from the hole, then insert a grommet. If you don't, there's a good chance the wires will chafe through on the metal edges

If you've got several wires to go through, as we did, tape them together into a makeshift "loom", which will make it much easier to poke the wires through

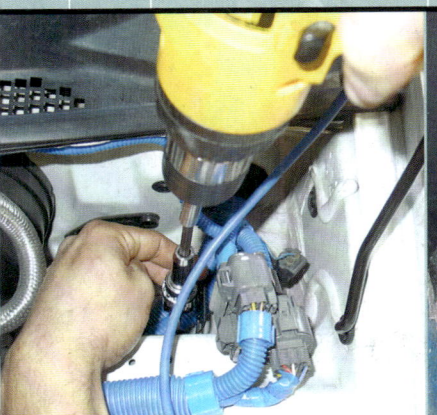
**03**

**04**

**05**

**06**

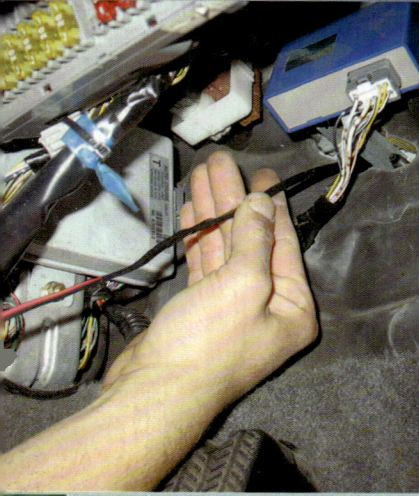

**07** After moving inside the car, with the help of an assistant, the alarm wiring was soon poked through. It's worth sealing any holes you make in the firewall (with silicone), to reduce the chance of water getting in. Make sure any wires running into the engine bay from the firewall run down and not up - this will minimize chances of water getting into your passenger compartment

**08** Slip in the siren and tighten the bolts

**09** All alarms worth having will have an LED to indicate the alarm status, and to hopefully deter thieves. The easiest option for mounting an LED is to pick one of the blank switches (if your vehicle is equipped with one), pry it out of the dash . . .

**10** . . . and drill it for the LED holder

The best way to connect to any existing wiring without cutting it is to solder on your new alarm wires. It's permanent, won't come loose, and doesn't mess up the original circuit. Strip a little insulation off your target wire and the end of the alarm wire. Twist one around the other, if possible **15**

**16** Now bring in the soldering iron, heat the connection, and join the wires together with solder (be careful not to burn yourself, the dash, or the surrounding wires!)

**17** Remember - whatever method you use for joining the new wires (and especially if you're soldering) - insulate the new connection big-time. The last thing you want is false alarms, other electrical problems, or even a fire, caused by poorly-insulated connections.

**18** Many alarms require you to link into the turn signal circuit, so the lights flash during arming and disarming. On our vehicle, the turn signal circuit could be accessed at the fuse panel. After temporarily reconnecting the battery and switching on the indicators, we test with our meter, and find this to be true

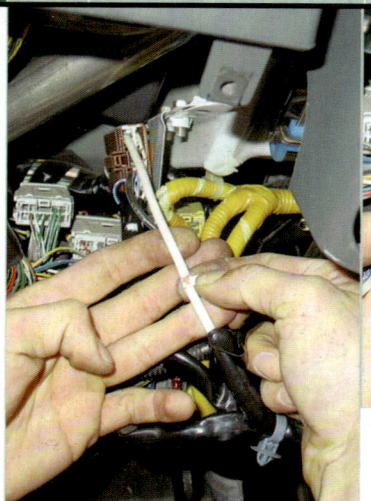

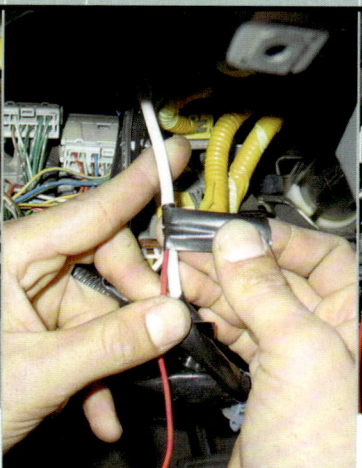

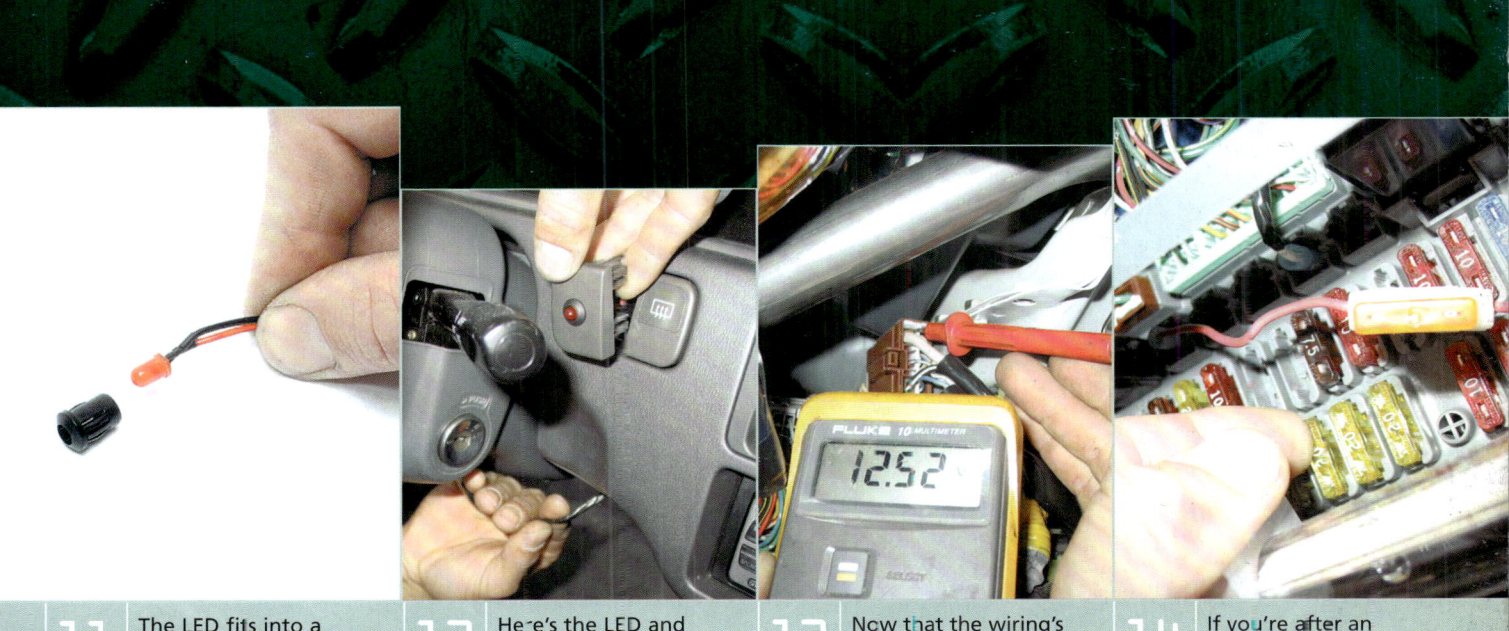

**11** The LED fits into a holder, which then fits into the hole. Assemble the LED and holder before installing

**12** Here's the LED and holder being installed

**13** Now that the wiring's more or less in the right place, it's time to start connecting it up. Power and grounds can be sourced from the fuse panel. When you've found a likely suspect, use a 12-volt test light (available at just about any auto parts store) or voltmeter to confirm your suspicions. We found power at the back of a connector for the steering column

**14** If you're after an ignition power circuit, probe the wire with the voltmeter or test light tip (or push it carefully into the back of the wiring connector) and attach the clip to a good ground (like one of the door pin switch screws) - check that it's a switched circuit by temporarily reconnecting the battery and turning the ignition on and off, which should turn power on and off. It's best to tap into the fused side of any wire - to check for this, pull the fuse from the fuse panel, and make sure your chosen wire goes dead

The control unit requires its own ground. Find a spot to mount it to the vehicle chassis. Be sure to sand off any paint so that the connection is made directly to metal **19**

Next on our wire target list - the power locks. With luck, finding the doors "lock" and "unlock" trigger wires shouldn't be difficult. The most likely place to find them is in the driver's door harness. More stripping and soldering had these wires joined to the relevant ones **20**

So come on - does it work? Most alarms require you to "program in" the remotes before they'll work. Test all the alarm features in turn, remembering to follow the alarm's instructions. Set the anti-shock sensitivity with a thought to where you live and park - will it be set off every night by the neighbor's cat, or by kids playing football? Finally, and most important of all - next time you park, remember to set it ! **21**

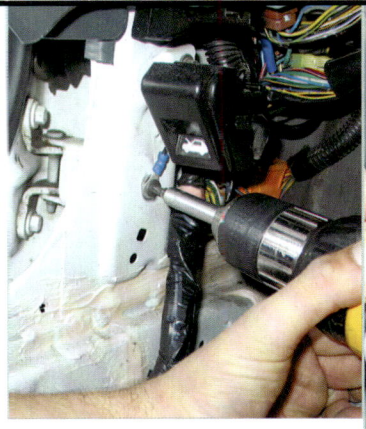

# Remote
# Power locks

Security

If your ride doesn't have power locks, don't despair - there are several kits out there to help you towards your goal. Hopefully, the details below, together with your kit's instructions, will help you out.

**01** First, remove the door trim panel. Most door panels are secured by a few screws, and push-in plastic fasteners around the perimeter of the panel (if necessary refer to the Haynes Automotive Repair Manual for your vehicle). Carefully peel back the plastic sheet from the door, ideally without ripping it

**06** . . . then, it's going to get a trim

**07** Connect the rods with the supplied clamp . . .

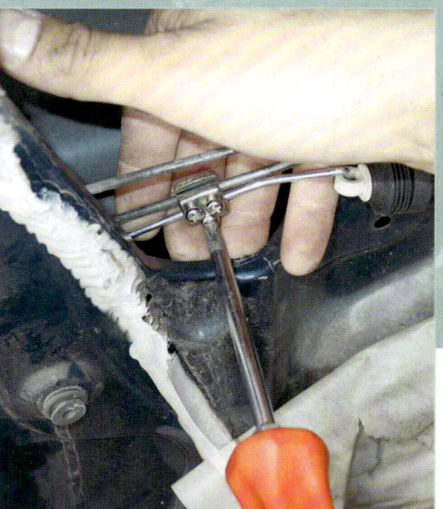

**08** . . . then fasten the clamp screws tight

  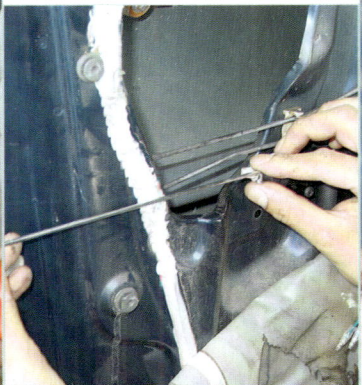 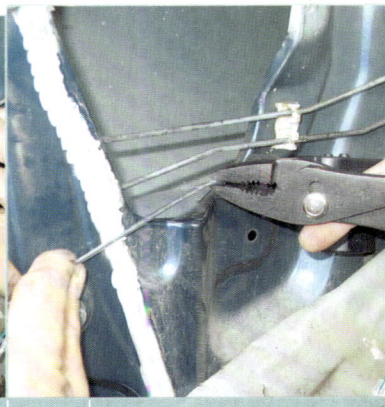

**02** The new lock solenoids must be mounted so they work in the same plane as the door lock buttons. What this means is it's no good having the lock solenoid plungers moving vertically, to work a button and rod which operate horizontally! Try it in place, and see where it can be mounted. Looks like we need to drill holes for this one . . .

**03** . . . then, once the holes are drilled, screws mount it to the door.

**04** The kit contains several items which look like bike spokes - these are your new lock operating rods, which join the door lock button operating rod to the lock solenoid

**05** This mounting location is going to require the solenoid rod to be bent a little . . .

**09** That's the mechanical side done, all that's left to do now is the wiring

**10** You've got to feed the solenoid wires through the door and into the car . . .

**11** . . . normally there's a handy rubber boot at the door edge you can pry out and feed the wires through into the passenger compartment

**12** Once you've managed that, you can connect the wires to your alarm system's control unit "trigger inputs" and give it a try

# Glossary of terms

## A

**Air dam** - A panel across the bottom of a car's front end, designed to reduce the air pressure beneath the vehicle for a better ground effect. Air dams were originally used only on race cars, but are now used on a wide variety of sporty street vehicles as well.

**Airfoil** - An aerodynamic device used to improve traction by increasing the down force on either end of the vehicle. In cross-section, an airfoil is basically an inverted wing; instead of providing lift as in an airplane, the airfoil pushes the car closer to the ground. The use of airfoils (also called wings) increases the cornering capability of a vehicle and improves stability at speed, but at the expense of additional aerodynamic drag.

**Air gap** - Space between spark plug electrodes, starting motor and generator armatures, field shoes, etc.

**Air pressure** - Atmospheric pressure (14.7 psi).

**Air scoop** - An aerodynamic device or opening used to duct cool outside air to some part of the vehicle, generally the carburetor or throttle body, the brakes, the radiator or an oil cooler.

**Allen wrench** - A hexagonal wrench which fits into a recessed hexagonal hole.

**All-wheel-drive (AWD)** - A vehicle drivetrain with every wheel under power. On a four-wheeled vehicle, all-wheel-drive generally refers to a full-time four-wheel-drive system with a center differential.

**Ambient air temperature** - The temperature of the surrounding air.

**Analog gauge** - A gauge with a sweep (moving) needle that points to visible increments printed on the face of the instrument (as opposed to a *digital gauge*, which displays on numerical *digit*, or value, at a time).

**Analog instrument** - A display which shows some physical quantity, such as mph, voltage or fuel supply, with a movable needle on a dial. Most expert drivers feel that the variable position of the needle makes and analog instrument easier to read at a quick glance than a digital instrument.

**Aspect ratio** - The ratio of section height to section width on a tire.

**Atmospheric pressure** - The pressure exerted by the earth's atmosphere at any given point, and altitude, above or below sea level. The atmospheric pressure is calculated by multiplying the mass of the atmospheric column of the unit area above the given point and of the gravitational acceleration at the given point. It's also the common term used to denote a value of standard or normal atmospheric pressure equivalent to the pressure exerted by a column of mercury 29.92 inches (760mm) high.

**Axleshaft** - A single rotating shaft, on either side of the differential, which delivers power from the final drive assembly to the drive wheels. Also called a *halfshaft*.

## B

**Balance shaft(s)** - The rotating shaft or shafts, incorporating eccentric counterweights, designed to counter-act the natural vibration of other reciprocating parts, such as the pistons, connecting rods and crankshaft.

**Balancing** - The process of checking every engine part for conformity to its specified dimensions. The specified working clearances for all moving parts are also checked. Balancing improves engine performance, smoothness and reliability. Also referred to as *blueprinting*.

**Black smoke** - Incompletely burned fuel in the exhaust.

**Block** - The lower part of the engine containing the cylinders; the block is the basic framework of the engine.

**Block deck** - The cylinder head gasket surface.

**Blowby** - The leakage of the compressed air-fuel mixture or the burned gases from the combustion chamber past the piston rings and into the crankcase. this leakage results in power loss and oil contamination.

**Blower** - A pump-like device which forces air into the cylinders at higher-than-atmospheric pressure. Because of this higher pressure, the cylinder gets more air per intake stroke, which means it can burn more fuel, which means more horsepower. There are two types of blowers - A turbocharger uses some of the waste heat energy in the exhaust gases to drive a compressor and pump the air; a belt-driven supercharger uses engine power to pump air. The term also refers to the *blower motor fan* assembly in the heating/air conditioning system.

**Blue smoke** - Caused by blowby allowing crankcase oil in the combustion chamber due to bad rings, valve seals or other faulty components.

**Bottom end** - A term which refers collectively to the engine block, crankshaft, main bearings and the big ends of the connecting rods.

**Brake balance** - The ratio of front-to-rear breaking force.

**Brake bleeding** - Procedure for removing air from lines of a hydraulic brake system.

**Brake booster** - A mechanical device (usually air, vacuum or hydraulically actuated) that attaches to the brake system and multiplies the driver's force input to reduce the effort normally required to stop the vehicle. Such braking systems are commonly referred to as *power-assisted, vacuum-assisted, hydraulically-assisted* or simply *power brakes*. In most vehicles, the boost comes from intake vacuum.

**Brake caliper** - The component of a disc brake that converts hydraulic pressure into mechanical energy.

**Brake cylinder** - A cylinder in which a movable piston converts pressure to mechanical force to move brake shoes against the breaking surface of the drum or rotor.

**Brake disc** - The component of a disc brake that rotates with the wheels and is squeezed by the brake caliper and pads, which creates friction and converts the energy of the moving vehicle into heat. Also referred to as a brake *rotor*.

**Brake drum** - The component of a drum brake that rotates with the wheel and is acted upon by the expanding brake shoes, which creates friction and converts the energy of the moving vehicle into heat.

**Brake dust** - The dust created as the brake linings wear down in normal use. Brake dust usually contains dangerous amounts of asbestos.

**Brake "fade"** - A condition in which repeated severe applications of brakes cause expansion of brake drum or loss of frictional ability or both, which results in impaired braking efficiency.

**Brake fluid** - A compounded liquid for use in hydraulic brake systems, which must meet exacting conditions (impervious to heat, freezing, thickening, bubbling, etc.).

**Brake flushing** - A procedure for removing fluid from a brake system and washing out sediment.

**Brake horsepower (bhp)** - The power produced by the engine (as measured at the output shaft) that is available for driving the vehicle. It's called brake horsepower because the shaft power is usually measured by an absorption dynamometer or *brake*.

**Brake lines** - The rigid metal tubing connecting the master cylinder to the brake calipers and/or wheel cylinders in a hydraulic brake system. Flexible brake hoses usually bridge the gap between the rigid metal lines and calipers/wheel cylinders to allow for the up-and-down motion of the suspension.

**Brake pads** - On disc-brake systems, the replaceable friction pads that pinch the brake disc when the brakes are applied. Brake pads consist of an organic or metallic friction material bonded or riveted to a rigid backing plate.

**Brake shoe** - The crescent-shaped carrier to which the friction linings are mounted and which force the lining against the rotating drum during braking.

**Brake system cleaner** - A type of solvent designed exclusively for cleaning brake system components. It will not destroy plastic, rubber or synthetic rubber components and it dries quickly, without leaving a residue.

**Break-in** - The period of operation between installation of new or rebuilt parts and the point in time at which the parts are worn to the correct fir. The time or mileage period during which the rough edges and friction between newly assembled moving parts and surfaces are gradually reduced. Generally calls for moderate loads and driving at reduced and varying speed for a specified mileage to permit parts to wear to the correct fit.

**Butt connector** - A solderless connector used to permanently join two wire ends together.

## C

**Caliper** - The non-rotating part of a disc-brake assembly that straddles the disc and contains the hydraulic components that pinch the disc when the brakes are applied. A caliper is also a measuring tool that can be set to measure inside or outside dimensions of an object; used for measuring things like the thickness of a block, the diameter of a shaft or the bore of a hole (inside caliper).

**Camber** - In wheel alignment, it is the outward or inward tilt of a wheel at it's top.

**Camshaft** - A rotating shaft on which a series of *cam lobes* operate the valve mechanisms. The camshaft is driven by gears or sprockets and a timing chain. usually referred to simply as the *cam*.

**Caster** - In wheel alignment, the backward or forward tilt of the steering axis. The angle between the steering axis and the vertical plane, as viewed from the side. Caster is considered positive when the steering axis is inclined rearward at the top.

**Catalytic converter** - A muffler-like device in the exhaust system that catalyzes a chemical reaction which converts certain air pollutants in the exhaust gases into less harmful substances.

**Center of gravity** - Point of a body from which it could be suspended, or on which it could be supported, and be in balance. For example, the center of gravity of a wheel is the center of the wheel hub.

**Chassis** - A French word meaning framework of a vehicle without a body and fenders. Generally speaking, the suspension, steering and braking components of a vehicle are all regarded as part of the chassis.

**Check Engine light** - A light on the instrument panel that lets the drive know of any detectable engine management system malfunctions. Also used as an emissions maintenance reminder light on some vehicles. Often, when this light is on, a trouble code is stored in the computer.

**Closed loop fuel control** - The normal operating mode for a fuel injection system. Once the engine is warmed up the computer can interpret an analog voltage signal from an exhaust gas oxygen sensor and alter the air/fuel ratio accordingly through the fuel injectors.

**Compressor** - An air conditioning component which pumps, circulates and increases the pressure of refrigerant vapor. Also, the part of a turbocharger that compresses the intake air or air/fuel mixture.

**Control head** - The dashboard mounted assembly which houses the mode selector, the blower switch and the temperature control lever of the heating, air conditioning and ventilation system.

**CV joint boot** - The flexible, accordion-pleated rubber dust boot which encloses the constant velocity joint and the end of the axleshaft attached to it. The CV joint boot prevents dirt, dust, mud and moisture from entering the CV joint.

# D

**Disc brake** - A brake design incorporating a flat, disc-like rotor onto which brake pads containing lining material are squeezed, generating friction and converting the energy of a moving vehicle into heat.

**Displacement** - The total volume of an engine's cylinders, usually measured in cubic inches, cubic centimeters or liters. The total volume of air-fuel mixture an engine is theoretically capable of drawing into all cylinders during one operating cycle. Also refers to the volume swept out by the piston as it moves from bottom dead center to top dead center. One liter equals 1000 cubic centimeters, which equals 61 cubic inches.

**Distributor** - In the ignition system on a spark-ignition engine, a mechanical device designed to switch a high voltage secondary circuit from an ignition coil to the spark plugs in the proper firing sequence. On diesel engines, a valve, often rotary in design, which conducts a vapor or fluid to a number of outlets. For example, diesel engine oil distributors.

**Double-overhead cam (DOHC)** - An engine that uses two overhead camshafts, one for the intake valves and one for the exhaust valves. The cams are driven by a timing chain or by a timing belt.

**Double-wishbone suspension** - Another name for a double-A-arm suspension. A suspension system using two wishbones, or A-arms to connect the chassis to the spindle or knuckle.

**Dry sump** - A lubrication system in which the engine's supply of oil isn't contained in the crankcase (sump), but is pumped to the engine from an external container. Allows the crankcase to be reduced in size and the engine to be installed lower in size and the engine to be installed lower in the chassis, and eliminates the oil starvation most conventional oiling systems suffer when subjected to the acceleration, braking and cornering forces generated by a racing vehicle.

**Dynamometer** - A device for measuring the power output, or brake horsepower, of an engine. An engine dynamometer measures the power output at the flywheel.

# E

**Engine block** - The iron or aluminum casting which encloses the crankshaft, connecting rods, connecting rods and pistons.

**Engine displacement** - The sum of piston displacement of all engine cylinders.

# F

**Firewall** - The insulated partition between the engine and the passenger compartment.

**Flywheel** - A heavy, usually metal, spinning wheel in which energy is absorbed and stored by means of momentum. On cars, this heavy metal wheel that's attached to the crankshaft to smooth out firing impulses. It provides inertia to keep the crankshaft turning smoothly during periods when no power is being applied. It also serves as part of the clutch and engine cranking systems.

**Foot-pound** - A unit of measurement for work, equal to lifting one pound one foot.

**Foot-pound (tightening)** - A unit of measurement for torque, equal to one pound of pull one foot from the center of the object being tightened.

**Four-cycle engine** - An engine in which a power stroke occurs every other revolution of the crankshaft. A cycle is considered 1/2 revolution of the crankshaft. The four strokes are intake, compression, power and exhaust. Also known as an *Otto cycle*, for the German Nicolaus August Otto, who built and developed the four-stroke cycle engine.

**Frame** - The structural load-carrying members of a vehicle that support the engine and body and are in turn supported by the wheels.

# G

**Ground (GND or GRND)** - The negatively charged side of a circuit. A ground can be a wire, the negative side of the battery or even the vehicle chassis. The connection made in grounding a circuit. In a single-wire system, any metal part of the car's structure that's directly or indirectly attached to the battery's negative post. Used to conduct current from a load back to the battery. Self-grounded components are attached directly to a grounded metal part through their mounting screws. Components mounted to ungrounded parts of a vehicle require a ground wire attached to a known good ground. Often, a single electrical ground is used as a common ground for a number of electric circuits in one area on the vehicle. The voltage potential of a ground should always be zero, or very near zero.

# H

**Halfshaft** - A rotating shaft that transmits power from the final drive unit to the drive wheels, but usually refers to the two shafts that connect the wheels to the final drive with independent rear suspension or front-wheel drive rather than the axleshafts of a live rear axle.

**Horsepower** - A measure of mechanical power, or the rate at which work is done. One horsepower is the amount of power required to lift 550 pounds one foot per second. One horsepower equals 33,000 ft-lbs of work per minute. It's the amount of power necessary to raise 33,000 pounds a distance of one foot in one minute.

# I

**Ignition system** - The system responsible for igniting fuel in the cylinders. Includes the ignition module, the coil, the coil wire, the distributor, the spark plug wires, the plugs, and a voltage source.

**Independent suspension** - A suspension design in which the wheel on one side of the vehicle may rise or fall independently of the wheel on the other side. Thus, a disturbance affecting one wheel has no effect on the other wheel.

**Intercooler** - A radiator used to reduce the temperature of the compressed air or air/fuel mixture before it enters the combustion chamber.

**Internal combustion engine** - An engine that burns its fuel within cylinders and converts the power of this burning directly into mechanical work.

# K

**Knurl** - A roughened surface caused by a sharp wheel that displaces metal outward as its sharp edges push into the metal surface. To indent or roughen a finished surface.

# L

**Lateral acceleration** - Sideways acceleration created when a vehicle corners. As a result of this lateral acceleration, centrifugal force acts on the vehicle and tries to pull it outward. The tires develop an equal and opposite force acting against the road to counteract this outward force. The side thrust generated by the tires in any corner is proportional to the mass and the velocity squared, inversely proportional to the radius of the corner. Steady-state lateral acceleration is usually measured on a *skidpad*, a flat smooth expanse of pavement with a circle marked on it.

**Lean** - A term used to describe an air/fuel mixture that's got either too much air or too little fuel.

**Limited slip differential (LSD)** - A differential that uses cone or disc clutches to lock the two independent axleshafts together, forcing both wheels to transmit their respective drive torque regardless of the available traction. It allows a limited amount of slip between the two axleshafts to accommodate the differential action. This design doubles the number of drive wheels in low-traction situation.

**Lower arm** - The suspension arm which connects the vehicle chassis to the bottom of the steering knuckle.

**Lubrication system** - The series of passages in the engine block and cylinder head that carries oil to all the bearing surfaces of the crankshaft, connecting rods, cylinder walls, camshaft(s), valve train, etc. The lubrication system also includes the oil pump pickup, the screen or filter, and the pump itself.

**Lug nuts** - The nuts used to secure the wheels to a vehicle.

# M

**Manifold** - Any device designed to collect, route and/or distribute air, air/fuel mixture, exhaust gases, fluids, etc. In air conditioning, a device which controls refrigerant flow for system test purposes by means of hand valves which can open or close various passageways connected together inside the manifold. Used in conjunction with manifold gauges and service hoses.

**Master cylinder** - In brake systems, a cylinder containing a movable piston actuated by foot pressure, producing hydraulic pressure to push fluid through the lines and wheel cylinders and force the brake linings or pads against a drum or disc. In hydraulic clutch systems, a similar device is used to push hydraulic fluid into a slave cylinder which activates the clutch release arm with a rod.

# N

**Normally-aspirated** - An engine which draws its air/fuel mixture into its cylinders solely by piston-created vacuum, i.e. not supercharged or turbocharged. Also referred to as Naturally Aspirated.

# O

**Overdrive** - Any arrangement of gearing which produces more revolutions of the driven shaft than the driving shaft. On some vehicles, this is achieved by adding a small gearbox behind the transmission;

on others, the overdrive gear is integral with the main transmission. In either case, an overdrive gear provides a taller gear in addition to the three or four lower gears. The advantages of overdrive include reduced fuel consumption, lower engine noise and reduced engine wear.

**Overhaul** - To completely disassemble a unit, clean and inspect all parts, reassemble it with the original or new parts and make all adjustments necessary for proper operation.

**Overhead cam (ohc) engine** - An engine with the camshaft(s) located on top of the cylinder head(s) instead of in the engine block. This design eliminates pushrods; some designs also dispense with the rocker arms too. The advantage of an ohc engine are quicker and more accurate valve response because of the shorter path between the cam(s) and the valves.

**Oversteer** - A handling characteristic that necessitates less steering lock as the vehicle speed increases around a constant-radius turn. An oversteering vehicle breaks away at the rear, so the driver must countersteer with the front wheels and possibly apply opposite lock to keep the vehicle from spinning.

# P

**Pad** - Disc brake friction material generally molded to metal backing, or shoe.

**Panhard rod** - A locating link running laterally across the vehicle, with its upper end attached to the body and its lower end attached to a live axle, beam axle or DeDion axle. The Panhard rod provides lateral location of the axle. Also known as a *track bar*.

**Pinion** - A small gear which engages a larger geared wheel or rack. Pinions are used in rack-and-pinion steering gearboxes and in the differential ring-and-pinion set.

**Piston** - The partly-hollow, cylindrical part attached to the connecting rod, that moves up and down in the cylinder as the crankshaft rotates. When the fuel charge is fired, the piston transfers the force of the explosion to the connecting rod, then to the crankshaft.

**Port injection** - A fuel injection system in which the fuel is sprayed by individual injectors into each intake port, upstream of the intake valve.

**Power** - The rate at which work is done. If work is expressed in foot-pounds and time in seconds, the unit of power is one foot-pound per second. This unit is inconveniently small, so a larger unit called *horsepower* is commonly used.

# Q

**Quartz halogen bulb** - A bulb with a quartz envelope holding the tungsten filament and filled with an inert gas containing iodine or another of the five halogen gases. The gas serves to remove the tungsten deposits from the bulb wall and redeposit them on the filament, thus preventing blackening of the bulb surface and reduction in light output. This kind of cycle requires very high filament and operating temperatures, in turn necessitating the use of quartz instead of glass but producing more lighting power per watt of electrical power.

# R

**Rack-and-pinion steering** - A steering system with a pinion gear on the end of the steering shaft that mates with a rack (think of a geared wheel opened up and laid flat). When the steering wheel is turned, the pinion turns, moving the rack to the left or right. This movement is transmitted through the tie-rods to the steering arms at the wheels.

**Relay** - An electromechanical device which enables one circuit to open or close another circuit. A relay is usually operated by a low current circuit, but it controls the opening and closing of another circuit of higher current capacity.

**Roll** - A rotating motion about a longitudinal center line through the vehicle that causes the springs on one side of the vehicle to compress and those on the other side to extend.

**Rollbar** - A hoop of tubular steel installed behind the driver and extending above his head and across the vehicle. The rollbar helps protect the driver from injury if the vehicle rolls over.

**Roll cage** - A tubular steel structure incorporating a rollbar plus additional bars along the doors, windshield header, roof rails, etc. built into some racing vehicles to help protect the driver from injury if the vehicle rolls over, is impacted by another vehicle or crashes. Adding a roll cage usually increases chassis strength and stiffness, making for more predictable and consistent handling characteristics.

**Roll center** - That point about which the body rolls when cornering.

**rpm** - Engine speed, measured in crankshaft *revolutions per minute*.

# S

**Shock absorber** - A hydraulic and/or pneumatic device which provides mechanical or hydraulic friction to control the excessive deflection of the vehicle's springs. Also referred to as a *damper*.

**Stabilizer bar** - A transverse bar linking both sides (either front or rear) of the suspension, generally taking the form of a torsion bar with rubber bushing mounts on the chassis that allow it to turn freely. The ends of the bar are connected to or shaped as lever arms with attachments to the suspension linkages at each side via balljoint or rubber-bushed pivot links. The effect on a bump that both wheels take equally is to allow the wheels to move the same amount without deflecting the stabilizer bar. However, individual wheel movement or body roll will force the bar to twist as the lever arms are moved in different directions or amounts, thereby adding the bar's own spring rate to that of the vehicle's springs. The stabilizer bar's main function is to reduce roll, but it influences overall handling characteristics as well. Installing a front stabilizer bar increases understeer; installing one at the rear increases oversteer. Also referred to as an *anti-sway bar*, an *anti-roll bar* or simply a *roll bar*.

**Strut** - A type of front suspension system devised by Earle MacPherson at Ford of England. In its original form, this layout used a simple lateral link with the stabilizer bar to create the lower control arm. A long *strut* - an integral coil spring and shock absorber - was mounted between the body and the steering knuckle. Many modern MacPherson strut systems use a conventional lower A-arm and don't rely on the stabilizer bar for location.

**Subframe** - A partial frame that is sometimes bolted to the chassis of unit-body vehicles. It can be used to support the engine, transmission and/or suspension instead of having these components bolted directly to the main body structure. This more expensive design generally results in better road isolation and less harshness.

**Supercharger** - A mechanically-driven device that pressurizes the intake air, thereby increasing the density of charge air and the consequent power output from a given engine displacement. Superchargers are usually belt-driven by the engine crankshaft pulley.

# T

**Timing** - Delivery of the ignition spark or operation of the valves (in relation to the piston position) for the power stroke.

**Toe-in** - The amount the front wheels are closer together in front than at the rear when viewed from the front of the vehicle. A slight amount of toe-in is usually specified to keep the front wheels running parallel on the road by offsetting other forces that tend to spread the wheels apart.

**Torque** - A turning or twisting force, such as the force imparted on a fastener by a torque wrench. Usually expressed in foot-pounds (ft-lbs).

**Track** - The distance from the center of one front (or rear) tire (or wheel) to the other front (or rear) tire (or wheel) with the vehicle set to its normal ride height and wheel alignment specifications.

**Traction** - The amount of adhesion between the tire and ground.

**Turbocharger** - A centrifugal device, driven by exhaust gases, that pressurizes the intake air, thereby increasing the density of the charge air, and therefore the resulting power output, from a given engine displacement.

# U

**Unit body** - A type of body/frame construction in which the body of the vehicle, its floor pan and the chassis form a single structure. Such a design is generally lighter and more rigid than a vehicle with a separate body and frame.

# V

**Valve clearance** - The clearance between the valve tip (the end of the valve stem) and the rocker arm. The valve clearance is measured when the valve is closed.

**Valve duration** - The length of time, measured in degrees of engine crankshaft rotation, that the valve remains open.

# W

**Wheelbase** - The longitudinal distance between the centerlines of the front and rear axles.

**Wing** - An aerodynamic device, usually shaped like an upside-down aircraft wing, attached to a vehicle to induce downforce on either the front or rear end.

# Safety First

Regardless of how enthusiastic you may be about getting on with the job at hand, take the time to ensure that your safety is not jeopardized. A moment's lack of attention can result in an accident, as can failure to observe certain simple safety precautions. The possibility of an accident will always exist, and the following points should not be considered a comprehensive list of all dangers. Rather, they are intended to make you aware of the risks and to encourage a safety conscious approach to all work you carry out on your vehicle.

## Essential DOs and DON'Ts

**DON'T** rely on a jack when working under the vehicle. Always use approved jackstands to support the weight of the vehicle and place them under the recommended lift or support points.

**DON'T** attempt to loosen extremely tight fasteners (i.e. wheel lug nuts) while the vehicle is on a jack - it may fall.

**DON'T** start the engine without first making sure that the transmission is in Neutral (or Park where applicable) and the parking brake is set.

**DON'T** remove the cooling system pressure cap from a hot cooling system - let it cool or cover it with a cloth and release the pressure gradually.

**DON'T** attempt to drain the engine oil until you are sure it has cooled to the point that it will not burn you.

**DON'T** touch any part of the engine or exhaust system until it has cooled sufficiently to avoid burns.

**DON'T** siphon toxic liquids such as gasoline, antifreeze and brake fluid by mouth, or allow them to remain on your skin.

**DON'T** inhale brake lining dust - it is potentially hazardous (see **Asbestos**).

**DON'T** allow spilled oil or grease to remain on the floor - wipe it up before someone slips on it.

**DON'T** use loose fitting wrenches or other tools which may slip and cause injury.

**DON'T** push on wrenches when loosening or tightening nuts or bolts. Always try to pull the wrench toward you. If the situation calls for pushing the wrench away, push with an open hand to avoid scraped knuckles if the wrench should slip.

**DON'T** attempt to lift a heavy component alone - get someone to help you.

**DON'T** rush or take unsafe shortcuts to finish a job.

**DON'T** allow children or animals in or around the vehicle while you are working on it.

**DO** wear eye protection when using power tools such as a drill, sander, bench grinder, etc. and when working under a vehicle.

**DO** keep loose clothing and long hair well out of the way of moving parts.

**DO** make sure that any hoist used has a safe working load rating adequate for the job.

**DO** get someone to check on you periodically when working alone on a vehicle.

**DO** carry out work in a logical sequence and make sure that everything is correctly assembled and tightened.

**DO** keep chemicals and fluids tightly capped and out of the reach of children and pets.

**DO** remember that your vehicle's safety affects that of yourself and others. If in doubt on any point, get professional advice.

### Steering, suspension and brakes

These systems are essential to driving safety, so make sure you have a qualified shop or individual check your work. Also, compressed suspension springs can cause injury if released suddenly - be sure to use a spring compressor.

### Airbag

Airbags are explosive devices that can cause injury if they deploy while you're working on the car. Follow the manufacturer's instructions to disable the airbag whenever you're working in the vicinity of airbag components. Never use airbag system wiring when installing electronic components. When in doubt, check your vehicle's wiring diagram.

### Asbestos

Certain friction, insulating, sealing, and other products - such as brake linings, brake bands, clutch linings, torque converters, gaskets, etc. - may contain asbestos or other hazardous friction material. Extreme care must be taken to avoid inhalation of dust from such products, since it is hazardous to health. If in doubt, assume that they are harmful.

### Fire

Remember at all times that gasoline is highly flammable. Never smoke or have any kind of open flame around when working on a vehicle. But the risk does not end there. A spark caused by an electrical short circuit, by two metal surfaces contacting each other, by a tool falling on concrete, or even by static electricity built up in your body under certain conditions, can ignite gasoline vapors, which in a confined space are highly explosive. Do not, under any circumstances, use gasoline for cleaning parts. Use an approved safety solvent.

Always disconnect the battery ground (-) cable at the battery before working on any part of the fuel system or electrical system. Never risk spilling fuel on a hot engine or exhaust component. It is strongly recommended that a fire extinguisher suitable for use on fuel and electrical fires be kept handy in the garage or workshop at all times. Never try to extinguish a fuel or electrical fire with water.

### Fumes

Certain fumes are highly toxic and can quickly cause unconsciousness and even death if inhaled to any extent. Gasoline vapor falls into this category, as do the vapors from some cleaning solvents. Any draining or pouring of such volatile fluids should be done in a well ventilated area.

When using cleaning fluids and solvents, read the instructions on the container carefully. Never use materials from unmarked containers.

Never run the engine in an enclosed space, such as a garage. Exhaust fumes contain carbon monoxide, which is extremely poisonous. If you need to run the engine, always do so in the open air, or at least have the rear of the vehicle outside the work area.

### The battery

Never create a spark or allow a bare light bulb near a battery. They normally give off a certain amount of hydrogen gas, which is highly explosive.

Always disconnect the battery ground (-) cable at the battery before working on the fuel or electrical systems.

If possible, loosen the filler caps or cover when charging the battery from an external source (this does not apply to sealed or maintenance-free batteries). Do not charge at an excessive rate or the battery may burst.

Take care when adding water to a non maintenance-free battery and when carrying a battery. The electrolyte, even when diluted, is very corrosive and should not be allowed to contact clothing or skin.

Always wear eye protection when cleaning the battery to prevent the caustic deposits from entering your eyes.

### Household current

When using an electric power tool, inspection light, etc., which operates on household current, always make sure that the tool is correctly connected to its plug and that, where necessary, it is properly grounded. Do not use such items in damp conditions and, again, do not create a spark or apply excessive heat in the vicinity of fuel or fuel vapor.

### Secondary ignition system voltage

A severe electric shock can result from touching certain parts of the ignition system (such as the spark plug wires) when the engine is running or being cranked, particularly if components are damp or the insulation is defective. In the case of an electronic ignition system, the secondary system voltage is much higher and could prove fatal.

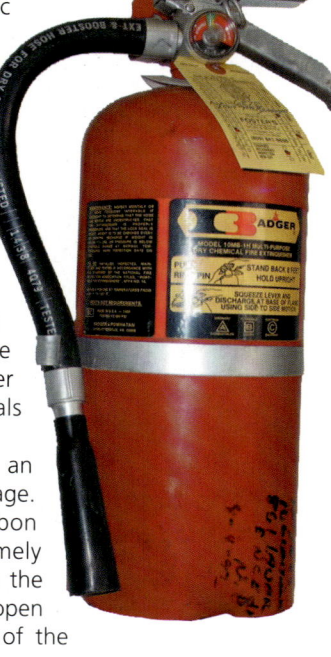

# Source List

**AEM (Advanced Engine Management)**
2205 126th St., Unit A
Hawthorne, CA 90250
(310) 484-2322
www.aempower.com

**APC**
22324 Temescal Canyon Rd.
Corona, CA 92883
(909) 898-9840
www.4apc.net

**A'PEX Integration**
(intercoolers, intakes, blow-off valves more)
330 West Taft
Orange, CA 92865
(714) 685-5700
www.apexi.com

**B&M Racing and Performance Parts**
(fuel system and many other parts)
9142 Independence Ave.
Chatsworth, CA 91311
(818) 882-6422
www.bmracing.com

**Blitz**
(intakes, turbo components, other parts)
4879 East La Palma Ave., Suite 202
Anaheim, CA 92807
(714) 777-9766
www.blitz-na.com

**Competition Cams**
(cams, valvetrain parts, ZEX nitrous kits)
3406 Democrat Road
Memphis, TN 38118
(888) 817-1008
www.zex.com

**Comptech USA**
(blower kits, Honda/Acura performance parts)
4717 Golden Foothill Parkway
El Dorado Hills, CA 95762
(916) 933-1080
www.comptechusa.com

**Clutch Masters**
267 E. Valley Blvd.
Rialto, CA 92376
(909) 877-6800
www.clutchmasters.com

**Crane Cams**
530 Fentress Blvd.
Daytona Beach, FL 32114
(386) 258-6174
www.cranecams.com

**Dart Industries**
(race cylinder heads and blocks)
353 Oliver Street
Troy, MI 48084
(248) 362-1188
www.dartheads.com

**DC Sports**
(cold air intakes, exhausts, other parts)
1451 East 6th Street
Corona, CA 92879
(909) 734-2020
www.dcsports.com

**Edelbrock Corp.**
(intake components, nitrous)
2700 California Street
Torrance, CA 90503
(310) 781-2222
www.edelbrock.com

**Flexalite**
(FAL fans)
P.O. Box 580
Milton, WA 98354
(253) 922-2700
www.flex-a-lite.com

**Fluidyne**
(aluminum radiators)
2505 East Cedar St.
Ontario, CA 91761
(800) 358-4396
www.fluidyne.com

**Focal America, Inc.**
ORCA Design and Manufacturing Corp.
1531 Lookout Dr.
Agoura, CA 91301
(818) 707-1629
www.focal-america.com

**Grant Products**
700 Allen Ave.
Glendale, CA 91201
(818) 247-2910
www.grantproducts.com

**GReddy Performance Products**
(large catalog of performance parts)
9 Vanderbilt
Irvine, CA 92618
(949) 588-8300
www.greddy.com

**Grillcraft Sport Grilles**
11651 Prairie Ave.
Hawthorne, CA 90250
(310) 970-0300
www.grillcraft.com

**Gude**
(camshafts, valvetrain, ported heads)
29885 2nd St., Suite Q
Lake Elsinore, CA 92530
www.gude.com

**Holley Performance Products**
(Airmass Exhaust, Holley Ignition, NOS, Earl's)
1801 Russellville Road, P.O. Box 10360
Bowling Green, KY 42102-7360
(800) Holley-1
www.holley.com

**Hondata**
(engine management electronics)
2341 W. 205th St, #106
Torrance, CA 90501
(301) 782-8278
www.hondata.com

**Innovative Turbo Systems**
845 Easy Street
Simi Valley, CA 93065
(805) 526-5400
www.innovativeturbo.com

**Jackson Racing**
(supercharger kits and more)
440 Rutherford Street
Goleta, CA 93117
(888) 888-4079
www.jacksonracing.com

**Jacobs Electronics**
2519 Dana Drive
Laurinburg, NC 28352
(800) 782-3379
www.jacobselectronics.com

**JE Pistons**
15312 Connector Lane
Huntington Beach, CA 92649
(714) 898-9763
www.jepistons.com

**Jet Performance Products**
(Computer chips)
17491 Apex Cir.
Huntington Beach, CA 92647
(714) 848-5515
www.jetchip.com

**K&N Engineering**
(air filters, intake kits)
P.O. Box 1329
Riverside, CA 92502
(888) 949-1832
www.knfilters.com

**Lokar Motorsports**
10924 Murdock Drive
Knoxville, TN 37932
(865) 966-2269
www.lokarmotorsports.com

**Midnight Performance**
(import tuning shop, products)
3324 Monier Circle, #1 and 2
Rancho Cordova, CA 95742
(916) 852-6887
www.midnightperformance.com

**Moore Performance**
(racing driveline components)
3740 Greenwood Street
San Diego, CA 92110
(619) 296-9180

>

# Source List

**MSD**
(ignition products)
1490 Henry Brennan Dr.
El Paso, TX 79936
(915) 857-5200
www.msdignition.com

**Neuspeed**
(full range of performance parts, accessories)
3300 Corte Malpaso
Camarillo, CA 93012
(800) 423-3623 Toll free
(805) 388-7171 Technical
(805) 388-8111 Distribution
www.neuspeed.com

**Nitrous Express (NX)**
1808 Southwest Parkway
Wichita Falls, TX 76302
(888) 463-2781
www.nitrousexpress.com

**NOS**
(see Holley)

**ProDrive**
(driveline components)
6530 Alondra Blvd.
Paramount, CA 90723
(888) 340-4753
www.prodriveusa.com

**Racers Against Street Racing (RASR)**
A coalition of auto manufacturers, aftermarket parts companies, professional drag racers, sanctioning bodies, race tracks and automotive magazines devoted to promoting safe and legal alternatives to illegal street racing on a national level. The message is simple: *If you want to race, go to a racetrack!*
www.racersagainststreetracing.org

**RC Engineering**
(injectors, injection specialists)
1728 Border Avenue
Torrance, CA 90501
(310) 320-2277
www.rceng.com

**SAVV Mobile Multimedia**
Mobile video
15348 Garfield Ave.
Paramount, CA 90723
(562) 529-7700
www.savv.com

**Scosche**
1550 Pacific Ave.
Oxnard, CA 93033
1-800-621-3695
www.scosche.com

**Split-Second**
(engine management electronics)
1949 East Deere Avenue
Santa Ana, CA 92705
(949) 863-1359
www.splitsec.com

**SSP Street Sound Plus**
2751 Thousand Oaks Blvd.
Thousand Oaks, CA 91362
(805) 557-1054

**STR**
(racing intakes)
1161 California Ave.
Corona, CA 92881
(909) 272-2150
www.strspeedlab.com

**Tanabe**
(Japanese exhaust systems)
see your sport compact tuner or dealer

**Turbo Specialties**
(turbo kits)
17906 Crusader Avenue
Cerritos, CA 90703
(562) 403-7039

**Turbonetics**
(turbochargers)
2255 Agate Court
Simi Valley, CA 93065
(805) 581-0333
www.turboneticsinc.com

**Veilside USA**
(performance and appearance parts)
1250 E. 223rd St., #105
Carson, CA 90745
(310) 835-5684
www.veilside.com

**Vortech Engineering**
(supercharger kits)
1650 Pacific Avenue
Channel Islands, CA 93033
(805) 247-0226
www.vortechsuperchargers.com

**Whipple Superchargers**
3292 N. Weber
Fresno, CA 93722
(559) 442-1261
www.whipplesuperchargers.com

**Woodview**
5670 Timberlea Blvd.
Mississauga, Ontario, Canada
L4W 4M6
(800) 797-DASH (3274)
www.woodcorp.com

**ZEX**
(nitrous oxide kits)
3406 Democrat Road
Memphis, TN 38118
(888) 817-1008
www.zex.com

## A special thanks to:

- APC (American Products Company), Grillcraft, Grant Products, Woodview, Lokar Motorsports, Nuespeed and MSD for supplying many of the custom and performance parts seen throughout this book.
- Phil Weitzl (Universal Products)
- Robin Girard (Woodview)
- Nathan Perkins and Manuel Gomez (Scosche)
- Kimon Bellas (ORCA Design & Manufacturing Corp./Focal America, Inc.)
- Jaime (Dracula) Palafox and Hector Galvan at SSP (Street Sound Plus), Thousand Oaks for all the Mobile Entertainment installations.
- Dave Klienbach
- Ramon Cuguas

# HAYNES REPAIR MANUALS

**ACURA**
- 12020 Integra '86 thru '89 & Legend '86 thru '90
- 12021 Integra '90 thru '93 & Legend '91 thru '95

**AMC**
- Jeep CJ - see JEEP (50020)
- 14020 Mid-size models '70 thru '83
- 14025 (Renault) Alliance & Encore '83 thru '87

**AUDI**
- 15020 4000 all models '80 thru '87
- 15025 5000 all models '77 thru '83
- 15026 5000 all models '84 thru '88

**AUSTIN-HEALEY**
- Sprite - see MG Midget (66015)

**BMW**
- *18020 3/5 Series not including diesel or all-wheel drive models '82 thru '92
- 18021 3-Series incl. Z3 models '92 thru '98
- 18025 320i all 4 cyl models '75 thru '83
- 18050 1500 thru 2002 except Turbo '59 thru '77

**BUICK**
- *19010 Buick Century '97 thru '02
- Century (front-wheel drive) - see GM (38005)
- *19020 Buick, Oldsmobile & Pontiac Full-size (Front-wheel drive) '85 thru '02
- Buick Electra, LeSabre and Park Avenue; Oldsmobile Delta 88 Royale, Ninety Eight and Regency; Pontiac Bonneville
- 19025 Buick Oldsmobile & Pontiac Full-size (Rear wheel drive)
- Buick Estate '70 thru '90, Electra '70 thru '84, LeSabre '70 thru '85, Limited '74 thru '79
- Oldsmobile Custom Cruiser '70 thru '90, Delta 88 '70 thru '85, Ninety-eight '70 thru '84
- Pontiac Bonneville '70 thru '81, Catalina '70 thru '81, Grandville '70 thru '75, Parisienne '83 thru '86
- 19030 Mid-size Regal & Century all rear-drive models with V6, V8 and Turbo '74 thru '87
- Regal - see GENERAL MOTORS (38010)
- Riviera - see GENERAL MOTORS (38030)
- Roadmaster - see CHEVROLET (24046)
- Skyhawk - see GENERAL MOTORS (38015)
- Skylark - see GM (38020, 38025)
- Somerset - see GENERAL MOTORS (38025)

**CADILLAC**
- 21030 Cadillac Rear Wheel Drive all gasoline models '70 thru '93
- Cimarron - see GENERAL MOTORS (38015)
- DeVille - see GM (38031 & 38032)
- Eldorado - see GM (38030 & 33031)
- Fleetwood - see GM (38031)
- Seville - see GM (38030, 38031 & 38032)

**CHEVROLET**
- *24010 Astro & GMC Safari Mini-vans '85 thru '02
- 24015 Camaro V8 all models '70 thru '81
- 24016 Camaro all models '82 thru '92
- 24017 Camaro & Firebird '93 thru '00
- Cavalier - see GENERAL MOTORS (38016)
- Celebrity - see GENERAL MOTORS (38005)
- 24020 Chevelle, Malibu & El Camino '69 thru '87
- 24024 Chevette & Pontiac T1000 '76 thru '87
- Citation - see GENERAL MOTORS (38020)
- 24032 Corsica/Beretta all models '87 thru '96
- 24040 Corvette all V8 models '68 thru '82
- 24041 Corvette all models '84 thru '96
- 10305 Chevrolet Engine Overhaul Manual
- 24045 Full-size Sedans Caprice, Impala, Biscayne, Bel Air & Wagons '69 thru '90
- 24046 Impala SS & Caprice and Buick Roadmaster '91 thru '96
- Impala - see LUMINA (24048)
- Lumina '90 thru 94 - see GM (38010)
- *24048 Lumina & Monte Carlo '95 thru '01
- Lumina APV - see GM (38035)
- 24050 Luv Pick-up all 2WD & 4WD '72 thru '82
- Malibu '97 thru '00 - see GM (38026)
- 24055 Monte Carlo all models '70 thru '88
- Monte Carlo '95 thru '01 - see LUMINA (24048)
- 24059 Nova all V8 models '69 thru '79
- 24060 Nova and Geo Prizm '85 thru '92
- 24064 Pick-ups '67 thru '87 - Chevrolet & GMC, all V8 & in-line 6 cyl, 2WD & 4WD '67 thru '87; Suburbans, Blazers & Jimmys '67 thru '91
- 24065 Pick-ups '88 thru '98 - Chevrolet & GMC, full-size pick-ups '88 thru '98, C/K Classic '99 & '00, Blazer & Jimmy '92 thru '94; Suburban '92 thru '99; Tahoe & Yukon '95 thru '99
- *24066 Pick-ups '99 thru '02 - Chevrolet Silverado & GMC Sierra full-size pick-ups '99 thru '03, Suburban/Tahoe/Yukon/Yukon XL '00 thru '02
- 24070 S-10 & S-15 Pick-ups '82 thru '93, Blazer & Jimmy '83 thru '94,
- *24071 S-10 & S-15 Pick-ups '94 thru '01, Blazer & Jimmy '95 thru '01, Hombre '96 thru '01
- *24072 Chevrolet TrailBlazer & TrailBlazer EXT, GMC Envoy & Envoy XL, Oldsmobile Bravada '02 and '03
- 24075 Sprint '85 thru '88 & Geo Metro '89 thru '01
- 24080 Vans - Chevrolet & GMC '68 thru '96

**CHRYSLER**
- 25015 Chrysler Cirrus, Dodge Stratus, Plymouth Breeze '95 thru '00
- 10310 Chrysler Engine Overhaul Manual
- 25020 Full-size Front-Wheel Drive '88 thru '93
- K-Cars - see DODGE Aries (30008)
- Laser - see DODGE Daytona (30030)
- 25025 Chrysler LHS, Concorde, New Yorker, Dodge Intrepid, Eagle Vision, '93 thru '97
- *25026 Chrysler LHS, Concorde, 300M, Dodge Intrepid, '98 thru '03
- 25030 Chrysler & Plymouth Mid-size front wheel drive '82 thru '95
- Rear-wheel Drive - see Dodge (30050)
- *25035 PT Cruiser all models '01 thru '03
- *25040 Chrysler Sebring, Dodge Avenger '95 thru '02

**DATSUN**
- 28005 200SX all models '80 thru '83
- 28007 B-210 all models '73 thru '78
- 28009 210 all models '79 thru '82
- 28012 240Z, 260Z & 280Z Coupe '70 thru '78
- 28014 280ZX Coupe & 2+2 '79 thru '83
- 300ZX - see NISSAN (72010)
- 28016 310 all models '78 thru '82
- 28018 510 & PL521 Pick-up '68 thru '73
- 28020 510 all models '78 thru '81
- 28022 620 Series Pick-up all models '73 thru '79
- 720 Series Pick-up - see NISSAN (72030)
- 28025 810/Maxima all gasoline models, '77 thru '84

**DODGE**
- 400 & 600 - see CHRYSLER (25030)
- 30008 Aries & Plymouth Reliant '81 thru '89
- 30010 Caravan & Plymouth Voyager '84 thru '95
- *30011 Caravan & Plymouth Voyager '96 thru '02
- 30012 Challenger/Plymouth Saporro '78 thru '83
- 30016 Colt & Plymouth Champ '78 thru '87
- 30020 Dakota Pick-ups all models '87 thru '96
- *30021 Durango '98 & '99, Dakota '97 thru '99
- 30025 Dart, Demon, Plymouth Barracuda, Duster & Valiant 6 cyl models '67 thru '76
- 30030 Daytona & Chrysler Laser '84 thru '89
- Intrepid - see CHRYSLER (25025, 25026)
- *30034 Neon all models '95 thru '99
- 30035 Omni & Plymouth Horizon '78 thru '90
- 30040 Pick-ups all full-size models '74 thru '93
- *30041 Pick-ups all full-size models '94 thru '01
- 30045 Ram 50/D50 Pick-ups & Raider and Plymouth Arrow Pick-ups '79 thru '93
- 30050 Dodge/Plymouth/Chrysler RWD '71 thru '89
- 30055 Shadow & Plymouth Sundance '87 thru '94
- 30060 Spirit & Plymouth Acclaim '89 thru '95
- *30065 Vans - Dodge & Plymouth '71 thru '03

**EAGLE**
- Talon - see MITSUBISHI (68030, 68031)
- Vision - see CHRYSLER (25025)

**FIAT**
- 34010 124 Sport Coupe & Spider '68 thru '78
- 34025 X1/9 all models '74 thru '80

**FORD**
- 10355 Ford Automatic Transmission Overhaul
- 36004 Aerostar Mini-vans all models '86 thru '97
- 36006 Contour & Mercury Mystique '95 thru '00
- 36008 Courier Pick-up all models '72 thru '82
- *36012 Crown Victoria & Mercury Grand Marquis '88 thru '00
- 10320 Ford Engine Overhaul Manual
- 36016 Escort/Mercury Lynx all models '81 thru '90
- 36020 Escort/Mercury Tracer '91 thru '00
- 36022 Ford Escape and Mazda Tribute
- 36024 Explorer & Mazda Navajo '91 thru '01
- 36028 Fairmont & Mercury Zephyr '78 thru '83
- 36030 Festiva & Aspire '88 thru '97
- 36032 Fiesta all models '77 thru '80
- *36034 Focus all models '00 and '01
- 36036 Ford & Mercury Full-size '75 thru '87
- 36044 Ford & Mercury Mid-size '75 thru '86
- 36048 Mustang V8 all models '64-1/2 thru '73
- 36049 Mustang II 4 cyl, V6 & V8 models '74 thru '78
- 36050 Mustang & Mercury Capri all models Mustang, '79 thru '93; Capri, '79 thru '86
- *36051 Mustang all models '94 thru '03
- 36054 Pick-ups & Bronco '73 thru '79
- 36058 Pick-ups & Bronco '80 thru '96
- *36059 F-150 & Expedition '97 thru '02, F-250 '97 thru '99 & Lincoln Navigator '98 thru '02
- *36060 Super Duty Pick-ups, Excursion '97 thru '02
- 36062 Pinto & Mercury Bobcat '75 thru '80
- 36066 Probe all models '89 thru '92
- 36070 Ranger/Bronco II gasoline models '83 thru '92
- *36071 Ranger '93 thru '00 & Mazda Pick-ups 94 thru '00
- 36074 Taurus & Mercury Sable '86 thru '95
- *36075 Taurus & Mercury Sable '96 thru '01
- 36078 Tempo & Mercury Topaz '84 thru '94
- 36082 Thunderbird/Mercury Cougar '83 thru '88
- 36086 Thunderbird/Mercury Cougar '89 and '97
- 36090 Vans all V8 Econoline models '69 thru '91
- *36094 Vans full size '92 thru '01
- *36097 Windstar Mini-van '95 thru '03

**GENERAL MOTORS**
- 10360 GM Automatic Transmission Overhaul
- 38005 Buick Century, Chevrolet Celebrity, Oldsmobile Cutlass Ciera & Pontiac 6000 all models '82 thru '96
- *38010 Buick Regal, Chevrolet Lumina, Oldsmobile Cutlass Supreme & Pontiac Grand Prix (FWD) '88 thru '02
- 38015 Buick Skyhawk, Cadillac Cimarron, Chevrolet Cavalier, Oldsmobile Firenza & Pontiac J-2000 & Sunbird '82 thru '94
- 38016 Chevrolet Cavalier & Pontiac Sunfire '95 thru '01
- 38020 Buick Skylark, Chevrolet Citation, Olds Omega, Pontiac Phoenix '80 thru '85
- 38025 Buick Skylark & Somerset, Oldsmobile Achieva & Calais and Pontiac Grand Am all models '85 thru '98
- *38026 Chevrolet Malibu, Olds Alero & Cutlass, Pontiac Grand Am '97 thru '00
- 38030 Cadillac Eldorado '71 thru '85, Seville '80 thru '85, Oldsmobile Toronado '71 thru '85, Buick Riviera '79 thru '85
- *38031 Cadillac Eldorado & Seville '86 thru '91, DeVille '86 thru '93, Fleetwood & Olds Toronado '86 thru '92, Buick Riviera '86 thru '93
- 38032 Cadillac DeVille '94 thru '02 & Seville - '92 thru '02
- 38035 Chevrolet Lumina APV, Olds Silhouette & Pontiac Trans Sport all models '90 thru '96
- *38036 Chevrolet Venture, Olds Silhouette, Pontiac Trans Sport & Montana '97 thru '01
- General Motors Full-size Rear-wheel Drive - see BUICK (19025)

\* Listings shown with an asterisk (*) indicate model coverage as of this printing. These titles will be periodically updated to include later model years - consult your Haynes dealer for more information.

Haynes North America, Inc., 861 Lawrence Drive, Newbury Park, CA 91320-1514 • (805) 498-6703

# HAYNES REPAIR MANUALS

**GEO**
- Metro - see CHEVROLET Sprint (24075)
- Prizm - '85 thru '92 see CHEVY (24060), '93 thru '02 see TOYOTA Corolla (92036)
- 40030 Storm all models '90 thru '93
- Tracker - see SUZUKI Samurai (90010)

**GMC**
- Vans & Pick-ups - see CHEVROLET

**HONDA**
- 42010 Accord CVCC all models '76 thru '83
- 42011 Accord all models '84 thru '89
- 42012 Accord all models '90 thru '93
- 42013 Accord all models '94 thru '97
- *42014 Accord all models '98 and '99
- 42020 Civic 1200 all models '73 thru '79
- 42021 Civic 1300 & 1500 CVCC '80 thru '83
- 42022 Civic 1500 CVCC all models '75 thru '79
- 42023 Civic all models '84 thru '91
- 42024 Civic & del Sol '92 thru '95
- *42025 Civic '96 thru '00, CR-V '97 thru '00, Acura Integra '94 thru '00
- 42040 Prelude CVCC all models '79 thru '89

**HYUNDAI**
- *43010 Elantra all models '96 thru '01
- 43015 Excel & Accent all models '86 thru '98

**ISUZU**
- Hombre - see CHEVROLET S-10 (24071)
- *47017 Rodeo '91 thru '02; Amigo '89 thru '94 and '98 thru '02; Honda Passport '95 thru '02
- 47020 Trooper & Pick-up '81 thru '93

**JAGUAR**
- 49010 XJ6 all 6 cyl models '68 thru '86
- 49011 XJ6 all models '88 thru '94
- 49015 XJ12 & XJS all 12 cyl models '72 thru '85

**JEEP**
- 50010 Cherokee, Comanche & Wagoneer Limited all models '84 thru '00
- 50020 CJ all models '49 thru '86
- *50025 Grand Cherokee all models '93 thru '00
- 50029 Grand Wagoneer & Pick-up '72 thru '91 Grand Wagoneer '84 thru '91, Cherokee & Wagoneer '72 thru '83, Pick-up '72 thru '88
- *50030 Wrangler all models '87 thru '00

**LEXUS**
- ES 300 - see TOYOTA Camry (92007)

**LINCOLN**
- Navigator - see FORD Pick-up (36059)
- *59010 Rear-Wheel Drive all models '70 thru '01

**MAZDA**
- 61010 GLC Hatchback (rear-wheel drive) '77 thru '83
- 61011 GLC (front-wheel drive) '81 thru '85
- 61015 323 & Protegé '90 thru '00
- *61016 MX-5 Miata '90 thru '97
- 61020 MPV all models '89 thru '94
- Navajo - see Ford Explorer (36024)
- 61030 Pick-ups '72 thru '93
- Pick-ups '94 thru '00 - see Ford Ranger (36071)
- 61035 RX-7 all models '79 thru '85
- 61036 RX-7 all models '86 thru '91
- 61040 626 (rear-wheel drive) all models '79 thru '82
- 61041 626/MX-6 (front-wheel drive) '83 thru '91
- 61042 626 '93 thru '01, MX-6/Ford Probe '93 thru '97

**MERCEDES-BENZ**
- 63012 123 Series Diesel '76 thru '85
- 63015 190 Series four-cyl gas models, '84 thru '88
- 63020 230/250/280 6 cyl sohc models '68 thru '72
- 63025 280 123 Series gasoline models '77 thru '81
- 63030 350 & 450 all models '71 thru '80

**MERCURY**
- 64200 Villager & Nissan Quest '93 thru '01
- All other titles, see FORD Listing.

**MG**
- 66010 MGB Roadster & GT Coupe '62 thru '80
- 66015 MG Midget, Austin Healey Sprite '58 thru '80

**MITSUBISHI**
- 68020 Cordia, Tredia, Galant, Precis & Mirage '83 thru '93
- 68030 Eclipse, Eagle Talon & Ply. Laser '90 thru '94
- *68031 Eclipse '95 thru '01, Eagle Talon '95 thru '98
- 68035 Mitsubishi Galant - 1994 through 2003
- 68040 Pick-up '83 thru '96 & Montero '83 thru '93

**NISSAN**
- 72010 300ZX all models including Turbo '84 thru '89
- 72015 Altima all models '93 thru '01
- 72020 Maxima all models '85 thru '92
- *72021 Maxima all models '93 thru '01
- 72030 Pick-ups '80 thru '97 Pathfinder '87 thru '95
- *72031 Frontier Pick-up '98 thru '01, Xterra '00 & '01, Pathfinder '96 thru '01
- 72040 Pulsar all models '83 thru '86
- Quest - see MERCURY Villager (64200)
- 72050 Sentra all models '82 thru '94
- 72051 Sentra & 200SX all models '95 thru '99
- 72060 Stanza all models '82 thru '90

**OLDSMOBILE**
- 73015 Cutlass V6 & V8 gas models '74 thru '88
- For other OLDSMOBILE titles, see BUICK, CHEVROLET or GENERAL MOTORS listing.

**PLYMOUTH**
- For PLYMOUTH titles, see DODGE listing.

**PONTIAC**
- 79008 Fiero all models '84 thru '88
- 79018 Firebird V8 models except Turbo '70 thru '81
- 79019 Firebird all models '82 thru '92
- 79040 Mid-size Rear-wheel Drive '70 thru '87
- For other PONTIAC titles, see BUICK, CHEVROLET or GENERAL MOTORS listing.

**PORSCHE**
- 80020 911 except Turbo & Carrera 4 '65 thru '89
- 80025 914 all 4 cyl models '69 thru '76
- 80030 924 all models including Turbo '76 thru '82
- 80035 944 all models including Turbo '83 thru '89

**RENAULT**
- Alliance & Encore - see AMC (14020)

**SAAB**
- *84010 900 all models including Turbo '79 thru '88

**SATURN**
- *87010 Saturn all models '91 thru '02

**SUBARU**
- 89002 1100, 1300, 1400 & 1600 '71 thru '79
- 89003 1600 & 1800 2WD & 4WD '80 thru '94

**SUZUKI**
- 90010 Samurai/Sidekick & Geo Tracker '86 thru '01

**TOYOTA**
- 92005 Camry all models '83 thru '91
- 92006 Camry all models '92 thru '96
- *92007 Camry, Avalon, Solara, Lexus ES 300 '97 thru '01
- 92015 Celica Rear Wheel Drive '71 thru '85
- 92020 Celica Front Wheel Drive '86 thru '99
- 92025 Celica Supra all models '79 thru '92
- 92030 Corolla all models '75 thru '79
- 92032 Corolla all rear wheel drive models '80 thru '87
- 92035 Corolla all front wheel drive models '84 thru '92
- 92036 Corolla & Geo Prizm '93 thru '02
- 92040 Corolla Tercel all models '80 thru '82
- 92045 Corona all models '74 thru '82
- 92050 Cressida all models '78 thru '82
- 92055 Land Cruiser FJ40, 43, 45, 55 '68 thru '82
- 92056 Land Cruiser FJ60, 62, 80, FZJ80 '80 thru '96
- 92065 MR2 all models '85 thru '87
- 92070 Pick-up all models '69 thru '78
- 92075 Pick-up all models '79 thru '95
- *92076 Tacoma '95 thru '00, 4Runner '96 thru '00, & T100 '93 thru '98
- *92078 Tundra '00 thru '02 & Sequoia '01 thru '02
- 92080 Previa all models '91 thru '95
- *92082 RAV4 all models '96 thru '02
- 92085 Tercel all models '87 thru '94

**TRIUMPH**
- 94007 Spitfire all models '62 thru '81
- 94010 TR7 all models '75 thru '81

**VW**
- 96008 Beetle & Karmann Ghia '54 thru '79
- *96009 New Beetle '98 thru '00
- 96016 Rabbit, Jetta, Scirocco & Pick-up gas models '74 thru '91 & Convertible '80 thru '92
- 96017 Golf, GTI & Jetta '93 thru '98 & Cabrio '95 thru '98
- *96018 Golf, GTI, Jetta & Cabrio '99 thru '02
- 96020 Rabbit, Jetta & Pick-up diesel '77 thru '84
- 96023 Passat '98 thru '01, Audi A4 '96 thru '01
- 96030 Transporter 1600 all models '68 thru '79
- 96035 Transporter 1700, 1800 & 2000 '72 thru '79
- 96040 Type 3 1500 & 1600 all models '63 thru '73
- 96045 Vanagon all air-cooled models '80 thru '83

**VOLVO**
- 97010 120, 130 Series & 1800 Sports '61 thru '73
- 97015 140 Series all models '66 thru '74
- 97020 240 Series all models '76 thru '93
- 97040 740 & 760 Series all models '82 thru '88
- 97050 850 Series all models '93 thru '97

**TECHBOOK MANUALS**
- 10205 Automotive Computer Codes
- 10210 Automotive Emissions Control Manual
- 10215 Fuel Injection Manual, 1978 thru 1985
- 10220 Fuel Injection Manual, 1986 thru 1999
- 10225 Holley Carburetor Manual
- 10230 Rochester Carburetor Manual
- 10240 Weber/Zenith/Stromberg/SU Carburetors
- 10305 Chevrolet Engine Overhaul Manual
- 10310 Chrysler Engine Overhaul Manual
- 10320 Ford Engine Overhaul Manual
- 10330 GM and Ford Diesel Engine Repair Manual
- 10340 Small Engine Repair Manual, 5 HP & Less
- 10341 Small Engine Repair Manual, 5.5 - 20 HP
- 10345 Suspension, Steering & Driveline Manual
- 10355 Ford Automatic Transmission Overhaul
- 10360 GM Automatic Transmission Overhaul
- 10405 Automotive Body Repair & Painting
- 10410 Automotive Brake Manual
- 10411 Automotive Anti-lock Brake (ABS) Systems
- 10415 Automotive Detailing Manual
- 10420 Automotive Eelectrical Manual
- 10425 Automotive Heating & Air Conditioning
- 10430 Automotive Reference Manual & Dictionary
- 10435 Automotive Tools Manual
- 10440 Used Car Buying Guide
- 10445 Welding Manual
- 10450 ATV Basics

**SPANISH MANUALS**
- 98903 Reparación de Carrocería & Pintura
- 98905 Códigos Automotrices de la Computadora
- 98910 Frenos Automotriz
- 98915 Inyección de Combustible 1986 al 1999
- 99040 Chevrolet & GMC Camionetas '67 al '87 Incluye Suburban, Blazer & Jimmy '67 al '91
- 99041 Chevrolet & GMC Camionetas '88 al '98 Incluye Suburban '92 al '98, Blazer & Jimmy '92 al '94, Tahoe y Yukon '95 al '98
- 99042 Chevrolet & GMC Camionetas Cerradas '68 al '95
- 99055 Dodge Caravan & Plymouth Voyager '84 al '95
- 99075 Ford Camionetas y Bronco '80 al '94
- 99077 Ford Camionetas Cerradas '69 al '91
- 99083 Ford Modelos de Tamaño Grande '75 al '87
- 99088 Ford Modelos de Tamaño Mediano '75 al '86
- 99091 Ford Taurus & Mercury Sable '86 al '95
- 99095 GM Modelos de Tamaño Grande '70 al '90
- 99100 GM Modelos de Tamaño Mediano '70 al '88
- 99110 Nissan Camioneta '80 al '96, Pathfinder '87 al '95
- 99118 Nissan Sentra '82 al '94
- 99125 Toyota Camionetas y 4Runner '79 al '95

\* Listings shown with an asterisk (*) indicate model coverage as of this printing. These titles will be periodically updated to include later model years - consult your Haynes dealer for more information.

Haynes North America, Inc., 861 Lawrence Drive, Newbury Park, CA 91320-1514 • (805) 498-6703